The Civil War Journal of
Lt. Russell M. Tuttle,
New York Volunteer Infantry

The Civil War Journal of Lt. Russell M. Tuttle, New York Volunteer Infantry

RUSSELL M. TUTTLE

Edited by GEORGE TAPPAN

McFarland & Company, Inc., Publishers
Jefferson, North Carolina, and London

LIBRARY OF CONGRESS CATALOGUING-IN-PUBLICATION DATA

Tuttle, Russell M., 1840–1908.
    The Civil War journal of Lt. Russell M. Tuttle, New York Volunteer Infantry / edited by George H. Tappan.
    p.   cm.
    Includes bibliographical references and index.

    ISBN 0-7864-2331-5 (softcover : 50# alkaline paper) ∞

    1. Tuttle, Russell M., 1840–1908.   2. United States. Army. New York Infantry Regiment, 107th (1862–1865) — Biography. 3. United States — History — Civil War, 1861–1865 — Personal narratives.   4. United States — History — Civil War, 1861–1865 — Regimental histories.   I. Tappan, George H.   II. Title.
E523.5107th.T87   2006
973.7'7447092 — dc22   2005036404

British Library cataloguing data are available

©2006 George H. Tappan. All rights reserved

No part of this book may be reproduced or transmitted in any form or by any means, electronic or mechanical, including photocopying or recording, or by any information storage and retrieval system, without permission in writing from the publisher.

On the cover: The Battle of Antietam, Sketch by A. R. Waud, *Harper's Weekly*, October 11, 1862

Manufactured in the United States of America

McFarland & Company, Inc., Publishers
  Box 611, Jefferson, North Carolina 28640
  www.mcfarlandpub.com

Contents

Editor's Note   1

List of Maps   5

1. War! War!! War!!!   7
2. In the Service of the United States   15
3. The Maryland Campaign   26
4. Back Across Virginia to Join Hooker   59
5. Fairfax Station, Virginia   64
6. Hooker's Campaign of the Spring of 1863   81
7. One Year of Service Is Passed   89
8. Shelbyville, Bedford County, Tennessee   105
9. On the March   119
10. After the Battle   126
11. August 13, 1864   147
12. Entered Atlanta   152
13. The Siege of Atlanta   157
14. "Going South to Seek Salt Water"   166

15. Entered Savannah	174
16. Goodbye Savannah	179
17. Homeward Bound	217
Epilogue	225
Appendix A. History of the Tuttle Family	227
Appendix B. A Note on the 107th New York Volunteers	228
Appendix C. "Health of the Volunteers"	229
Index	231

Editor's Note

The text of this book was transcribed from a handwritten manuscript found in a collection of personal items from my wife's family. Those who might have known how it came to us are no longer living; perhaps it arrived with a collection of old books from an estate sale many decades ago. I came across it by accident in a box in my garage.

The manuscript is a collection of 5½ × 7¾ inch pages with a threaded binding enclosed by a portion of a Hornellsville High School diploma, a printer's reject, as a cover. The text appears to have been compiled from the author's diary, his army notebook, and portions of letters he wrote home or received while in military service during the U.S. Civil War, from 1862 to 1865. It begins with the announcements of war on page 60 of his diary during his junior year at the University of Rochester, 1861 (he calls this part of his diary "the college annals"). There were also several separately bound additions providing more intimate comments on his life, thoughts and opinions during his service. I have taken the liberty of splicing them into the army notebook. Unfortunately, 150 pages of these notes, covering the earliest days of his enlistment, have not been found.

The author's name was not given, but the mystery gradually unfolded when his first name, Russell, and subsequently his father's name, Rufus Tuttle, eventually appeared in the text. This prompted a natural curiosity to discover who this young man was, and where he was from. What emerged was the story of a very normal, well educated young man who, in missing home, friends, and family, recorded his day-by-day thoughts, feelings, and activities in his writings.

Russell Mumford Tuttle was born in Almond, Allegany County, New

York, on January 12, 1840, the son of Rufus and Mellinda Mumford Tuttle. Young Tuttle was much affected by the onset of the War of the Rebellion while in his junior year at Rochester. After receiving the sad news of the death of a friend wounded in battle, he felt pressed to do his duty for his country. After graduation he enlisted in the service as a private citizen on August 11, 1862. Russell Tuttle was mustered in as an orderly sergeant in K Company of the 107th Regiment, New York Volunteers, in which his uncle, Allen N. Sill, was captain.

Over the next three years he served with the Army of the Potomac, seeing tough action in Maryland and Virginia, the Siege of Atlanta, the March to the Sea, and the return through the Carolinas and Virginia to discharge at Elmira, New York, on June 19, 1865. During the course of his military career he was commissioned second lieutenant March 1, 1863, and first lieutenant August 1, 1864; he was brevetted captain at discharge.

With the exception of minor editing for presentation, and a few difficulties interpreting some words, the text is a true copy of the original. Words of which we are unsure and a few needed to complete the sense are enclosed in brackets. I have taken the liberty to format paragraphs to give the reader an occasional break, and have indicated proper names of periodicals, ships, and foreign words in italics.

Russell Tuttle usually placed commas and periods outside quotation marks. The publisher elected to place them inside the quotation marks in accordance with current American practice.

Some name spellings vary. The name of Tuttle's friend Binny is also spelled Binni or Binnie. We see both Doc and Dock. The name of Tuttle's future wife, Ervilla, is first given as Arvilla, and then as Villie. These variants remain, without correction or comment.

An appendix provides a short history of the Tuttle family. Additional appendices detail the wartime journey of the New York Volunteers and the chronic disease and poor health that plagued soldiers in the Civil War — something upon which Tuttle often commented in his writing.

This effort would not have come about without the encouragement of Alice Taychert, director of the Hornell Public Library, Hornell, New York, who has been instrumental in researching historical material on the author, and has provided valuable help at every turn.

I am also deeply indebted to good friends Hugh Hay-Roe and Earl Watkins for the many hours they dedicated to identification of certain words that were difficult to interpret and to proofing of the text; to Clark McCollough for his valuable assistance with computer technology and scanning the photos and illustrations; and to Heather Greenfield and Will Tuthill for cover design suggestions.

I also feel indebted to young Russell Tuttle for leaving us his remarkable diary of events, thoughts, and impressions captured during those three difficult years of dedication to the cause of his country. His beautifully sensitive descriptions of the countryside, flowers, and birds singing in the woods, intermingled with the tragic loss to sickness and the horrors of the maimed and dead, have brought me close to this young man. His recognition of the fine qualities of people he met along his route, as well as his appreciation of the more beautiful towns and cities he passed through, helped me share with him some of my own day-to-day feelings of this world we live in. After spending a year with him on this project, I felt obliged to prepare his work in a form that could be shared with a larger public.

My wife's brother and sister, Dr. Willard H. Sutton of Glastonbury, Connecticut, and Mme. Marion Attali of Paris, France, have donated the original Tuttle manuscript to the Hornell Public Library. In 2008, the Hornell Public Library will celebrate its sesquicentennial, and Russell Tuttle as one of its founders.

George Tappan
Kingwood, Texas
January 2006

List of Maps

Rochester, Hornellsville, Elmira, New York	9
The Potomac Campaign	22
Harper's Ferry–Antietam–Sharpsburg–Boonsboro	32
Hooker's Campaign of the Spring of 1863	56
Rail Route, Virginia to Tennessee	94
Tennessee–Georgia Campaign	96
Tennessee, Shelbyville to Chattanooga, *Harper's Weekly*, September 5, 1863	100
North Georgia, Resaca to Atlanta, *Harper's Weekly*, July 2, 1864	124
March to the Sea and Northward through the Carolinas	171
Marching Northward through North Carolina	194
Marching Northward through Virginia and Homeward	219
March Route, Chattanooga to Washington	221

War! War!! War!!! [From the College Annals] p 60
1861 Junior year.

to all the talk just now. Very exciting news is just now arriving from Charleston. Our Fort Sumter has been attacked, and taken, that is taken! Our people are all in excitement, though they are of course unable as yet to tell how much reliance to place in the dispatches. Strange to say there are some even here who seem to rejoice at the news, — who are traitors enough to laugh when they hear of the defeat of the stars and stripes — Let them laugh if they will. Fort Sumter may be taken, But the End is not yet.

15th — All along the route, returning to Rochester from vacation home, I heard nothing else talked about but the taking of Fort Sumter & the President's proclamation calling for 75,000 men. It is nothing but War now, and all are of the one opinion that the government must be sustained But what a terrible and bloody conflict is upon us! To day the news of the fall of Fort Sumter is confirmed and the city is wild with

War! War!! War!!!

| From the College annals | 1861 | Junior Year |

It's all the talk just now. Very exciting news is just now arriving from Charleston. Our Fort Sumter has been attacked, and later, that it is taken! Our people are all in excitement, though they are of course unable as yet to tell how much reliance to place in the dispatches. Strange to say there are some men here who seem to rejoice at the news, who are traitors enough to laugh when they hear of the defeat of the stars and stripes. Let them laugh if they will. Fort Sumter may be taken, But the end is not yet.

Monday, April 15th: All along the route, returning to Rochester from vacation home, I heard nothing else talked about but the taking of Fort Sumter and the President's proclamation calling for 75,000 men. It is nothing but war now, and all are of the one opinion that the government must be sustained. But what a terrible and bloody conflict is upon us!

Today the news of the fall of Fort Sumter is confirmed and the city is wild with excitement. In the evening the Rochester Light Guards Zonar were out in public parade, and were immensely cheered.

April 16th: The war is the all-engrossing matter just now. People can think or talk of nothing else. The President's proclamation meets with a hearty response from the north, while the Border states indignantly refuse to comply with its demands. Since the Border states act as they do matters look worse than ever. The war bids fair to be one of the most fierce and bloody of any on record. Maryland and Delaware alone remain true. The most we can expect of Kentucky and Tennessee and indeed of Maryland I fear, is that they will remain neutral in the fight.

April 17: Nothing particular new from threat of war, but all over the country the people are preparing for a mighty struggle. Prof. Quimby is very excited. He is surely going into the fight. Rochester University will lose one of the best teachers, and I am not sure but that she will yet have to lose one of her students.

Thursday, April 18: The Pres. said as we gathered together this morning, we had met in troublous times, but exhorted us to keep calm, and do our duties here faithfully, and if sterner duties should here after call us, to be prepared for them.

In the evening there was a great meeting at the City Hall, in fact two meetings for one room couldn't hold them all. Songs were sung, speeches made, resolutions adapted, cheers given, and withal the most enthusiastic meeting held that Rochester ever saw. Prof. was present and made a flaming war speech. He is greatly excited. Speeches were also made by Mayor Nash and others.

A noticeable feature of the meeting was the presence of a Kentuckian. He spoke in both meetings and was loudly applauded as was the state of Old Kentucky.

April 19th, Friday: It is hard work to try to study. The war absorbs all my attention to it, is so much excitement to me. I fear I will be sick if I am not careful. Prof. Quimby is full of interest now. Walked over to his house after dinner. He is especially anxious today about the Arsenal at Harpers Ferry. He says that the North is deficient in arms.

Evening: Very exciting news comes tonight of a great riot at Baltimore. The Massachusetts troops had to force their way through the city. Several were killed in the fight! This opens the Ball. Even Maryland must be subdued by force. The war is imminent. I am really fearful that the Rebels will take Washington yet. (Wrote to Luin Thacher)

Saturday, April 20: In the Junior class this morning we started a Student Military Company. My name heads the list. Twenty six have already signed their names. This is merely to drill, and not to volunteer at present. But we want to be prepared for what may be necessary. The *Hornellsville Tribune* comes telling of the patriotism and the prosperity of the town. Good for the Light Guards! I almost want to go back and enlist with them.

Prof. Quimby, Noble Man! is getting up a regiment here. Has four companies already started and has an office in the City Hall for the reception of arms. His recruiting office is at 141 State Street. God bless him.

Sunday, April 28: The week just begun finds the country in a much better condition than did the last. Then Washington was in imminent danger. It is now considered out of danger, and will soon be protected by thousands of faithful troops. The Federal Government warmly seconded by the United North is making great preparations with great dispatch for carrying on a

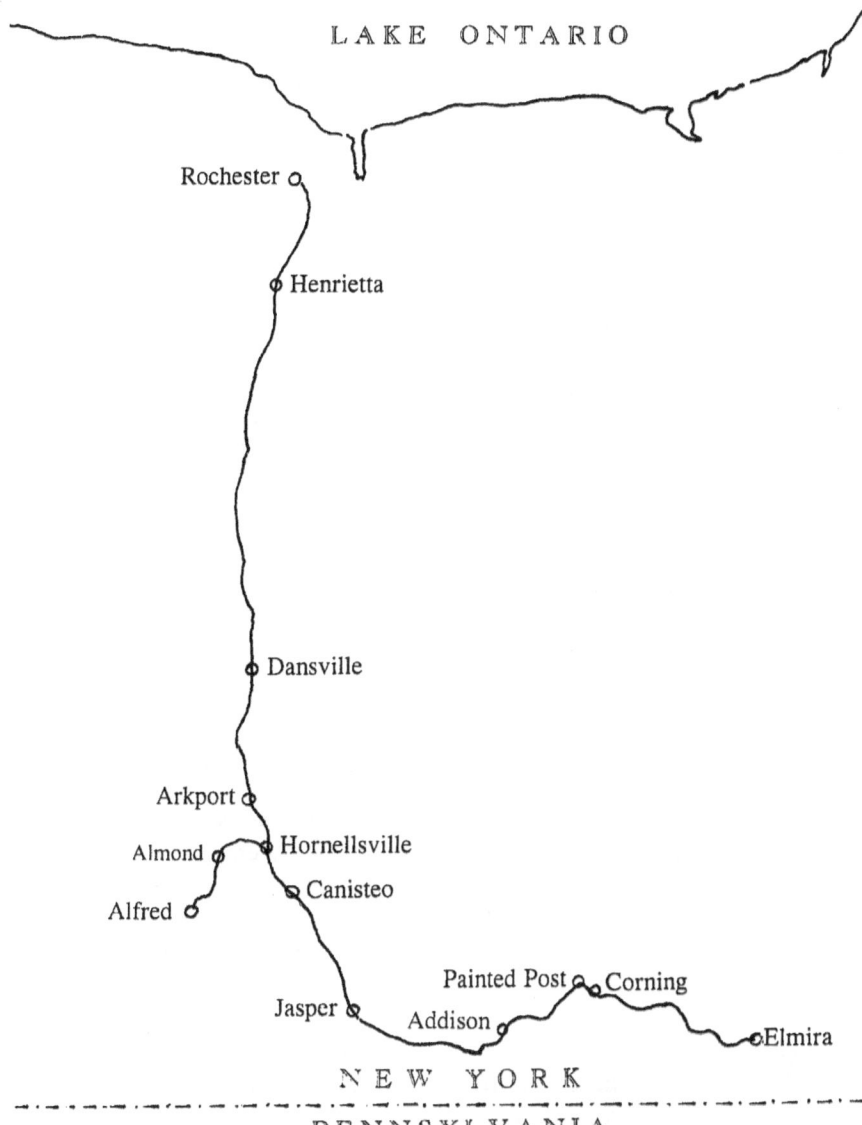

Rochester, Hornellsville, Elmira, New York

rigorous war. And the South seems to be doing its best to oppose us. Maryland has been strongly, more than strongly secession, and now again in some portions they dare to express union sentiments. And federal troops will soon have her completely under subjection, Maryland will probably be compelled to stay in the Union. Fort Pickens is not taken, and will not be, and with Forts Monroe and McKinley in our possession Virginia and Maryland are at our mercy, so everything is brightening up before us as a nation.

April 28: In Rochester the war spirit is by no means cooled down yet. The "Quimby Regt." is about full, and will start for Elmira this week. Younger, Webster, Gould, Burbank, Prof. Gilbert, and Savage are among the enlisted and I guess Pattengill also. We have formed a Student's Company now numbering sixty for drill. Mason Captain, Gardner First Lieut., and Tuttle Ensign. At Hornellsville they are stirring also. The Canacadeas have volunteered and they are going to get up another company also. The Cornet Band have volunteered their services to the 60th Rgt.

Prof. Maxon and Williams of Alfred and several students have gone to Washington to fight for the defense.

Evening: This has been a day long to be remembered in Rochester. Tomorrow the Rochester Regiments are to depart for the war, and this is the last Sabbath which many of them, probably will ever spend here. The company of Capt. Taylor marched up and attended our church in a body. Dr. Shaw preached a most impressive sermon on the war and at its close the members of the company from our church were each presented with a Bible. There were three who were members of our congregation and SS. A large American flag was hung up behind the pulpit. I never saw so many people in that church before. It was absolutely full. The scene was withal a sad one for many of the friends who were there.

Monday, April 29: Got a letter from Mother beseeching me not to enlist. It seems that I caused her much pain and anxiety by my letter. Well, I shall not enlist until I am certain that it is necessary. Mother says that Father has signed $25 for the support of the families of volunteers, and has promised Uncle Allen that he will support his family if he should be called to go to war.

Tuesday, April 30: Wrote to Carrie and informed her that I am not going to enlist, this time at least. Yesterday afternoon attended a flag raising at the Curtis Female seminary.

Received a letter from Father in a somewhat different strain from that of Mother's. He would say, if Mother and Caroline were willing, "go and enlist," but on their account I think I better not say so. At any rate he hopes I will be able to remain in College through my Junior year and in Sept., he says we will see what can be done. Well, that is sensible I think. At the class prayer meeting, Brown, Tousy, Leonard, Owen, Younger, Tuttle, West. Alf Younger made a very impressive farewell to his classmates, stating that it was a feeling of supreme duty that led him to go into the war.

Saturday, May 4th: In the afternoon I went down to St. Luke's Church with P — and witnessed the raising of the American Flag over that church, the first flag raised over a church in the city. Speeches were made by Dr. Claxton, Alfred Ely, and Roswell Hart. Went to the Valley Depot to see two companies off. It was an affecting scene to see some of their leave takings.

There were some fine looking men in the ranks and it was sad indeed to see them bidding good bye to their man and dear friends.

The Hornellsville Tribune brings news. The chief of which is the enlisting of several of my Alfred friends. The pride of Alfred has gone. The best students and the finest young men. I know all but one of the list. First and nearest of all is my old friend and true friend, my correspondent for life Luin Thacher. Brown, Dexter, Sanders were also good fellows, and good friends, while I am well acquainted with Maxon, Bacon, Todd, and Kenyon. Five of this number are fraternity brothers. Well, may God go with them and bless them and help them to be good soldiers, both for themselves and for the country, as I am quite certain they will be. I learn that by the death of Col. Wheiting, Mr. Craw of Hornellsville becomes the Col. of the 60th Regt. Mr. C. has been active in getting the volunteer companies up at Hornellsville, and has drilled them constantly. He is full of enthusiasm in the cause and will make a good Col.

Sunday, May 5th: At the Y.P.M. Dr. Shaw's son, just returned from Nashville, Tenn., made some very interesting remarks. He came home because he would not fight against the stars and stripes. In the evening went to Plymouth Church and heard Mr. Edwards preach a patriotic sermon. Capt. Wauser's Company, in which are Ed Gould, Younger, Webster, and Burbank, attended in body. They were each presented with a Testament and a copy of the Book of Psalms. Two large banners were hung up behind the pulpit and the choir sang America and the Star Spangled Banner. The church was crowded just as full as possible.

Friday, May 10th: The American flag hoisted upon a staff erected in front of the College and a sword purchased by the students for a parting gift to Prof. Quimby was presented.

This was indeed a big thing, and would have been even bigger if it had not rained. But we had a big time after all. A large number was out with many ladies from the High School, Miss Curtis, and the city generally. The exercises were of the deepest interest to the students for Prof. Quimby is dearer to us than any other man in the faculty. May God go with him and bless him in our prayer. He is one of the noblest and best of men I ever saw and the loss of his services is a great one for the University.

In the evening I went with Geo. Gardner to take to Prof. Quimby, his sword, which was left at the Arcade for exhibition. We found there Col. Gardner and Miss Carrie and Drs. Kendrick, Cutting. The time spent in their company was most interesting to us. Col. Gardner talks like an old hero as he is. His daughter seems to sympathize somewhat with the South, and had to stand the argument and ridicule of the rest. Geo. & I were both delighted with Mrs. Quimby. I never saw her before. She is a splendid woman, in every way worthy of, I am sure of her noble husband.

There is something so noble about her that our admiration was at once gained.

Monday, May 13: Capt. Wauser's Company set off for Elmira this morning. The best looking Company that has yet gone, though rather young. The people turned out in goodly numbers to see them off. Among them the University boys, for Younger and Webster and Gould and Burbank went in this company. There was the usual public parade, the usual crowd of friends and spectators, and the cars moved away. How many such scenes are going on throughout the land! We are not used to such scenes and the very strangeness of such scenes makes the pain of parting greater for those who send away and those who are sent.

Tuesday, May 14: Had a letter from Luther Howell. It is two months since I wrote him. He says not a word as to what college society he has joined. His letter is all of the War. He belongs to a students Company called the "Amherst Boys." They tendered their services to the state but were not fortunate enough to be among the accepted ones. They are still drilling and ready to go.

Tuesday, May 21: Luin is still in the barracks at Elmira. He is in the Southern Tier Regt., Mr. N. M. Crane is Lieut. Col., and of which the Hornellsville Company is a part. He is sorry for me that I could not enlist, and at the same time congratulates me. He would not have enlisted had he known then as much on the subject as he now knows, and yet he does not regret the step. For he believes he did right.

Drill at Butt's Hall in the afternoon and as Capt. Updike was not there I had to take command. Made myself fairly hoarse in the operation.

1862

August 1st: Painting. Letter from Enos. Good news. Enos wants me to study for the ministry, but thinks I would do equally well as a journalist.

Saturday, August 2nd: Painting yet — awful hot — Russell's Panorama.

Sunday, August 3: Church. Sermon on election. Took a little class at SS. Eve — Mr. Waldo's last sermon — He is to have a summer vacation.

Monday, August 4th: A letter from Sheldon. He is traveling for his health among the Berkshire hills. Awful hot. Beautiful eve. I am not well tonight, yet that does not wholly prevent me from enjoyment of this fine moonlit evening. Sister Carrie went down to my Aunt Jane's to spend the evening and as it was but a few steps I accompanied her, and as we passed along I was reminded of the lines:

1. War! War!! War!!!

"Under the moon in the village street
Gossiping groups in the shadows meet;
Seated at dusky doorways there
Red-lipped maidens taste of the air.
Whispering now of their lovers eyes
Blue as the beautiful summer skies,
Whispering now of their flatteries sweet
As autumn's fruitage dropped in the heat;
Until their cadence a trembling tune
Soft as their pulses under the moon."

Tuesday, August 5th: Letter from Ben Ride.
After the lost spectacles up Crosby Creek with Father!
Thoughts of enlisting. Ben writes: Bro. Webster received a shot in the leg, below the knee, at the time and place stated in the resolutions, and from the effects of that wound died in one of our hospitals. The Upsilon Chapter is fully conscious of having lost one of its noblest members. Like all of our combatant heros, he has served his country faithfully and effectively. He was the first to fall. *Resquiescat in pace.* This is sad news indeed. Webster was a splendid fellow, one of the best we ever had in our chapter, and as a soldier he had won for himself great admiration and regard. How many precious lives are sacrificed to this unholy Rebellion. What a fearful account will have to be rendered by somebody for all this! My heart is full of grief for poor Webster. He was one of my best friends. I wish I could take his place and avenge his death. But he was not unprepared to die, and I know he is in Heaven now where wars and fighting never come.

Wrote to Cooper at Rochester. Told him I wanted to enlist now since hearing of Webster's death.

Wednesday, August 6th: Did not go to W. E. Prayer M. Staid at Aunt Jane's. Uncle Allen has gone to Elmira on Military business, and she

Gen. Robert B. Van Valkenburgh

is "heartsick" thinking of the time when he will go to where the real business of war is carried on.

Thursday, August 7th: About concluded to enlist. Hot days.

Friday, August 8th: Wrote to James. Enlistment papers. Learned from J.W. Robinson, who writes from Harrison's Landing, Va., that my friend and former correspondent, Wesley Northup 1st Sergeant Co. G, 1st Regt. Minn. Vols. died of fever in Hospital near Yorktown, Va. May 16, 1862.

Talking a great deal with Father about enlisting. Am getting the War fever strong.

Saturday, August 9th: Letter from G.K. Gilbert. Fools errand to Elmira. After a great deal of talking about going into the service, I went down to Elmira to see if Col. Van Valkenburgh could not give me a place. I hardly knew what myself. Of course I found no place for me, always excepting that of private soldier.

So I came home. Carl Gilbert is to be the principal of an academy at Jackson, Michigan.

Sunday, August 10th: A.M. Methodist Church.

Evening: Presbyterian Church, and heard Mr. Wakeman. Today I did listen to the sermon and tried to worship my God as his children should.

2

In the Service of the United States

Monday, August 11, 1862: Hornellsville to Elmira. Went down with Uncle Allen to help him make out his papers. A world of writing was to be done, and spent a day or two to do it all in. Had given up the expectation, tho not the wish, of going into the service with this Regiment, but went down to do what I could in helping it off, and perhaps something would turn up for me yet.

At the depot I bade good bye to Lydia Thacher, who had come down to see off her brother Eugene, and told her I was "going to war" but she would not believe me. At Elmira I found that James Pinch, who was to have been Orderly Sergeant, might not after all if the boys continued their wish for another man, but the other man had not yet been agreed upon. Upon Uncle Allen's offering to make me that other man, then I wanted him to make me 2nd Serg, I agreed to enlist. Then I telegraphed up to Father, "I can have a good position in Sill's Company. Can I go? Ask Mother?," and in due time the answer came.

Sgt. Eugene Q. Thacher Co. K 107th New York Volunteers

"Ma says you must act your own judgement, and satisfy yourself. I say go. Rufus Tuttle." That did the business. My enlistment papers were forthwith made out. In the meantime I was very busy with the interminable muster rolls of the Company.

Camp of 107th N.Y.V. Elmira, N.Y., Aug 9, 1862*: "I am writing this in the barrack and no very elegant accommodations I can assure for such business. This you know is the first Regiment organized under the first call for 300,000 more, and it will proceed to Washington in a day or two. (But before I go any further, let me say that I am not going alone. They won't take me if I wanted to even so bad. I have found that out today to my perfect satisfaction, So keep your heart easy.) These barracks are those occupied by the 27th Regt. where Wauser, Gould, and poor Webster were. I see the numbers 27 and 64 in many places around, those regiments having been here. The 64th was here but a few months since, and now the 107th Company, in which my uncle is, is about ready to go. We are very proud here that this district sends the first regiment from the State, under the late call.

Volunteer Regiment on Parade at Camp, Elmira, New York, *Harper's Weekly*, August 17, 1861.

*What follows is Tuttle quoting one of his own letters written two days before. Such quotes appear throughout the journal, usually identified with a note regarding the letter's recipient—for example, "To Father."

The Col. (Van Valkenburgh) who is quite a politician and a M.C. [member of congress] has received quite a flattering notice from the President, and has been promised the best arms and quarters for his regiment to be found when they get there."

Elmira again, Aug 11th 1862:

I told you the other day that I would not enlist because I could not be accepted here. That was a false alarm. My papers are made out, I have been examined by the surgeon and pronounced perfectly sound and able to endure military service, and now I only await a telegraph "Yes" from home, and to be sworn in by the U.S. mustering officer, and I shall be "in" for it for "three years or during the war." I said some time ago that I should not enlist, but the reasons which led to that decision are now removed and I feel it my duty to go. I cannot ignore any reason why I ought not to go. But I cannot stop now to make any long explanation. Only this much will tell it all. I feel it to be my duty to go and therefore I shall not wait to be drafted. I enlist as a private soldier, tho' of course I stand a good chance for some non commissioned office. This regiment goes to Washington on Wednesday it is thought.

Tuesday, August 12th: There was no little grumbling in the Company when it became known that I was to be Orderly. Threats of shooting even were made against both the Captain and myself. But no notice was taken of any such manifestations. Yet I was sorry to come into the Company under such unfavorable circumstances. Busy at the rolls.

To Father: "We were up till after midnight last night making out enlistment papers. Our Company is now full and running over."

I have had my first meal and my first night in camp. Attended roll call at five o'clock this morning, and are now waiting the coming of the adjutant to be mustered into the service of Uncle Samuel. I am bound to go through now. I was duly mustered in with twenty or thirty others by Adjutant Smith, now chosen Major of the Company.

Wednesday, August 13: Today we received our "Bounty" from the state, $50, and from the U.S. $25 with a $2 premium, making in all $77, and I was clothed in Uncle Sam's uniform, for the first time. Father came down to see me today. Well he did for to go home was impossible. He saw me put on my soldier clothes and looked rather dubiously at the rough uniform and the knapsack I had to carry. He staid around some time watching the busy confused crowds around the barrack, more like Bedlam than anything he had ever seen, and at length concluded to go. I walked as far as the entrance gate with him, but could go no further without a pass, and bid him good bye there.

It was a solemn parting, tho' hurried, little was said, but much was thought. Bert Plimpton's wife was there too, and her sister Mrs. Miller. The

Sgt. Albert M. Plimpton Co. K, 107th New York Volunteers (W. L. Sutton, photographer)

latter sewed upon my coat sleeves my Orderly Sergeant's chevrons. Today was the day set for our departure for Washington, but we can hardly get away until tomorrow. We sat up until two o'clock last night making out enrollment papers, and have to be up early in the morning besides. Just think I shall be compelled to go off without even seeing and bidding good bye to my folks.

I am very very busy, never so much so in my life, can hardly find time to eat.

The adjutant came and said that Co. K must have another muster roll made out. That was a three hours work, but I had to do it in one, and was complimented by the Col. for my feat. When I returned to the Captain's barrack I found them deserted and the whole regiment out on the parade ground ready to start. I had often heard of breaking up camp, but never knew what it was like until now. The regiment is under orders to start for Dixie at 11 o'clock, and we are now waiting for the time to come. The men are singing "Glory Hallelujah." We have two days rations in our haversacks.

I was up all night last night, and of course will have to be up for many hours now. When will I ever get any sleep! I don't know. We marched down town, all through it, and then on the cars, and about midnight the 107th Regiment took its leave of Elmira.

Thursday, August 14: Elmira to Baltimore.

Left Elmira about 1 o'clock A.M. Then when morning broke we were in Pennsylvania, a very mild but picturesque country. Reached Williamsport about 8, where we were enthusiastically received. Then on through Harrisburg, York, and to Baltimore. We went through some of the most beautiful country I ever saw. I did not know that Pennsylvania had any such places in it.

The scenery along the Susquehanna was particularly fine. Handkerchiefs were waved at us all the way, and wherever we stopped the people brought us cake and fruit, and what we wanted most; water to drink. Our march through Baltimore was splendid. We were astonished at the enthusiastic reception that met us. When it was late in the evening the streets were full of people, houses illuminated, flags flying. (etc etc.) Our march through the city was one succession of cheers, and we stopped and gave an extra cheer when we came to the street where the Massachusetts men were shot down.

At the Soldier's Home we were given a fine supper at the expense of the loyal Baltimoreans. It must have been nearly morning when we were once more on our way.

Friday, August 15th: Baltimore to Washington.

How emotional it was to see the places I had so often read of, the Relay House, Annapolis Junction, the Long Bridge at Washington etc., and yet everything was peculiar Southern and was of course strange to me. I was about bushed when we reached Washington. I had had only four or five hours of sleep out of seventy. The only sleep I had on Thursday night was on Friday morning as we were coming into Washington in the blazing hot sun on the top of an iron roofed flat car. But arrived at Washington site and I went up to see Dr. Jamison, surgeon 86th N.Y. who stopped at the house of the Swiss Consul. There I had something to drink, a good dinner, a bed, a short sleep. Lucky for me! Took quite a liking to the young man, the Consul's son.

We went back to the depot in time to see the review of the regiment by President Lincoln and Secretary Seward. A miserable supper at the Soldier's Rest, and then we marched into Dixie. We left with Mr. Seward our

The mile long bridge across the Potomac, Washington to Alexandria, *Harper's Weekly*, May 18, 1861. The bridge was of wood with a quarter mile central section of masonry. It had a draw at either end.

magnificent prize banner, presented to us by Gov. Morgan for being the first N.Y. regiment under the new call.

We had not finished our march when we reached Washington, but were ordered at once into Virginia seven miles distant. We thought it was rather tough, but we did it, and I stood the jaunt better than some of the rugged farmers boys in the regiment. Fortunately I did not have a very heavy knapsack. Arrived here at "Camp Seward," as it has been, between Forts Albany and Richardson. We found that the only quarters that had been provided to us consisted of a big field, but it was a most beautiful warm summer evening, so we built a few camp fires, wrapped up in our blankets, laid down in the stubble, and enjoyed one of the sweetest and most refreshing sleeps that ever blessed my eyelids. My first and not unpleasant experience in the fields.

Saturday, August 16: Busy all day long in laying out camp, pitching tents. A tents etc. . This is the order in which our companies come: from right to left of regiments: B, F, D, K, C, I, G, A, H, E, 1,6,4,9,5,10,7,2, Baldwin, Miles, Slocum, Sill, Fox, Colby, Laman, Wilkinson, Clark, Morgan. Capt. Laman laid out the camp. Am still quite unpopular in the company for taking the position of Orderly. I see it now as I am entering upon my duties.

But I will outlive it, I hope.

Sunday, August 17: Today we are just beginning to live. Drew regular rations for the first time, and are gradually working into the routine of camp

Left: Lt. Col. Allen N. Sill, Co. K, 107th New York Volunteers, Hornellsville, N.Y. (Moulton & Larkin, photographers). *Right:* Capt. E. S. Baldwin 141st. Regt., New York Volunteers (Brady's National Portrait Galleries)

life. We have not done anything yet in the way of military drill. This is Sunday, but nobody seems to know it. Everything goes on just as usual. But I am going to try not to forget my Lord and Master even here. What should I do, especially now, should he forget me?

But Sunday was observed. In the afternoon the regiment was called together in the peach orchard near our camp, and Chaplain Crane made some remarks. He read to us the 27th Psalm and made it the basis of his remarks. There was singing and prayer also.

Thursday, August 21: It seems a long time since I arrived here. We had our first mail today. But I was not among the favored. It is night and the soldiers are gathered around the camp fire or in their tents waiting for tattoo and evening roll call. Our regiment band has been giving us some beautiful music, while the boys are singing "Gloria Hallelujah" and other camp songs through all the company tents. Mike Sherron, who is the character of our company, is telling a story in front of my tent, while I hear in the distance the voice of prayer and praise from a prayer meeting in front of the Chaplain's tent. So are all things mixed together here. So it is ever in a soldier's life I guess. This morning Lt. Rutter came with an order from the Col. detailing me for extra duty. I had to prepare duplicate receipts for the whole regiment; for all the ordnance and ordnance stores received. This I had to obey of course, for I am my own master no longer.

Late at night we had orders to move to Fort Lyon, at six in the morning, are promised that we shall see service very soon, and I have been issuing ammunition (40 pounds to a man) this evening. A great many troops are leaving Washington today and tomorrow and something must be up but we poor soldiers know nothing of what is going on.

Saturday, August 23: From Fort Albany to Fort Lyon.

We had a long march (for raw recruits) by a round about way, from Arlington by or near Manson Hill, Baileys Crossroads, Fairfax Seminary, Port Ellsworth, etc, to this most extreme outpost in this direction from Washington. Our parade ground overlooks the Potomac, and from it we have one of the finest views I ever saw, the Potomac visible for miles, Alexandria in the foreground and Washington in the distance, its capitol and everything in full view. Our camp is splendidly located, we have continually such fine breezes from up the river. The Rochester Regiment (108th) took possession of Camp Seward a few days after we left. We arrived here about one PM and rested in the field in the blazing sunshine until the baggage wagons brought us our camp equipage and we went to work pitching our tents. The Orderly's tents at the head of the street went up first, but we had not begun to ditch around it when the Captain brought around our mail. I sat right down in my tent and read my letters, amid all the confusion and hubub of the tent pitching. Hired a nig boy.

The Potomac Campaign

Sunday, August 24: Last night an order came to rush us forward to Manassas. But I guess it was countermanded. McClellan's Army is rapidly reinforcing Pope. All night and today great transports have been coming up the river and discharging troops here who are immediately sent on to the scene of action. How hard they looked, the officers in torn and dirty blouses, boots torn to pieces, and hardly any uniform about them to distinguish their rank.

Not far from our parade grounds, on the river bank is the old Fairfax mansion. Built by Lord Fairfax long before the Revolution. Here Washington spent most of his time when young and from here he started off on his first surveying trip. I went over

Maj. Gen. George B. McClellan (F. Guterunst)

this evening with the Captain and took supper there. Had a good cup of tea! How old and queer the house looked!

Two companies of this regiment have been detailed for artilleryists in the Fort, from which the 69th N.Y. Militia leave today for home. They are being instructed in Artillery drill. All day long the trains of the Alexandria R.R. have been carrying thousands of troops and bringing in wounded and prisoners from Culpepper and vicinity.

Tuesday, August 26: McClellans Army continues to come in. Some go on to the front and some are camping around us.

My good friend Sheldon writes me. "One glance at the envelope which enclosed your letter, and at its post-mark was sufficient to tell the story. I knew that you had enlisted before I broke the seal. It was right-manly and noble and patriotic in you and also your present position is as honorable as any you could possibly occupy, yet I hope and at the same time feel confident that your ability will soon secure for you a more lucrative one. While I cannot but feel sad that one who is so near to me is exposed to peculiar danger, yet as a classmate and brother I feel proud of you. May God spare your life and return you to your home crowned with many a laurel is my earnest prayer." Sheldon writes that Pattengill thinks of enlisting, that Will Ely is assistant surgeon in 108 NY., Ira Clark in the 140th, and Willie Orr 2nd Lieut. in the 113th, adding verily the γψιλον chapter of ψγ is not made up of cowards.

Wednesday, August 27:—the great scare! My letter to N. will best tell the story—all excepting that about the Band which made a precipitate retreat on Washington and were never heard of afterwards. The leader could not wait, even for his wife, but left word for her to come on after him. He was going to Washington. But the letters: All is excitement in camp. This afternoon the long roll sounded and we have been ready for action ever since. At dress-parade this afternoon we were told that the enemy had succeeded in getting in behind Gen. Pope and was close upon us. We are ordered in the rifle pits in front of the fort tonight and warned to receive the greybacks as best we can, should they make their appearance. This afternoon on the parade ground our review was stopped and we were drilled for a long time on loading and firing and the bayonet exercise. For all the afternoon McClellan's men have been hurrying out of Alexandria in all directions to meet the rebels. Our Major says that they have captured all our artillery in the fort; and that infantry fighting is now our only resource. I hardly think it can be possible that we can be in such danger, yet of course I am ready for anything that may come up. But one feeble Brigade is in advance of us, yet the fort is behind us. Of course I know nothing of what is before us. We may be having a grand scare, and we may be in real danger. Time will prove all. Oh the scare! Oh the ridiculous camp rumors! Oh the gas of our Major—

Thursday, August 28: The camp is filled with all kinds of rumors today, of great disaster to Gen. Pope and of important movements all around us. The truth is we are in perfect ignorance of everything that is going on even within a few miles of us, and cannot believe anything we hear. Still one knows from the movements of troops, etc, that something of great moment is on foot. I have seen lots of Union refugees hurrying by toward Washington today, driven from their homes by the advancing foe.

There has been all day long one continuous line of baggage wagons coming in and another of soldiers going out on the Alexandria pike. There seems to be no end either of men or of baggage trains.

The Potomac presents an animated scene, too. Large numbers of transports loaded with troops came up the river this morning, the deck of one steamer bursting with field artillery, and two great black gun boats have taken their position just before us. Large numbers of boats have come down from Washington, too, all bringing troops. I went over to the camp of the 27th today and saw Charlie Pacvek. He told me all about the boys I knew, and about poor Webster especially. Ed Gould is sick in a house not far distant. We have had no less than three orders to march today, and in as many directions. I made a visit to Fort Lyon yesterday. It is one of the largest forts in this vicinity, and is yet unfinished. It has only thirty guns mounted, when it should have a hundred more.

How the troops are passing down from Washington today. I hear a train every few minutes, and they have been coming in boats and every other way. But the Manassas Gap R.R., which was so busy a day or two ago is unused now. The Rebs have captured the trains and torn up the track.

Friday, August 29: Fort Lyon to Fort Craig

We are now where we first encamped, a little above Washington and I know not how far distant from the river. We had a tough march for me. I was never so nearly used up as when we at last arrived here, but I was sick when we started. We did not march more than ten miles I guess.

Saturday, August 30th: We are near enough to Bull Run to hear distinctly the cannonading which has been going on all the morning. It cannot be many miles from us to where they are fighting. How briskly they are fighting! It is almost one continuous roar of artillery. I cannot realize that they are having a battle so near me that I can hear it. I have just been told that we may be ordered forward at noon, and then perhaps I may see one. Yet there is small chance when McClellan's and Pope's men are all ahead of us.

Sunday, August 31st: We have been Brigaded with the 13 N.Y., 35th Mass., and the 124 Penn. Col. Van Valkenburgh commands the Brigade of (53d) Whipples Div. Brigade.

Monday, September 1st: From Fort Craig to Fort Albany.

Moved camp today and are once more at our old camp ground.

Extracts: Your letter was only half read when the longroll sounded (some of Smith foolishness) and we were shortly out in line of Battle and posted on both sides of the road leading to Centerville. It was a scene, that road, and all the others leading toward Bull Run, long trains of wagons miles in length driving into Washington, immense droves of cattle hurried along, families moving in behind the line of forts for safety. All the houses in our forts were ordered to be cleared today, and the troops from the various camps taking position at various points.

It is a beautiful evening out. Our men who have been digging rifle pits all day were ordered out about a half hour ago to keep at it all night. I have just been out listening. I could hear the tumult in the roads in all directions. The drums beating, forts behind us, the bugle calls from the camp of the Potomac Army which has fallen back near us, the works of men in the trenches, etc.

Busy times in camp. Battalion, Company, and Squad. Occasional visits upon "old soldier" friends in other regiments. Writing much to my friends at home, and enjoying beautiful southern evenings, the fine views of the river and the capital in front. All this filled these days of my young soldier's life. My troubles broken out at different times and in various ways. But I was all the time getting the better of them, was becoming less and less unpopular as "Orderly." The trial was made to depose me. A petition was gotten up for a new selection of non-commissioned officers in the company but the trial came to grief as the powers were on my side. There was a kind of belief that when real campaigning came, I would play, so the matter was perhaps left by common consent for time to settle. One week passed.

3

The Maryland Campaign

Saturday, September 6th: Fort Albany via Georgetown to Tennallytown.

Moonlight and romance. It was late in the morn when we broke camp and started off in high march order.

Marching orders, bound we knew not whither, but rumors said up the Potomac. A fine moonlit evening and good roads made the marching not unpleasant. A woman belonging to a man in Co. D accompanied us marching along in the march with her feller. Going by the Arlington house we passed the Pennsylvania bucktails, a remnant weak and small, by forts whose garrisons thought we were the whole Brigade, across the Aqueduct Bridge at Georgetown, through that University town, and out to Tennallytown where we arrived at about eleven, and were put to bed in a big field.

Sunday, September 7th: Tennallytown to Rockville Md.

We had lain about an hour when we were rousted out again, (we tho't there was another scare) and marched to Rockville reaching there about ten A.M. We encamped in a beautiful grove, The Montgomery Co. Fair Grounds and awaited further orders, taking what rest we could in the meantime. Before long the 108th Rochester regiment marched in and rested near us. I went over to see who I could see and found my classmate Will Ely, Sam Porter, Ed Pierce, etc.

Monday, September 8: This morning we were routed out of our fine camp and marched out here a couple of miles or so, to the Stone House near Rockville when McClellan had arrived in town and wanted our comfortable place for his H'd Quarters. We are now a part of his Army in Gordon's Brigade of Williams' Division of Banks' Corps. Our provisional Brigade

Maj. Gen. Ambrose E. Burnside, Commanding Army of the Potomac (Brady's National Portrait Gallery).

organization was broken up, and the 107th N.Y. and 13 N.J., two new regiments, are joined to the old 3rd Brigade consisting of the 2d Mass. 3rd Wis, and 27th Ind. of the 1st Div. of Mansfield's Corp, afterward known as the 12th A.C. [Army Corps]. The 108th was put under Gen. Sumner's command and thus became permanently a part of the 2nd Corp. Since beginning this I saw a fellow from the 33rd N.Y. and at once started off to about a mile to see Ed Armstrong. Found him looking well and hearty and had a real good visit with him. Also with Jim McNair, a Capt. in that regiment. While I was there marching orders came and I left them, (Slocum's Division was next to them. These hills are covered for miles with the concentrated armies of McClellan, Pope, Banks, and Burnside.) and found my way to the 27th N.Y. First I found Charlie Reekok, and then Ed Gould. While I was visiting with them the 108th came along and we captured Will Ely. Ed, Will, and I had a $\psi\gamma$ meeting. Franklin's Division marched by just then and McNair stopped a moment. Richardson tarried a while too, and we had a little Rochester University Alumni meeting. Ed Gould says I have a terrible trial before me if I try to live a Christian life in the army. He never knew but one man who did it, and that was Lt. Webster. He told me all about Webster, who was certainly one of the noblest souls that ever lived. I wish I could be like

Gen Nathaniel P. Banks Jr. (Charles D. Fredricks & Co.).

him. Could I live the life he lived I would be almost willing to meet the same fate.

Tuesday, September 9th: Rockville to Middlebrook, Md.

After waiting for orders nearly all day, we were at last jerked out and marched to double quick time, almost until dark. We bivouacked in line of battle across a gully, somewhere near Middlebrook. We marched most of the time in fields and woods, as the roads were filled with artillery and ambulances, But it was a splendid night. A hundred thousand men are marching southward in twelve columns, these are the second from the Potomac, and from every hill top, and stealing through every valley could be seen the seemingly endless columns of troops.

Wednesday, September 10th: Camped on the hill side.

We have been marching all day long, and have now halted for the night. I am tired and hungry, and must cook what little food is left for supper. We drew only a day's rations when we left Rockville, and have used them nearly all up. Many around me have just eaten their last hard crackers. I have four crackers left, a little coffee, and a spoonful of sugar. It is dark, but the many camp fires light up these woods, and it is a busy scene. The *Baltimore Clipper* has just appeared in camp and the boys are reading them aloud to the troops around the camp fires. One is reading at my elbow and I am both listening and writing. The papers tell us that the

Anxious for news when a paper arrives. From *Harper's Weekly*, July 20, 1861.

Rebels are in force within a few miles of us, 150,000 strong. Well, we shall soon see I guess.

Thursday, September 11th: Damascus, Md.

We have been marching again today, northward still, but not very far. After all our marching we have come about fifty or sixty miles. Received a mail once more. Was about sick on the march but wouldn't give up, so I came in all right at night

Friday, September 12: Gainsville, Md.

Are getting nearer to the Rebels at any rate. Have heard firing all day, but it is distant and seems to recede.

Saturday, September 13th: Monocucy River & Frederick, Md.

After marching fifteen or twenty miles to get five, we have at last arrived at this Secesh* town. But the Rebels are gone, of course, tho' our men under Burnside are pressing them closely. Last night the Rebels were in considerable force here. Now we can only hear the guns and see the smoke where our men are hurrying up their rear guard. We reached here about noon and are now resting. An immense number of men in the field around Frederick. The Rebels are in hearing distance now, but they won't be very long. We have had some interesting talks with the citizens since we came here. They have great stories to tell about the Rebels.

Sunday, September 14: Sunday was an eventful day. We were roused up early, three day rations distributed, ammunition inspected, and told to prepare for a long march. Just as we were coming into Frederick city the bells were ringing for church, the first that I had heard since I left home. (I lost my ring this morning, but it was found in the straw.) I have called the town Secesh, but it is not entirely so. A great number of American flags met our view on every street. And indeed I forgave the town all its secession, when I remember the splendid half slices of bread and butter, real bread and butter, which my Captain found somewhere. Our march through Frederick was a triumphal progress, but there was work ahead.

Frederick and South Mountain, Md:

A long and weary march over the hills, from Frederick, brought us into the Middletown valley, by far the most beautiful valley I ever saw, and everything throughout its length and breadth looked so peaceful and quiet, that one could not think of war in such a place. And yet long lines of troops filing across it as far as the eye could reach, and for miles along the mountain side beyond it. Our men were shelling the Rebels out of the woods. This was the Battle of South Mountain. The people were out in their yards looking at the fight. The shells looked finely when they burst. Especially after dark. We had a wearisome march that night, away up the

---

*Secesh: a slang reference for "Secessionist" in common usage at the time.

Middletown, Maryland, *sketch by A. R. Waud, Harper's Weekly*, October 25, 1862.

valley, to the extreme right, and then back again to reinforce Burnside on the extreme left. After marching all day it came tough to keep at it until after midnight. More than half of the regiment fell out. When our company stacked arms we had but about 8 stacks. We must have made over thirty miles.

Monday, September 15th: Boonsboro, Md.

We did not stop until nearly noon. Just as we were in line Gen. Burnside and staff rode by us, and of course received three hearty cheers, which he gracefully acknowledged. We were in the battlefield of the day before. The dead and wounded were still lying there in good numbers. Our march all day was full on the back of the fleeing Rebels, though so far in the rear that we had no fighting to do. All along the way we saw broken litters, cast away clothes, greasy and gray Rebel guns piled in stacks, and now and then Rebels themselves either lain decently by the roadside, or left seemingly where they fell. Prisoners, lots of them, were huddled together in barnyards or wherever they could be kept. Just before reaching Boonsboro, Gen McClellan and staff passed us. As he passed within two or three feet of me, I had a good chance to look at him. A perfect wave of cheers followed him

Boonsboro, Maryland. South Mountain in the background, *sketch by A. R. Waud, Harper's Weekly*, October 25, 1862.

along the whole line. He uncovered his head in acknowledgment of every cheer. I hope you may never be shocked by the sight of a Rebel soldier, especially a dead one. Never thought that so much dirt, grease, rags, and vermin could be gathered together on one man, as these prisoners carried. But when they have been slain in Battle, clothes have been torn off, their mangled and distorted bodies covered with soot, powder and blood, I cannot describe the sight.

Tuesday, September 16th: In the field near Weavers, Md.

This morning we were started out of our camp on the double quick with the promise that we should see the Rebs in a few hours at the most. The cannonading sounded very near, the signal flags were "talking" on every hill top and we believed what they told us. But we were merely marched into this field, took our place in the Brigade line, loaded our guns and then told to "rest" which we had been doing all day. An army of troops is around us, waiting like us to be ordered over the hills in front of us, to the battle which is now going on. Among them is Gorman's Brigade, and Patrick's also, in which is the 23d N.Y., many of them have been over to see us. Late in the evening we were marched around to the extreme right, crossed the Antietam Creek and took position in the reserve line. We were very quiet about it all, and in the darkness and silence lay down to sleep.

Wednesday, September 17: Antietam.

(The following hurried note written home was printed in the *Hornellsville Tribune* to my great annoyance and disgust.) "We were in the battle and it was a severe one too, the 107th. laid five hours under fire, between two batteries, we lay flat on our faces, and the bullets and shells passed over

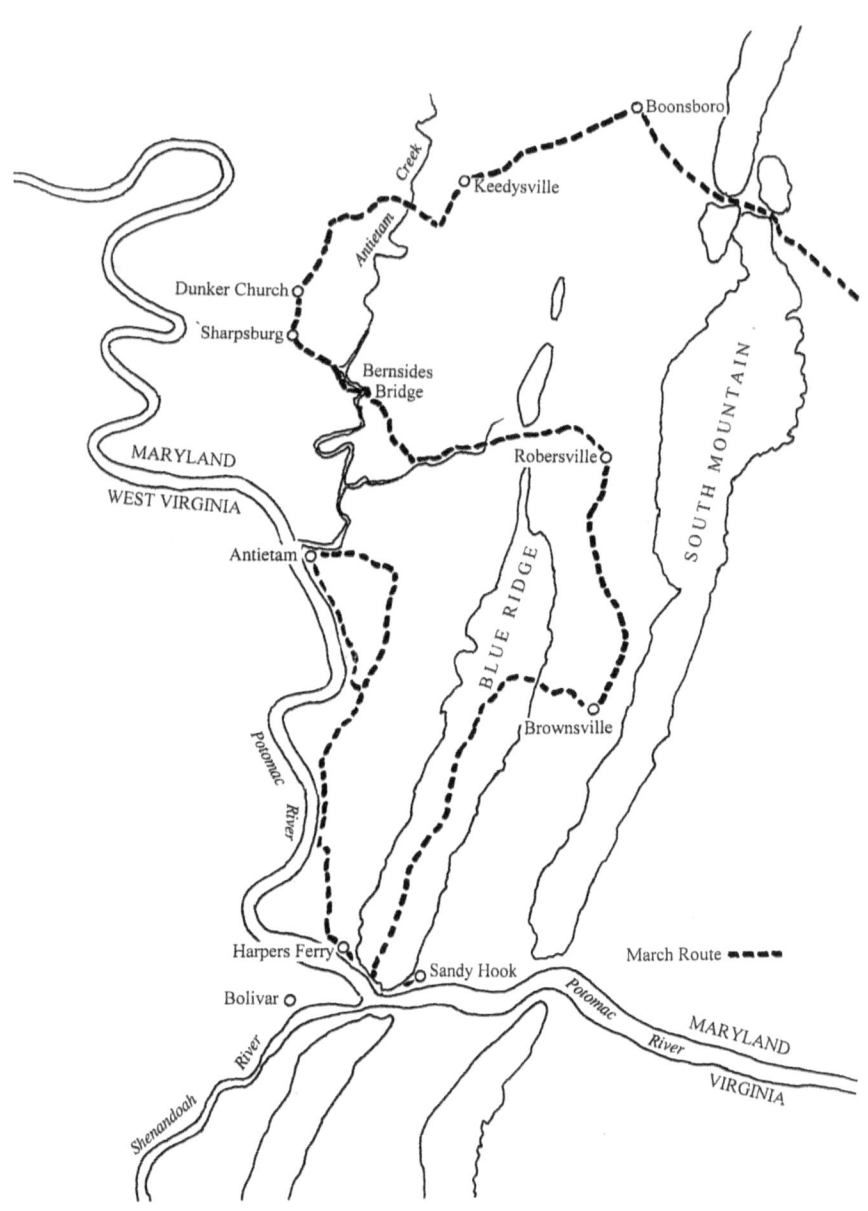

Harper's Ferry–Antietam–Sharpsburg–Boonsboro

us and on us in a perfect shower. We were very lucky however, not more than sixty being killed and wounded out of the whole regiment. One Captain was mortally wounded. Only three were wounded in Co. K though for a time we thought that Will Lamphere was killed. God has graciously spared my life through one severe engagement. We are drawn up in line of battle,

3. The Maryland Campaign

Brig. Gen. W. A. Gorman

waiting to go into the fight again this morning. We may not be as lucky again today. If I should fall, as I may, I have but one request to make, but one prayer, that we may all meet in Heaven. Could you see the dying and the dead and wounded strewn around us here, you would soon feel to pray for the soldiers who have gone forth to fight for their country. I want you all to pray for me. Our General says that we have done nobly. But we are called to go — Good bye — Russell."

Another account of the terrible battle near Sharpsburg, in which we were engaged, I will not attempt to give any description. Such a battle is one of those things which must be seen to be appreciated. The 107th, though in the very thickest of the fight was very lucky indeed losing only about sixty in killed

The Battle of Antietam, *sketch by A. R. Waud, Harper's Weekly*, October 11, 1862.

After the battle of Antietam, *sketches by A. R. Waud, Harper's Weekly,* October 11, 1862.

and wounded. Gen. Gordon complimented us highly, and from other regiments, as we went out of action we heard the remark, "You're a bully regiment and a lucky one." The 107th supported Battery "M" of the 1st N.Y. Artillery, and (behind us) Battery of 4th U.S. Artillery, exactly opposite the white school house of Dunker Church, where the battle raged so severely. How that house was riddled by shot and shell! And how the dead men were piled up around it when we marched by, a day and a half after the battle! It is a wonder that so few of us were killed. Each of us ought to give thanks to God for so signally preserving us. The Col. of the 46th Penn rode up to our Col. after the action and said he was glad to see him alive. "You saved Coleman's Battery and that hill today," he said. "When you rallied to defend that Battery as the Rebels were charging on it, my men were running like sheep." He said he didn't expect to see us come out alive. Our whole Brigade consisting of Mass 2nd, Wis 3rd, N.J. 13th, Ind 27 and N.Y.107th was in the fight and suffered more or less heavily. I have heard unfavorable remarks of the 108th from several sources. The accompanying account is from the New York Times.—I have not attempted to give any account of the battles except as I gave them in my letters at the time. The annexed account is from the N. Y. Tribune, Extra, Sept. 19th.—But I am getting into the old soldier's style of praising my own regiment. We have gained a good name I am sure. And I am free to confess if we have done well. I don't want to do any better. I don't want to go into another such battle, and yet we are ready to go anywhere we are ordered.

Thursday, September 18th: On the Battle Field.

It is now nearly two o'clock and the Battle has not been renewed yet. They have all day been taking care of the dead and wounded. But we cannot be still much longer. I write in great haste. One of the 23rd has just come and told us that Olin Brunell was killed yesterday. Gen. Mansfield who died this morning commanded our Corp.—*The Times* Editor thus sums up the battle and what followed.

We were not aware of the salutary reflections of the Rebels, and thus were in hourly expectation of a renewal of the fight. But the day wore away, and night came with no battle. It was a day of ghastly and horrible sights, the burying of the dead and bringing in of the wounded.

Friday, September 19th: Sharpsburg, Robersville, and Brownsville, Md.

Brig. Gen. George H. Gordon Commanding, 3rd Brig., 1st Div., 12th A.C. (Charles D. Fredricks & Co.).

Brig. Gen. Joseph K. F. Mansfield

Ordered to go to Harpers Ferry. We marched through the historical cornfield, dead men and horses everywhere, and struck the Sharpsburg road by the Dunker church, all around which the dead were lying in heaps. And on to the village of Sharpsburg, full of shell holes and wounded soldiers and marching troops. Took the river road and crossed the Antietam creek at Burnsides Bridge. More heaps of dead and more scenes of terrible fighting. Just after we crossed the bridge we met the 12th N.Y., which I had not seen since they left Elmira, by farm houses from which yellow flags fluttered and barns, which were also used as hospitals, and then to the road to Rossville. It was after dark when we passed through this loyal little town, but we had a glowing welcome from the people. Then a tiresome, tiresome, march I know not how many miles further, until we were told to halt and make ourselves as comfortable as possible right where we were.

Tumbled over the fence into a field and went to sleep. In the morning we found we were in the little burg of Brownsville.

Saturday, September 20th: Maryland Heights and Pleasant Valley, Md.

After the battle near Sharpsburg, Williams Division was ordered to Harpers Ferry to drive away the Rebels and hold this place. As we supposed that they held the Maryland Hills which overlook it, we had to climb the mountains from Brownsville, and advance along the ridge. Such a climb, and such a march I never want to take again. I never saw such rocks and ledges, and passes and defiles, as we had to climb up and over and through. But when we reached the heights we found that the enemy had left, and such tired men were very willing to be deprived of the fight they had come after. We were up on the mountain until evening, when we marched down into Harpers Ferry. The view from the hills was magnificent, the most extended by far that I ever saw. We could see for miles and miles up and down the Potomac Valley, and up that of the beautiful Shenandoah, where the great Rebel army was marching back. Could see fighting which was going on up at Shenandoah, etc, etc.

Brig. Gen. Alpheus S. Williams Commanding, 1st Div. 12th A.C. (Brady's National Photographic Portrait Galleries).

Sugar Loaf Mountain in Maryland was in plain view. As we marched along the mountain top, we passed over the recent battle ground, the trees were greatly cut, and scraped, and the log breast works hastily thrown up showed signs of desperate fighting. There were many graves of Carolinians and others, but alas, the Union Soldiers who had fallen afterwards were unburied. Swarms of buzzards were holding riot over their remains. Our men buried as many such as they could find.

Sunday, September 21st: Pleasant Valley, Md.

A Sabbath of quiet! Never was it so acceptable. Our men were all tired out. There is scarce a man in the regiment, who if he were at home, would not think himself ill, and wish to rest awhile. For three weeks we have not had a full day's rest. I hope they will let us remain here, at least, until tomorrow. In addition to our being tired out, we got out of both water and food while on the mountains yesterday, and some really suffered. A single hard cracker was a prize. I came down the mountain with only a lemon and a small apple in my haversack. It was funny to hear the boys tell what they dreamed of while resting on the mountain, of seeing rations distributed, of "finding a pie" etc. How anxiously we watched our supply train coming down the valley, and eagerly the boys snatched their rations when they did come, 24 crackers, a slice of bacon, tea, cupfull of ground coffee, and as much sugar, "three days rations."

Monday, September 22nd: Sandy Hook to Md. Heights, Md. From a letter of the 28th: Since I wrote you last we have once more changed our position. We were then in the valley east of the Maryland Heights. Last Monday we marched through Sandy Hook, by Harpers Ferry to this place, about four miles. We are now encamped on the mountainside, on the western slope of the Maryland Heights. Harpers Ferry, with the encampment of Sumners Corp. on the Bolivian Heights back of it, is below and across the river from us. The place presented a sad scene of desolation as we passed by it. The bridges destroyed and a great part of the village burned. We expected to have to wade the river there, as we saw many troops doing. But we turned up on this mountain, our Brigade, and I guess our whole Division. Since then a pontoon has been laid across the river by the 50th engineers. One of their Orderly Lue Taylor made me a visit the other day.

Friday, September 26:

(This is miserable paper, but the best I can get of our Sutler who is our only source) and so charges just what he pleases. Soldiers have many things to dampen their enthusiasm, sometimes to make them even desperate. They are fleeced by everybody from paymaster to Sutler. The Quartermaster and Medical Department are as bad as the rest. How much of the choice wine and liquors furnished by the government, or of the fillets etc. sent to hospitals by friends at home ever reaches the common soldiers do you think?

Top: Harper's Ferry and Maryland Heights, *photograph by Brady, Harper's Weekly*, October 4, 1862. *Bottom:* Sandy Hook. *Harper's Weekly*, August 10, 1861.

3. The Maryland Campaign

Washing clothes in the river. *Harper's Weekly*, July 20 1861.

I wish I could tell you how little! Quartermasters Department after the same fashion. Regimental baggage has been cut down to the lowest notch, five wagons to a regiment, two of which are kept for the Staff and the Doctors and the other three come along when the lazy teamsters get ready to bring them. We lost our overcoats, blankets, etc. in the last battle, had to throw them away when we went into the fight and ever since we have had to be on the ground with nothing to cover us, and the nights intensely cold. I was thinking but a night or two ago I would give anything if I could lie down on your front porch where the ivy leaves would shield me. Nearly all the regiment are sick, some dangerously so. Our Captain is very unwell, and the majority of our company are unfit for duty, and it is all from exposure which I believe to have been unnecessary. I wonder that my health is so good, and I am not perfectly well. But tents have come for the officers today and perhaps the men will be provided for ere long. Our Commission department is very good, much better than in most of the regiments near us. Our only trouble is a want of dishes in which to cook our food. We have to depend mostly on our little tin cups. But I will stop or you will think I am dissatisfied. Such is not the case. I had heard of all these little discomforts before I enlisted, and am not disappointed that they have come. But some of the boys are terribly homesick and disgusted.

Sunday, September 28: Date of letter to Carrie

After waiting over a week in total ignorance of the outside world, our mail was received last night, and the whole regiment was made glad by the reception of the long delayed news from home. I am quite well at present and will of course do my best to keep so. Went yesterday down to the Potomac, about a mile distant, and had a good wash. Changed my clothes for the first time since I left Virginia. All through our Maryland campaign we had had neither the time or the clothes for such a change. Sure I had taken off my shirt, and washed it and waited till it would dry, to put it on again. But I don't like such work.

Before yesterday I had had off my shoes but once, and my pants not at all, since we left Fort Albany, Sep. 6th. You can imagine what kind of life we have led. Yesterday I was in a house, and you cannot think how strange it seemed to sit down in a regular chair once more and write on a table. I find that my enlistment was a very remarkable event, judging from the astonishment it caused in many of my friends. What is there about me I wonder that makes it so extraordinary that I should enlist? Some tell me I could have done better. Perhaps, but I am satisfied with my place. Many fear that I cannot endure it. Well, so I feared. But I have done much better than I expected. Of course, I have not been well all the time. But I have never yet been a day off duty, which hardly another man in the company can say, and I stand it better than nine tenths of the men, or officers, too.

Luin Thacher writes: "I think you might have done better than you have, but patriotism is more fully shown and displayed by those in the ranks than by those who wear shoulder straps. You will find some rough times, and some as happy and joyous days as you ever experienced. If you only have a good set of boys and a good leader all will be well. The position of Orderly Sergeant is not an enviable one. Still you will have no difficulty."

Younger writes: "They said you were not in the army and had no intention of going there. All right if you can stay at home. For one I am the happiest man in Christendom. For more than a year I mourned my inability and it chafed my every day more sorely, and every night with deeper anguish, the thought that I could not aid our nation in her peril. And constantly the wish grew stronger and the prayer more earnest that I might have strength again to fight until I merely asked that I might do a soldiers duty and meet a soldiers fate. My prayer is answered, and I am again a soldier. The broad earth is my couch. The blue sky my counterpane, my right hand my pillow, and my tired sword my couch companion."

Crandall writes: "Russell you perfectly surprised me when you enlisted. It makes me ashamed to stay at home, and think of you such a frail little fellow as you taking up a musket. I never thought you had any fight in you, although it was fairly proven that you could endure long marches in numerous instances."

Geo. Gardner writes: "Judge of my surprise when I learned a few weeks ago, that you were in the army, a soldier fighting in the field. Exposed to every danger and enduring every hardship. etc, etc."

Bob Turner writes: "Is your health good, and do you think you will be able to endure the hardships incident to camp life? I hope for the best for you, but you are pretty slender for that kind of business."

Younger writes: (in another letter) "and so you are in the army, Good for you! I don't know as I told you, but when I was told at Mrs. M...o* that you were not, I said rather bluntly, I don't believe it and I did not. You showed, permit me to say, a great amount of heroism in going in actually a private at this stage of the war. I have no fear but you will rise if allowed a fair chance and continued good health. etc."

Louise Langworthy writes: "foreboding, I think, my constitution not strong enough for a soldiers life. etc."

Tuesday, September 30th: Our company went out on picket duty today, excepting the sick, those on guard, the Captain who is very sick, the 2nd Lieut. who is officer of the day, and the Orderly who was kept at home to make out the monthly reports.

Of news I have none whatever to give. We are still encamped as when I last wrote, and see no indications of a speedy removal. A good part of our regiment is out every day, some on picket duty, and most on "fatigue," chopping up on the mountain, where they are building a fort I believe. (the place thus cleared was known as Slocum's Farm) A great many, an unusual number of our men are sick. We had so many hardships, exposures and privations of food and sleep during our Maryland Campaign that it has nearly used up our regiment. Our Surgeon complains bitterly of the hard treatment. It is not a wonder that I went through it all so well!

Wednesday, October 1:

Will I ever get this letter finished? I was busy yesterday, and have been so busy this morning that I have had no chance to think even. In addition to all my cares, I have to take care of a friend who lies in our tent very, very ill. It is Almen W. Burrill. I fear that he cannot live; and here he lies, his only bed, a blanket with a little straw beneath it. We do the best we can for him, but what can we do here? The hot sun, when it once gets up, is pouring down upon the tent, so that I cannot stay in here, and he is burning up with fever within. And his case is but one case of which there are very many in the regiment. Our men are sick in great numbers, and some are dying already. This hillside is the most unhealthy place to be found in all this section of the country "anywhere," said our surgeon yesterday. "Let us go to any place but this unless it be up onto the mountain where the dead bodies are."

Thursday, October 2nd: A dense fog, with a cold chill air, envelops the mountain this evening and I am reminded of the cool days of autumn at home when the last of the summer's fruitage is gathered in and we prepare once more for the coming of winter. Do you remember how pleasant the

---

*All ellipses are orginal to Tuttle's manuscript.

first fires of the season are, when we gather round them some chill evening or morning? The thought of just such a scene makes me almost wish this morning that I could be home for just a few minutes. But soon the mists will roll away up the mountainside and the sun will come out, burning and prostrating with a dry fever heat. I had hardly begun to write, when I saw a funeral procession passing by, so I followed it, the first funeral held in our regiment. The services were most impressive. Poor fellow.

"By stranger hands his dying eyes were closed. By stranger hands his decent limbs composed."

And he sleeps his last sleep of earth on this bleak hillside, so far away from his home and friends. I looked with the most perfect unconcern on the heaps of dead and dying I saw at Antietam, but I could not look at his white face as he laid in the rough box made for his coffin without being deeply moved. (Another interruption.)

When I had written thus far orders came to get our company in line and prepare for review at a moments notice. "The President is coming." Now we knew what that firing meant down at the Ferry this morning. In due time the president came, accompanied by quite a crowd of celebrities, greater and lesser. He carefully reviewed the different regiments of our Brigade. The 107th did not make a very big show as most of the men are up on the mountain chopping. How proudly our color bearer displayed our state Banner, the one through which a shell burst at Antietam. As the president turned back down the mountain road some choppers from the heights above raised a glorious cheer for him, which he acknowledged by waving his hat at them.

You read then of the repulses of the rebels when they attempted to take Cothrans Battery, what splendid charges they made! They came on in most perfect lines, the admiration of all who saw them, but they could not stand the terrible fire that met them. You should have seen the Rebel dead, as they lay just there after the Battle. They formed a line so straight as that of any Dress Parade. Few regiments would have remained on line as unwaveringly, and fallen in their places as did those men. They were North Carolinians I am told.

Sunday, October 5: The fever keeps on unabated. From ninety to a hundred cases are reported in hospital each day, from our regiment. Today Martin Sage of our company, the first man that we have lost, was buried. He died yesterday. The little regiment graveyard behind Mr. Unselds garden is filling up fast. I witnessed the burial of Sage, and then almost down sick myself, went over to Mr. Unselds and by the help of Uncle Allen engaged permission to sleep in their loft until I felt better. I shared Uncle Allen's bed, he being laid up with the fever. Lieut. Col. Diven was sick in the room downstairs and his wife with him, to take care of him.

Tuesday, October 7th: I am a little unwell. My turn seems to have come at last, and like the rest I must have my little run of camp fever and camp dysentery before I can hope to become acclimated. These two diseases are a most diabolical compound I assure you, when they come together. There is a great deal of sickness in camp, and those poor fellows who have no shelter, have it very hard. I betake myself to a home nearby where I have good accommodations.

Thursday, October 9th: For I was and am sick. Fever. Everybody in camp, almost, is having it, and I couldn't be an exception. Yet I am in hopes that we shall be able to break it up before it runs much longer. When one gets the fever nothing tastes good, nothing smells good, or looks good. I am just sick and disgusted with everything I see. Tea and toast form my only sustenance, and such tea as is furnished by our commission, I am getting so that I cannot eat that even. The last of duty I had was to attend the funeral of a comrade named Sage. I had to fall out of the procession and lie down by a tree while they were burying him.

The *World*'s correspondent, a college chap is writing by my side. His name is Hammond, a ΣΦ from the University of Vermont, Burlington.

Sunday, October 12th: Tomorrow morning Capt. Sill starts for the North, on a leave of absence for twenty days. I will send you a letter by him.

Of course you will want to know about my health. Much better I am grateful to be able to say. Uncle Sam has kept me waiting no short time for my pay, but I have got something out of him in the way of medicines opium, quinine, blue pill, and I don't know what all. Well, I have been real sick, and even now they haven't got the yellow out of my eyes and skin. But I am doing well, am excused from duty, and away from camp entirely, at a farmhouse where Uncle Allen staid when he was sick. Col. and Mrs. Diven are stopping here also. He has been sick too. You may thank her indeed for the interest she has taken in me, made me tea and crust, coffee, porridge, mustard plasters, etc, and has been very kind indeed.

So the time has passed. I will not deny that I have been very lonely, and I have thought of home and friends very often. Yet I have not been homesick. That is I have had no desire to go home. Think I would show my face at home now, when I have been away but two months? Guess not! But what pleases me most, for which I have cause for true gratitude is the prospect of returning health. I hope to be well very soon. But I find that I am weak yet, much more so than when the fever was on me, and I cannot write much at a time.

Monday, October 13th: Capt. Sill went home on leave, and Col. Van Valkenburgh returned to civil life.

A cold raw day, dark too, with the over head and the mists around us. It has seemed all the afternoon like twilight in the midst of a November rain and I am sitting up in my garret quarters all alone, as I have been for hours, now reading a little, now writing a little and resting a great deal. I am not lonesome for my thoughts and my memories keep me good company, and more than that I am so elated with the prospect of being well once more that the very acts of standing up straight and walking like somebody make me feel cheerful and joyful. I bless God for returning health, the choicest boon to mortals given, whose value I learn now more than ever having been deprived of it for a season. At home and among friends sickness might not be such a discomfort. But here when health is lost, all seems lost, and I no longer wonder at the perfect apathy with which the sick soldiers view the approach of death. And he is among us now, reaping the sick harvest with his dread and ghastly hand. Two of our men died last night and nine more the surgeon says are now at the very point of death.

It is raining, and I am led back through a world of memories by the music of the rain upon the roof. But I wish you could see the roof that is over me now, shingles of oak, two or three feet long and lapping at both the sides and ends. May have been in their place through more than one generation, and on the outside look worn-out and very old. But within though a little weather stained they seem good enough for a century yet. What a queer old house this is. Southern in all its features, white washed inside and out, and with verandahs all around it, And the folks who live here, they are farmers of the old camp. The old lady is very kind to me. I am the only enlisted man who has been allowed to remain here. But she took a liking to me, and being a good soul her motherly heart overflowed with pity when she saw how sick I was. The Capt. had been sick here, and when he went away he asked that I might take his place. The old man demurred, didn't want fever in the house, but the old lady said, "Yes, leave him. Will take care of him. I like that boy, he has had a good mother to bring him up. I know." So I found my place of refuge here. Do you think I'll ever forget that old lady?

Today the Capt. started home on a leave of absence. He goes to my home, my father and mother and sister. Did I wish to go with him? Honestly, no. But I sent lots of love to the dear ones there and make it for him a pleasant visit and a safe return. With our Captain went also our Col., the latter for good. He has been re-nominated for Congress and so resigned. We are all very sorry to lose him as he is a splendid officer.

Thursday, October 14: I am still better today almost well in fact, and hope to be able to return to duty very soon. Have I not cause to be thankful? Mrs. Unseld seems to be well acquainted with the 8 NY Cavalry. Calls them "Col. Babbit's men." She told me a long story about a difficulty she had with Capt. Moor.

Wednesday, October 15th: I am glad to say that I have entirely recovered my health, and when I get a little stronger will return to duty once more. That will be in a day or two I suppose. I cannot tell you how good I feel to be well again. Everything is bright and pleasant to me now.

You need have no fears for our comfort now. We now have all our property with us. Blankets, tents etc. and are living quite comfortable. Some are even putting up little log huts, as if we were going into winter quarters here.

A great many people from the North and some ladies are now visiting our camp. A soldier in the 125 Penn. took breakfast with us at the house the other day in company with his sister who had come to see him. I happened to be also at the table when they came and we became very well acquainted of course. Soldiers never wait to be introduced. He was the perfect counterpart of Elder Sawyer's son who we saw at Parma. And she was the sweetest, loveliest, interesting damsel I ever met.

Thursday, October 16: Good bye to farmers house, and returned to life in camp but not to duty yet.

Friday, October 17th: Visit to Harpers Ferry. I was detailed with six men to go over to Harpers Ferry and bury one of our Captains who had died in the hospital there. His name was Henry Brewer from Wheeler. We had to get some boards and make a box for a coffin, carry it over there two miles, by hand, dig a grave when we got there, and hold a funeral in whatever style we pleased. No mourner was present, save only the brother of the poor fellow who had gone. We buried him as tenderly as we could, quite decently in comparison with the treatment that others received. I could not see him buried without any ceremony at all, and so I made a brief prayer at the grave ere we filled it up. We buried him on the high bluff overlooking the Shenandoah. While on such an errand we had but little chance to see the town. We had a good long look at the Engine House which John Brown has made historical, as we had to wait sometime just in front of it for the wagon train to pass. Then to look at the ruins that encircle the town. One is astonished at their extent. It seems almost beyond estimate, the amount of property that has been destroyed there. I wonder that there was anything left of the place. All transit across the river is still by the pontoon bridge built by Stuart's Engineers. The railroad bridge is being rebuilt and a temporary trestle has been finished. But it will be a long time before the permanent structure is done. The iron bridge which the Rebels destroyed must have been a splendid one.— It was quite dark when we had finished our work at the grave, and then we had no little trouble in getting back to camp. Obliged to get a pass to cross the pontoon and then to hunt up a sergeant who could read it, our journey to camp was a series of challenges by sentries. In each case we were conducted to the officer in charge, back with him to whom was told our story, and who then would let us go on. Even in the day time it is very hard to get from our camp to the Ferry I presumed here with the pass I got at Harpers Ferry.

Saturday, October 18: Gladdened by a visit from Lieut. Prentiss of the 23rd and his father just from Hornellsville. They were on their way to the Regt. near Sharpsburg and accepted our hospitality for the night. They brought late news from Hornellsville, of the building there etc., and from the 141st of their fine location, easy times, and good condition, so unlike ours.

Sunday, October 19th: Carrie's Birthday.

I have not forgotten that this is my sister's birthday, and I have been wishing that I could send you a present, or at least celebrate the day in some way. I do celebrate it in this respect that today I report "to duty" in the camp. My strength as well as health is now fully recovered, and I think, and I expect soon to fall into the old routine of duty.

This is a most beautiful day very unlike the weather we have been having for the past two weeks. The air is mild and still, and now that the sun is up, the day is bright and pleasant. Somehow it is stiller than usual in camp today, and in this quiet tent I find it not so difficult as it commonly is to recognize that today is the Sabbath. Yet we have no regular services for our Chaplain is very sick in Washington, and his assistant, a soldier, who was once a minister is in our own hospital dangerously ill. We miss our Chaplain very much, not only in his ordinary duties, but especially when so many are sick and dying among us.

In the regiment and company all goes in about the same old track. More strict regulations are being enforced in relation to roll call and drills, and the commissioned officers have been ordered to procure Case's *Tactics*, just out of which they are to have a school of instruction. Our camp has been laid out anew, and we have had to change the position of our tents once more. Our two story bed made of stakes driven into the ground, had to be pulled up and our fireplace moved. Our fireplace is a square hole dug in the corner of the tent, and from which a covered trench leads out about two feet and opens into a barrel which is our chimney. Our stove draws quite well and is very useful these cold nights and mornings. Last night, when it was really quite cold and the wind blew almost a storm without, we gathered around our little fire place, suggesting the blazing hearth of some old farm house, and listened to Lieut. Prentiss recital of the campaign of the old 23rd. I believe if I am ever permitted to build a house for myself it will have an old fashioned big fireplace in it, But that is looking quite a ways ahead.

This is my sister's birthday. She is 17 today, though it hardly seems possible that she is that old. When I first went away to school she was but a little girl, and now she has become older than I am, I was going to say. It has been mild and spring like all day long and the day closed with a truly magnificent sunset. From our camp we can see over the Potomac and up the Shenandoah beyond Harpers Ferry and Bolivar, and for miles away into Virginia, a range of mountains higher than all others in sight, closing the view in the far distance. It added not a little to the scene to know that a hundred thousand Rebels are waiting for us this side of that mountain range beyond which the sun went down so grandly.

Friday, October 24: Carrie: The wind is blowing almost a hurricane tonight and our tents rock and swell as if they were going to blow away bodily. Today we had an inspection, most minute and careful, of our whole Brigade, — to which we were to bring out those who are perfectly well and able to march off into battle at a moments warning. Co. K took only 26 men. And tonight at dress parade a general order was read that no more clothing would be given out now than was actually necessary or that the men could carry with them for the impending movement.

T. (Thomas) K. Beecher has just paid our tent a visit of a minute or two. He has brought quite a mail from his regiment to ours. He says that his regiment has only been playing (at war) soldier so far, and we have a pretty hard time in comparison. One more of our company died last Tuesday. Like the other three he died of typhoid fever. His name was John W. Ryan of H'ville [Hornellsville] and his fathers name is Bullen.

Saturday, October 25: This morning we received orders to pack up everything, put up two days rations and be ready to march at ten o'clock. It came hard for the boys to leave their comfortable log huts, scarcely finished, but at ten o'clock we were ready with more luggage on our backs than we had ever carried before. Just then an order came, countermanding the marching orders until further notice came, so here we are, still in the same old place. Well, I feel more comfortable tonight in our warm close tent than I could by the road side or in some field, lying out in this driving storm. This was the time when Capt. Slocum and his Lieut's made themselves sick trying to eat up and drink up a boxfull of dainties just received from the north, and which they didn't want to leave behind.

Sunday, October 26: Our equivocal, or something worse, has come at last. It has been raining all day long, and we have been shivering over our little smoky fires, hardly venturing out when we are obliged to, to the various roll calls. We have but five or six a day to guard mounting, Sunday morning inspection, etc. They get us out often enough I assure you. I feel disgusted every time I hear the drumbeat, especially when it is now Reveille.

Wednesday, October 29: Was just making out muster rolls, a good weeks work when taken in addition to my regular duties, when one fine Wednesday evening we received orders to pack up and march immediately. Well we packed up, and we marched — marched from Maryland Heights way up the Potomac; then right about faced and marched down the Potomac (picking our way through the darkness and mud along the side of a road obstructed by the wagon trains which followed us!) to a point away below where we are now, and are encamped. It was about seven o'clock when we started and about two when we arrived. We were some tired when our march was ended, and somewhat enraged too, to think that so much of it had been unnecessary. We were quite cold too, as it was a very chilly night, But we tore a good farmers fence to pieces and laid out our sleeping accommodations on the damp ground, dispersed in great circles around our blazing fires. When we awoke in the morning we were covered with frost, our fires had long since gone out, and my feet, well they were cold! I just hopped around like a chicken with its head cut off.

Thursday, October 30th:

Again on the march we passed the Antietam iron works and continued about three miles, when the Brigade halted. After a while the 13th NJ, 27 Ind. and 2 Mass. went on to Sharpsburg, and we were sent back on the road we came, past the iron works again to the very place where we had encamped the night before! The boys swore a little harder than ever now. Found the 3rd Wis. here, where we should have been left in the morning as they were. We had marched four times by the iron works.

Saturday November 1st:

Lieut. Goodrich is out with a part of our company tonight on picket. As the Rebs are so very near we have to keep our lines strongly guarded, and closely watched, while those who remain in camp might be ready at any time to fall in to repel an attack. It is our particular duty to watch the Antietam Ford where Stewart's Cavalry once crossed.

We were mustered for pay yesterday, as we are every two months, but the coming of the paymaster is quite another thing, which we haven't seen yet. We expect the Capt. back tomorrow, or which day his time runs out. Those good things which that trunk contains have been anxiously looked for and talked about for some time.

Sunday November 2: Our Captain has not come yet. I have delayed writing for two or three days expecting he would be here. I trust he will not be long on the way. He is somewhat unpopular in the company and perhaps in a measure undeservedly so. Yet I think he will be welcomed back with pleasure.

Today has been a rather quiet day in camp for we have no drills on Sunday only guard mounting, Sunday morning inspection, and evening dress parade. They are fighting again today up the Shenandoah, perhaps at Sukim Gap. Even at this distance I can hear the cannonading quite plainly.

Monday November 3rd: We have found no permanent abiding place yet. We have changed camp five different times in as many different days. Tomorrow, we are told we must change again, and go down near the iron works. I can generally find time to write, even when on the march, but my leisure time has been all consumed in finishing up the Mus [Muster] and Pay Rolls, monthly reports, etc, etc. Just got through with them last night at a late hour working all day Sunday to accomplish it. Went to sleep resolved to have a good time all to myself today, writing letters as our company would be out on picket. But woe was me! This morning I found I was detailed as "Officer of the Guard," and so all day long I have had to remain at the gate of the guard house, an imaginary position on one side of our camp ground, an about as disagreeable duty as ever fell to me. Only commissioned officers should be put on such duty. But they have gotten on a trick lately of detailing Orderly Sergeants also, we who already have more business to attend to than any other man in the company, not excepting the Captain. I have made an agreement with the Sergeant of the Guard that if he will remain at the guard house and let me sleep until midnight, I will then take his place and excuse him till morning, etc.

Tuesday, November 4th: I have just been relieved from duty, as Officer of the Guard. Had about two hours sleep last night. Freed from guard duty I have to take the company in charge, for two of our commissioned officers are absent, and the third is officer of the day. So many of our commissioned officers are away, and so few men are fit for duty, that those who can and do remain in the harness have busy times indeed. It is wonderful how our regiment has dwindled away. We left Elmira over a thousand strong, and last Wednesday night when we started our march we could not muster two hundred and fifty. Many of course were about on various kinds of duty. Some have died, some deserted, a few have been discharged, and a large number are on the sick list.

These remarks are true in every particular, all except our being left behind when the Brigade marched. We marched, what few there were left of us, and are now doing our full share of picket duty with the rest of the Brigade. I have said that our lines have been very much weakened here. Our Brigade has taken the place of almost an entire Army Corp, Fitz, John Parlin's, Butterfield's Brigade was encamped where the 3rd Wis. and we are now. Martindale's Brigade was a little way up the river. In the 44th NY, in Butterfield's Brigade, I found an old Alfred friend. Nash, a Lieut. We had a good many talks before he left. Our regiment occupies the camp ground occupied by the 16th Mich., a new regiment which fought most desperately at South Mountain. They had arranged this camp most beautifully, with streets paved, rows of evergreens in front of the officers quarters, comfortable fireplaces built, and everything ready for us to set up our tents where they had taken theirs down. We have a much more pleasant location than at Maryland Heights. From my tent door I have a beautiful view off toward Sharpsburg, of a rolling country dotted with farm houses and fine groves, and behind all a ridge of the South Mountains covered to its summit with forests which look magnificent in their autumnal dress. While you are having your first taste of winter winds and snows we are in the most romantic period of autumn. The forests around us now do indeed look splendid with all their varied and gorgeous tints. How often, as I look at them am I reminded of the walks I used to take away down the river and below the Lower Falls.

It is a beautiful evening tonight, and its magic spell seems to have made everybody musical. Down in the company street the boys are chorusing "Glory Hallelujah" at the top of their voices. In the tent on my left some officers are enjoying the more refined airs, *Annie Laurie, Cottage by the Sea,* etc. while behind us, a lot of officers cooks and servants are discoursing some plantation melodies. Now the lieutenants have formed in line and marched up the street, probably to serenade some Captain and then go in to eat up the ginger cakes and drink his wine which came in his last box from home, unless he doesn't see it.

"Tattoo" has been beaten and I have been out to call the roll. What a splendid, splendid evening it is! Every man seems to be enjoying the scene. Our line officers have been in a regular train, chasing each other around the parade ground, going through a very peculiar Zouave Drill, etc. When the music came out to beat "Tattoo" they danced a cotillion or something else, but had to break up at last as the rules now require commissioned officers to be with their Companies at every roll call. All Quiet on the Potomac at last. Quite a strong wind seems to be springing up, and we may soon have a storm. Then, O Mud! Mud!

Wednesday, November 5th: They are laying out our camp anew this morning, preparatory for winter quarters. It now looks as if we were to remain here for some time. I am to have a spacious and majestic edifice erected at the head of "K" Street, which I am to occupy all by myself. From four to six are usually congregated in one tent, but I am to keep the pay, rations, and other property of the company, and so must have more room. I have just been down with our 2nd Lieut. laying out our street, Skimmeroon St. I suppose it will be called, as our company goes by the name of the Skimmeroon family. Co C next to us is the Steppenfield family. There were four brothers in the company, by the name of Steppenfield and they all deserted three or four nights ago while on guard.

I must tell you as I did Enos that physical strength and endurance, though very necessary, are not all that is needful to make a good soldier, and that in the faithful performance of the duties of my position I may accomplish as much for the success of the good cause as the strong men. Have you ever thought how much of the welfare of the company is dependent of the Orderly Sergeant? I furnish their food and clothing, in that they are taken care of when sick, that the duties which fall to the company are evenly distributed among the men, making out all the detail for every kind of service. In fact I have the company entirely in my hands except when out on parade, marches, or something of that kind. Our men come to me to borrow books and newspapers, envelopes writing paper and stamps, to get information in this thing, of help in that thing, to procure their pay papers, and to get their letters directed, to get their descriptive lists, applications for furlough etc. made out, and for a thousand other things too numerous to mention. Of course it makes me a kind of slave to the company, for I have to be always at my post and am always busy. Yet if by doing all this and keeping the company in good order both as to their behavior and their physical condition, I can make them better soldiers, and keep them the better prepared for whatever services may be required of them, am I not of as much value to the government as a Samson in strength? And I have done this. I say of myself I have succeeded in my position. Our company is in as good condition as any in the regiment, and are as well contented. Ours is the only company from which none have deserted. Therefore when my friends tell me that I ought not to have come to war, as almost all do, I will not admit it until my experience has been very different from what it has been thus far. We did not move down to the Antietam Iron Works to camp as no suitable place could be found there.

The Dunker church was almost exactly in front of our position, and the battery which we supported made more than one of those ugly looking holes in its walls and roof. Here the Rebels did make a desperate stand. Behind this church the dead lay in heaps, more thickly than in any other spot which I saw. And what was most sad to me was that the majority of them wore blue clothes. This was the only place I saw where the Rebel dead did not outnumber ours. This picture looks as natural as life and recalls most vividly the scenes of that terrible battle day. One of our shells went screaming through that house and into those woods! And how the Rebels swarmed there! It was from there that they advanced, in such a splendid line to charge on our battery. They came out into the open field about five rods in front of the church, when the battery opened on them with grape and canister. One of our men was telling me while on guard last night that he "never delighted in bloodshed," that he had to chuckle with a grim delight "to see the Rebs hop when the grape shots struck them." One convulsive spring into the air, and then they would drop, many of them never to rise again. When we marched along the road in front of this church two days after the Battle, the dead (all rebels) were lying there yet, full as many, as are represented in the picture. What a disgusting spectacle they were. Their bloated and blackened faces fairly sickening to look upon. About ten rods back and to the left of this church in the woods is a heap of rock, two or three feet thick and about six rods long forming a natural and most perfect breastwork. Behind this the rebels held their ground all day, and whenever our men would advance into the woods they would receive a murderous fire from this position. It was on this account that we had so many killed there, and that at this point the battle raged so fiercely all day long. Many a bullet sent from near that church whistled over our devolved heads, that day, but it was all right so long as they went over us. Many of them came among us, as our lists of killed and wounded bear sad record.

Friday, November 7: A day or two ago I was telling about the glories of autumn here, and that winter had not made its appearance. I'll take it all back. I have seen today all the winter I wish to see this year. The ground is covered with snow, and a driving storm is continually bringing down more, piling it up in our streets, and drifting it under the sills of our tents and into our doors. Cold, too. I should think it entirely too cold for snow. Our wash dish froze over as soon as it was left out in the cold this morning. In perfect accordance with military rule we have been commanded to move our tents today. The camp was laid out anew a day or two ago and our street was placed about a rod to the right of its old position. This required a change of all the tents of course, and today, when the storm came on, seems to be the chosen time for the removal. The officers quarters where I abide appeared to be right already, but the poor men have to suffer. I look out between the folds of our tent door, and shiver at the scene. They are in one mass of drifting, driving snow flakes, the earth is white with its snow covering. Some of the men are already working at their tents, some are shivering in their fireless tents, and some are by their fires in the street, cooking and eating their food while the snow is drifting over it and them. We had an inspection and review yesterday by Gen. Gordon and staff. It lasted from eleven until five. They made a minute inspection of our arms & accouterments, knapsacks etc., in the field, and then of our quarters in camp. I never shall tell how near this child came to getting a reprimand because his place was not found to be particularly clean. The Orderly of Co. C was sent to the guard house because of his dirty careless appearance generally. My gun doesn't go out again for inspection unless it has been cleaned up I reckon.

Monday, November 10th: The Captain has not made his appearance yet. This morning we were told that he had made application to have his leave extended.

The people of Chemung and Schuyler [counties in New York] have sent down four car loads of provisions for our regiment; potatoes, onions, turnip, beets, apples, etc. Four or five barrels of the good things were brought up to our company a few days ago. You ought to have seen the glad faces of the boys as their provisions from home are dealt out to them. Jimmie Doil of our company was in raptures when I gave him a hand full of potatoes, the first he had seen since he came into the service. Onions are especially sought for and especially recommended by our surgeon. Considering that half of our regiment is from Steuben [county], it is certainly very generous of the people of Chemung and Schuyler to furnish so well for us, these good things are divided equally through the whole regiment.

Lieut. Goodrich talks of resigning. He told me so the other night when we were together. And he wanted to know how much I would give for his shoulder straps. I began to think I have earned a commission.

Tuesday, November 11th: Fire! Fire! Fire! I push to the front door and see a bright light at the other end of camp in E or H Street. Somebody's barrel chimney has taken fire, and by it the tent covering of his hut has also been ignited. I return to my writing but the men are rushing down to the dress parade yelling, "fire! fire! fire! No 2 this way. Pull away boys. Yes, yes, yes, yes, break her down break her down — and it sounds so much like old times I cannot believe that I am not in old Rochester once more putting my head out of some university hall window, or running out to the gate to see where the fire is.

Wednesday, November 12th: The Captain has just made his appearance tonight. He looks very different from what he did when I saw him last. We were all most glad to see him and especially to see him looking so well, but his big trunk didn't come with him. Today Plimpton with six others of our company who have been complaining around camp lately, started off to General Hospital. Plimpton seemed to be very sorry to say good bye to us, but the rest seemed to be glad enough to get away. They think if they can only get to general hospital they will soon be discharged and sent home. About twenty are now absent in Hospital, from our company. Men who came just to secure their bounty and have long since become sick of this business, they will use any means for getting out of the service, and are a despicable set generally in my opinion. The Captain sends regards and says he feels as if he had "got home once more."

About midnight last night, orders came for us to be out in line of battle in twenty minutes!

What a time there was then for arms and clothes. We hurried out. Some of the companies were ordered off to strengthen the picket line, and the rest were ordered back to quarters warned to be ready to spring out at the first drum beat. Went to bed with clothes all on, even to ammunition belt and slept quietly till morning.

Thursday, November 13: Wadsworth is defeated we are told. I am sorry indeed for that. When men like Seymour and Mr. Woods can secure the popular vote of the Empire State it is a bad state of affairs I must say, bad. But they tell us never to despair of the Republic. And McClellan is removed. I cannot say whether I am glad or sorry. It seems to create here no excitement what ever. While I have heard few men approving, I have neither heard any condemning the act. All that I have seen, like Burnside about as well as McClellan, and are not dissatisfied with the change, as they would have been had Fremont or some such man been assigned to the place.

Friday, November 21st: I have been at work building for some days now. Today I am writing in my own house, a log hut, seven by ten, chinked and mudded up so that it is quite warm and comfortable with a tight cloth roof and a good fireplace in one end. A bright warm fire is blazing before me as I write and my house as I look around it is the very picture of comfort. My hut is made of hickory logs, as nice timber as you ever saw. In New York state it would be a sin to use such timber for anything less valuable than axe helves.

The Captain's trunk came today. He was out on picket when it came, but we were too anxious to get at the good things inside, to wait for his return. It would have done you good to have seen us gather around that trunk when it was opened, and to hear the remarks that were made as the various parcels and packages were taken out. We can never thank you enough for them. Two little pin cushions, very neatly made, require special acknowledgment. I found the paper on mine "From Jennie" with her compliments. Many thanks to "Jennie." Lieut. Goodrich is in a peck of trouble. He has heard already from home that he intends to resign.

Thursday, November 27th: Thanksgiving day has come and gone once more. It is now late in the evening, a beautiful evening, following one of the most glorious Indian Summer days that I ever saw. Our Thanksgiving services (for we have spent the day in camp) were held in the open air of course, and nothing could have been more appropriate to the occasion than this bright and beautiful day, and the splendid Indian Summer scene around us. We have kept Thanksgiving day in as good style as possible for us here. Had a good sermon and a good dinner, the two good things of a Thanksgiving day. I will not stop to tell you all the dainties we had at our dinner. A good share of them came in the boxes sent by our friends at the north, and the feast closed with a bottle of nice home made wine, marked Tuttle 1858, which I had received especially for the occasion. We drank to the health of our friends far away, who were ever in our thoughts.

Gen. Jackson (not Stonewall) came to our camp today and we had a general brushing up of our street and quarters for his especial benefit I suppose. A fancy dress parade in which all were required to appear in their very best closed the exercises of the day. The night was a scene of merry making by the officers where some were a little more merry than the day required. For myself I have everything to be thankful for in the year that has gone. Life, health, prosperity, friends. I have been through the greatest dangers and escaped unharmed. I have merited nothing I have received everything. Who could have more cause for thankfulness than I? If I have been called to endure hardship, to meet danger and death, to be prostrated with sickness, yet have I been given strength to endure those hardships. I have been kept and delivered from every danger, and I have been speedily restored to health. And if I have been deprived of the happiness and comforts of home, I have nevertheless the glad consciousness of being where duty calls me. I ought to be both contented and happy, and I believe I am so. Truly, oh my heavenly Father, "thou crownest the year with they goodness."

Friday, November 28: Today I went down to our picket lines. A heavy cannonading up the river somewhere led us over to the "lookout" and from there I went on down to the Potomac. You get a splendid view from the lookout, can see up the river for miles. The Potomac and the canal by its side runs along below you, and across the river there extends a landscape as fine perhaps as any Virginia can boast. If there are any Rebels over there, they keep out of sight. All looks as peaceful and as prosperous as if no war was ever heard of there. And on this side of the river boats are moving along the canal, and farmer wagons along the road, as be the days of profoundest peace. But blue overcoats and glistening guns are moving up and down the canal line as far as the eye can reach, and if you turn around you find some ugly looking Parrott guns at your side, and you know that war and strife are with you even in this scene of peace. I went down to the iron works, in ruins now, but which once employed over a thousand workmen, and then to the canal and to the aqueduct. It is under this aqueduct, which carries the canal over the Antietam Creek, that a road leads down to the Antietam Ford, but the way has been obstructed now. The trees have been felled across the creek in the arches of the aqueduct, and along the river bank a line of rifle pits have been dug.

A cold month, but one of quiet duty.

Saturday, December 6th: It is very cold today. The ground is covered with a dry fine snow, which melts not a bit under the sun of noonday and which the wind is whirling in clouds around our bleak encampment or driving it through the openings and crevices of our log huts. I have rarely seen a more tedious storm, even at home. Last night I found it rather cold on guard duty even when in the guard hut by a fire. How fared the poor fellows who were out on picket? I wonder.

Sunday, December 7th: It kept growing colder last night, and this morning it was freezing cold. The snow creaked under our feet as we walked, and the wind—I thought it would bite my ears off. Last night the wind blew terribly. More than one chimney went over, and I was fearful my canvas hut roof would go too. It came tough for the poor boys who had to go out on picket this morning. How the cold wind whirled through our ranks as we were in line at guard mounting! And many of the boys were without gloves or mittens.

Plimpton is chumming with me now. He is troubled still with his rheumatism and is looking for a discharge. He thinks he may get it. But give me health and they may keep their discharges.

Tuesday, December 9th: But I am a man of business and, especially now that I have hired out, my time is not my own. Big thing this soldiering is! One hundred and seventh Regiment of New York Volunteers! Don't

Hooker's Campaign of the Spring of 1863

it sound big? "Who wouldn't sell his farm and go for to do soldier?," is the exclamation I daily hear from our men. I wonder how many of them owned a farm? And then in the bitterest irony they repeat the familiar inducements to volunteers, fourteen dollars a month, good clothing, board, and medical attendance! Fourteen dollars a month and Congress promises to make it fifteen. I hope they wont for we will never get our pay then? Our boys begin to think we will never get our thirteen even. Biggest thing of all! Orders have come for us to be ready to march at a minute's notice! It lacks five minutes of three. It will take half a day to pack up all the food and effects I have collected in my house. Fare you well for a time.

"The wind is ready and the ship is fair."

Wednesday, December 10th: Antietam Ford to Maryland Heights, Md.

Broke camp in the morning, but did not march until afternoon. Many and diverse things were done to pass the time while waiting. A big snow ball fight between the right and left wings of the regiment where snow balls gave place in time to loaves of old bread, where gallant charges were made and batteries, and many prisoners were taken, was the great thing of the day. Nor shall I ever forget the accumulation of old bottles in front of the Adjutant's tent, the departure of the Keme Brigade for Smoketown Hospital etc., or the march at last, snow in the roads, and mud where the sun shone. We only went to Maryland Heights near our old camp, and stopped for the night. On the way we passed the former residence of old John Brown, and the school house where he taught. Slept nicely on my bed of leaves scraped up from the snow.

Thursday, December 11th: Through Harpers Ferry, Va., Sondan Co., Va. Bound south.

The old story again; long marchings and picturesque campings, only we can't see the picturesque always. Passed through Harpers Ferry this morning and found ourselves once more on sacred soil. Crossed on pontoons over both the Potomac and Shenandoah rivers. No winter quarters (I believe it) and mud! Such mud! With snow and ice in the woods. To march down a steep icy road with heavy canteen haversack ammunition belt, gun

Maj. Gen. Franz Sigel

etc to carry is quite a feat of pedestrianism. We had considerable grand and lofty tumbling accompanied by some very select swearing on starting out this morning.

Last night we encamped in the woods, appropriated a rail fence and built roaring big fires and made ourselves comfortable for the night. Our camp was a splendid scene, the woods all lit up with fires, through the midst of which ran the long line of glistening guns in stacks. The men were gathered around their fires cooking their suppers or feeding together as jolly a set of fellows as you often see. Above all, through the tree tops, was the bright full moon shining out of a cloudless sky, but if the sky was clear it was also cold, and we kept close to our fires. We started on the march again at three o'clock this morning. We are going down to join Sigel's command. Here after we "fights mit Sigel." I have just learned that our destination is Dumfries and Stafford Court House.

I gave my watch in charge of Lieut. Atwood at Harpers Ferry this morning. He is going home. Lieut. Goodrich is not very well. The rest of us are all right. Plimpton went off with the rest of our sick men to Smoketown Hospital.

Friday, December 12: Through Hillsboro to camp near Leesburg, Va.

Back Across Virginia to Join Hooker

Saturday, December 13: Through Leesburg, a twenty-two mile march, and encamped near Gum Spring, Va.

Sunday, December 14: Through Fairfax C.H. [Fairfax Court House] and to Fairfax Station. Used up.

Monday, December 15: To camp beyond the Occoquon at Wolf Run Shoals.

Tuesday, December 16: Rain. Two miles, and encamped. Eight miles yet to Dumfries. This morning I awoke in the woods, the rain coming down upon me in torrents, and I in a regular ague chill. We had crossed the Occoquon River last night, and climbed the high hill this side of it and encamped early in the evening after coming but a mile or two from the creek. But the rain came and rather interfered with the rest we expected to get. The water was pouring into my neck when I awoke and as I turned over when getting up the water ran into my mouth from the blanket which I had pinned up. We have come but two or three miles today, have been waiting in the field here several hours expecting to go on every moment. Have been drying our blankets, cleaning our guns and brushing ourselves up generally. Now I will try to write a letter.

We have had a great march from Antietam and it is not finished yet though we are drawing near to scenes of interest once more. Our old Corp under Slocum is on the move, and Heintzleman and Sigel are just ahead of us I suppose. There are only about 20,000 men in our Corp. The others are larger. Burnside will have a right smart heap of troops after a while I reckon.

Left: Gen. Henry Warner Slocum (J. McClees, artist). *Right:* Gen. Samuel P. Heinzleman (Brady's National Portrait Gallery).

Our march through Loudon County was full of interest and excitement. We had little skirmishes with the guerillas every day, and as for foraging it was rich! The country for miles around Leesburg is overflowing with good things, And no small amount of hay and corn, of sheep and hogs, chicken, turkeys, and cattle even were put under process of conscription. The people in all that section are inveterate "secesh," so we had no hesitation in taking what ere we wanted. At Leesburg we saw not a thing that looked like Union feeling, except on the part of the colored population. But we went proudly through that old Sodam with the Stars and Stripes flung to the breeze. Twenty thousand more for the big fight down here somewhere. The men we met were very mild and lonely, though probably they mounted their horses and were after us a half hour after our column passed them, but the women were very bitter on us. One stood with a club to guard her cellar door, but it did her no good, for an officer went in to reconnoiter. I saw a girl jerk a hoe away from a man who was digging carrots in her garden, and just such incidents were occurring all the time. George Paling, company cook, went into a house on a splendid farm to buy some bread. "Can't sell you any. If you want a little to eat we can give it to you, but we don't sell provisions to Lincoln's hirelings," etc. "Why you seem to be rather Secesh here," said Geo. "Yes Sir! We are that till we draw our last breath." "Then I shall have to conscript a little," was the reply, and he started out and shot a fine sheep belonging to the premises. Then teamsters took six more, and when the New Jersey boys came along they shot a heifer. Chaplain saw our Geo. with the sheep on his back and remarked, "It's no sin to take from such people. Won't you let me have a piece tonight?" He got it.

The guerillas bothered us generally, even rushing in upon our baggage trains, cutting out as many wagons as they could and making off with them. Our Cavalry chased them up and paid them well for their pains. One day the whole column was delayed two or three hours while our cavalry was retaking a sutler's wagon belonging to the 123rd New York. Several of our men who strayed away were undoubtedly picked up by these parties.

When we neared Bull Run the fences began to grow scarce. Until now a fence is a subject of special remark. " See! boys there's a fence." "Lets go into camp!" What a desolation is all this country! Even the houses are destroyed. I did not stand the march very well, almost gave out two or three times. I am getting used to it now, but it almost used me up in the process. We have dragged ourselves along under our heavy knapsacks foot sore and weary, until it seemed that we could not go another step, and then have lain and shivered all night, until the reveille has started us up again at four, three, or even two o'clock in the morning. This march has brought us the first real hardship I have seen. And today the mud is awful. It is almost impossible for our artillery and wagons to get along. And we are waiting now for our immense wagon train to come up. Well, I never saw such a time! You will never know what mud is until you see the real secesh soil moistened up. With all this we have an occasional snow storm for variety.

It is many days since we have seen any letters or even a paper, we know nothing of the outside world, and are in the greatest doubt as to whether Burnside has taken Richmond or Lee Washington.

Wednesday, December 17: Fairfax Station Va.

You will see that we have retreated after going almost to Dumfries. We turned and came right back to this place over one of the muddiest, crookedest, deepest, steepest, meanest roads I ever saw. Eleven miles is a good day's march over it. It is part corduroy part rock, and the rest mud. What in creation sent us back here? I don't know. Since the tenth we have made about fifteen miles a day. A look at your map will show our route. Sharpsburg, Harpers Ferry, Leesburg, Fairfax C.H., Fairfax Station, Dumfries on the Potomac, and back again to the Station. We are now eighteen miles from Alexandria, and nearly west of it. How long we will remain here is, of course, a mystery to us. We marched here several hours, now are under orders to "move" at a moment's notice, and yet may remain for some days. I hope so for these rail roads look like civilization once more. We are encamped in the woods near the depot and are making ourselves as comfortable as we can without our tents. We have cut down a hickory tree and have made a roaring fire, by the light of which I am trying to write. I found a Hornellsville man on the Alexandria train. Matt Hartman. I used to see him in the machine shop when I went to get the school taxes. He seemed to be delighted to see us.

Thursday, December 18: I saw a newspaper today, and read that Burnside had retreated across the Rappahannock, and that McClellan had been restored to his command. What a cheer went up from regiment to regiment in our Brigade at the latter intelligence. "McClellan's our man" was the watchword everywhere. The 29th Ohio and the 27th Va. regiments have been added to our Brigade. The former have a fine band.

Grange and Alexandria R.R.: Would you like to know its time table? On the door of the ticket office is put up this notice: "Trains leave when they get ready. Ask no questions."

Thursday, December 25: Christmas Day. It is not a happy Christmas day with us today. The most that I can say is that it is a contented one, and hardly that with most in camp. We have been moving our camp again today. This is the fourth camp we have occupied near Fairfax Station, and a great

"McClellan's Our Man," song of the Army of the Potomac, celebrating Gen. McClellan's return to his command. *Harper's Weekly*, August 2, 1862.

many are in the worst of humor over the perplexities and botherations which always attend a change of camp. We marched about two miles this morning, laid out our new camp ground, put up our tents and have just had our dinner, Christmas Dinner! which was no great affair today.

We had a grand review and inspection of our Division yesterday by Gen. Williams. Our own Brigade is a very large one, and Crawford's not much smaller. It is very tiresome for the men, more than a day's march. When I got back I was so tired that I just laid down by the fire, looked into the flames and blazing coals, and thought of friends far away, of Christmas Eves and Christmas trees until I fell asleep.

It was quite pleasant this morning, but it is now cold and dark. The Capt. and 1st Lieut. have gone to Alexandria today to spend Christmas with some Hornellsville friends who are living there at present. Of course I could not go. I am not an officer.

Sunday, December 28: To Wolf Shoals Va.

Monday, December 29: Return to Fairfax Station. We were all unaware of the cause that routed us out of camp that fine Sunday morning, but it seemed there was great danger impending somewhere.

A great number of the regiments were suddenly found to be unfit for duty, and had to be left behind. Capt. Damon was among the number and was placed in charge of the camp. We rested quietly on the bank of the Occoquon in bivouac through the night. It was a beautiful clear night, but keenly cold also, and there was little sleep for us as one lay and watched the twinkling stars. In the morning we marched back to Fairfax Station in a hurry, making the eight miles in two hours. We found that the Rebel Cavalry had been on a raid and had torn everything up at Burks Station. We had been sent to intercept them, but they didn't come our way.

Tuesday, December 30th: Brigade review in the field by Gen. Williams H'd Q'rs.

Fairfax Station, Virginia

A New Year begins and old things pass forever.

From Army Note Book   **Jan 3, 1863**   Day by Day

Saturday, January 3d: Fairfax Station, Va.
We have been busy building us another shanty. Today we have had a grand Division Review, and now tonight I feel like a fool. New Year's day was a splendid one, beautiful and bright, and the morning was fine. I celebrated the day working hard and all day long. How often I heard the remark among the boys, "This is the queerest New Year's I ever saw," and each would tell where he was a year ago, or two years ago today. That seemed to be the chief subject of conversation as we gathered around our fires in the evening. We are in winter quarters once more. Have been busy for a week in putting up our log huts. The boys call them "one-horse pig pens." Howard has gone on to visit the 142st. Goodrich has been in Washington for over two weeks now. There is a rumor that he has resigned. I shouldn't wonder if he should do so ere long.

Sunday, January 4th: Grand Review of 12th Army Corps. John Smith and wife came up from Alexandria and went over with Capt. Sill and I to see the sight.

Thursday, January 8th: Have been troubled with a bad cold for over a week now. It is getting no better fast and I am almost sick.

Saturday, January 10th: Miners Hill Va. to Alexandria Va.
Went to Alexandria by W.S.M.R.R. on a pass procured by Mr. Stowe, who is Depot Agent and a friend of John Smith. Rain.

Sunday, January 11th: Miners Hill, Va.

5. Fairfax Station, Virginia

Left: Maj. Joseph W. Robinson, M.D. 141st New York Volunteers (Newman, photographers). *Right:* 1st Lt. Miles W. Hawley Co. B, 141st Reg, 2nd Div. New York Volunteers (W. L. Sutton, photographer).

Went on to Miners Hill on an engine with John Smith and George Ferow, and saw the 141st. Met Joe Robinson, Miles Hawley, Capt. Russell, George Gray, Harris Sawyer, etc. Joe showed me a fine picture of Carrie.

Monday, January 12th: Running around Alexandria. Into an old church and looked at Washington's pew, saw the Marshall House, the old market and the Masonic Hall, etc. Sick. Went to a circus with Mr and Mrs Smith. Thus went my birthday. I am sitting in John Smith's office in the Round House. He is Master Mechanic. He has been here two years now. Am not feeling very well with my cold, and am keeping quiet at Mr. Smith's house to see if it won't help me. They are very kind and do their best for my comfort and entertainment. Smith has a fine position here. Is fairly giddy with being up so high. He gets nearly two hundred dollars per month and ranks as major, for everything is military here. This is a queer old town, dirty and apparently falling to pieces, full of everything that is bad, yet having much to excite interest and curiosity. An immense army business fills its streets now with life and activity, and it has many fine residences, some as costly and elegant as I ever saw. They belong mostly to the Secesh. When deserted by their owners, and are now used [by the] government as hospitals, many a poor sick soldier now occupies apartments more elegant than he ever saw before. The town is full of hospitals. Nearly every church and large house you see is in use. And the crowds in the streets are chiefly made up of soldiers and contrabands.

Tuesday, January 13th: Returned to camp at Fairfax Station. Capt. Colby has been made Major, Lt. Rutter Captain, Lindsey Lieut., and Ed Fay Serg. Major. Good.

Thursday, January 15th: I returned to camp a day or two ago feeling not a bit better than I left it. I am somewhat better today, so that I have been out on Company and Battalion drills, perhaps I'll be all right in the morning? I hope so.— The Doctor has just been in with an order from Head Quarters, requiring a report of all men in the company who are not able to march fifteen miles a day, and that such men be provided for, in case they should be left behind, and orders came but recently requiring us to provide ourselves with complete outfits of clothing, arms, etc. And when I came up from Alexandria the other day the train was loaded full with ammunition etc. And all the rest of our Corps have gone on to the front,

Left: Lt. George E. Gray 141st New York Volunteers (W. L. Sutton, photographer). *Right:* Harris Sawyer, Steward 141st Reg, New York Volunteers.

Left: Sgt. Maj. Ed Fay 107th New York Volunteers (Mountain and Larkin, photographers). *Right:* Lt. Col. Newton T. Colby 107th New York Volunteers (J. Sagar, photographer).

excepting our Brigade alone. And the ambulance train has been ordered to lay in a stock of wines.

And the surgeons are sharpening their instruments for immediate use. Now there's no use in talking. I guess what they are up to. They want to get us into a scrap. Capt. says, "let's not go" and we have about made up our minds that we won't go. But then if they are really going on to Richmond we want to go too. But seriously, things betoken a speedy movement here

Friday, January 16th: Very cold and stormy day. Indications of an impending movement multiply.

Saturday, January 17th: News came today of the acceptance of Lieut. Goodrich's resignation. Capt. Sill immediately put in a recommendation of Col. Diven for Howard to be 1st Lieut., and I to be 2nd Lieut. Good for me. The Col. rather wanted to put in somebody else at first.

Monday, January 19: The marching orders which we had been expecting so long came at last. Broke camp in the morning and crossed the Occoquon at Wolf Run Shoals. Our Co., (20 off. and 61 men) largest in the regiment.

Tuesday, January 20th: Wolf Run Shoals to Dumfries, Va. A good long march over a greasy road, brought us to Dumfries. What a looking place! I had long wished to see it, but one sight is enough. Old and tumbling to pieces, it must have been dead fifty years ago. Rainy and cold in the evening.

Wednesday, January 21st: A good many on getting up found that they had been lying in the water which had risen around their beds. Rainy and cold, but we started out. A mile or two brought us to the Quantico. Cold. Still raining. No bridge. Creek high and rising, crossing on a log and falling in, "such men laughing," log swept away at last, a merry waiting in the rain for a bridge. Thanks to Col. Diven a good bridge at last, over dry shod but wet through by the rain. Marched a mile or two to a camping place and put up for the night.

Rain, rain, rain.

Thursday, January 22: The muddy march from Dumfries. Tough march over hills, through mud, across ditches, jumping,

Top: Lt. Alonso B. Howard Co. K, 107th New York Volunteers. *Bottom:* Dumfries, Virginia, *sketch by A. R. Waud, Harper's Weekly*, August 24, 1863.

wading, climbing, struggling, through mud, no rations, mud so deep that wagons had to be lightened, our mess chest slung. Quite unwell by the time we reached camp. Major Colby over took us, with Parmeter, Campbell. I shall never forget this day of hardships.

Friday, January 23: Stafford C.H., Va.

Down sick when morning came—fever. Was put in an ambulance. Gave up my gun to Corporal Wright. Went into bivouac at Stafford C.H. Received a good mail. Took medicine and kept quiet.

Saturday, January 24: Feeling better. Getting rid of my fever attack. We were paid off last by paymaster Charles Campbell of Bath. Our company was called up for pay at about midnight. The boys used to complain of being called up in the middle of the night to eat, but all came up very readily to get their little green backs. He paid me only to the first of November, ult. I received $54.00.

Monday, January 26: Well enough to be around as usual. Stafford Court House is the Hd. Quarters of Gen. Sigel, who commands the Reserve Guard Division Army of the Potomac consisting of the 11th & 12th Corps, which are now encamped in this vicinity.

Went down with the Capt. to see the town. Was surprised at its insignificance. But two inhabitable houses in the place. One, a good one formerly owned by a northern man, was occupied by Gen. Sigel. Gen. Slocum took the other. The Court House, a poor affair, was filled with commissary stores, and the jail, a rough one, with prisoners. The brick clerk's office with slate roof and overgrown with ivy was the only pleasant sight I saw. Picked some of the ivy leaves and returned to camp.

Tuesday, January 27: Stafford Court House to Hope Landing Va.

Moved to camp near Hope Landing on the Aquia. Awful muddy roads, and we were sent out to make better ones. Before we got into bivouac it began to rain. We put up our tents in the storm and went to sleep wet and cold.

Wednesday, January 28: Life at "Valley Forge"

Stormed all day and at last it began to snow. . The snow was better than the cold rain. Misery! Misery! Sat in the tent almost all day with a canteen of hot water at my feet which were well nigh frozen. What would I have done out on guard! One of the worst evils of the no winter quarters system we find to be the smoke of the camp fires. It is almost unendurable. It is ruining our eyes, and we are almost ready to endure the cold rather than to be smoked out any more. It was a long time before I could get to sleep last night on account of my eyes. They were so inflamed and discharged so constantly when I tried to shut them.

Friday, January 30th: To Aquia Landing and Return.

Walked down to the Landing with the Capt. after a good meal. Got a poor one, yet ate it with relish. Had a fine walk down the beach. Saw all the sights, and were home by dark.

Saturday, January 31: A fine day and therefore worthy of notice. Col. Diven is at Washington attending to his congressional duties. He was with us through our march and earned quite a name for himself from the bridge he built over the Quantico. He took off his overcoat and went to work in the rain and saw the thing put through. Lt. Col. Smith has been away sick for some time, but is soon coming back I hear. The regiment is now under command of Major Colby — the best officer of the lot. The weather has moderated greatly and we are having pleasant sunny days again. With the birds singing in the woods, and the warm sun melting the snow away from the edges of the paths, it seems just like the coming of spring at home. We are anxious for the spring to come here, but we must expect a couple of months of rain first, yet it seems almost summer now. I have been running around today, through the woods and down to the landing, and out on the headland to look at the landscape. I took a kind of lazy delight in strolling along the sunny places, up and down the beach and by the sunny side of the fences. What a beautiful view one gets from the headland near our camp, of the Aquia Creek, for five miles down to its mouth, of the barracks and warehouses and tents at the landing there, with the boats and shipping there, of the Potomac River for miles above and below, and of the blue shores of Maryland beyond. The Aquia is really a bay up to this point, from two to four miles wide clotted with islands and fringed with coves and smaller bays. Houses are to be seen in romantic places along the shore, and altogether the view is very fine. This creek has been of interest all through the war. At its mouth the rebels maintained for a long time their blockade of the Potomac, and our gunboats had quite a fight with their batteries there, and it was up this creek that so many Rebel vessels escaped our cruisers. Aquia Landing is now the base of operations for the Army of the Potomac, and from it come the supplies for all of Hooker and Sigel's troops.

Hope Landing, four miles up the creek, is a mere sand bar running out into the river with only the ruins left of what was a landing, and perhaps two or three houses near it. The government is now building a kind of dock a little below this old landing. Capt. Sill and I took a walk down to the Aquia Landing yesterday. What a busy, busy place it is! All military. All new rough boards or tents. One brick railroad building, partially destroyed, was all that looked over a month old. But there is an immense business done there now. What enormous quantities of army stores. There was corded up on the dock a pile as large as our barn of wagon tongues alone, and everything like new in proportion. Immense storehouses were filled with army supplies, clothing, forage, etc. Trains from Falmouth were continually coming in and the bay was filled with boats and transports, soldiers innumerable, contrabands ditto, a sailor now and then, a few citizens, railroad men in the government employ, or men from the north on their way to visit friends in the army, make up the population.

Sutlers and Jews are robbing the soldiers on every corner.

The 107th is engaged at present in making corduroy roads down to the creek. There is a good corduroy running back from this landing which the Rebs built. We expect to join the Brigade at Stafford C. H. when our road work is done here. The boys say they didn't enlist to work out their road tax on these miserable Virginia mule roads. Howard was today appointed acting Quarter Master. QM Morgan is going to Washington for a few days. Howard has gained a point in getting even this temporary appointment. Uncle Allen has fallen away in weight to 184 pounds. I weigh twenty pounds more than before entering the service.

Sunday February 1: The boxes which we should have had at Antietam Ford, have come at last. Eugene's box had a carved knife for me.

Maj. Gen. Joseph Hooker (Brady's National Portrait Gallery).

Thursday, February 5th: Gen. Wells of Howard has been with us a day or two visiting his son. He went home this morning not very well pleased with the soldiering, I guess. Gen. Colby, wife, and father are here also. Sunday, February 8th: Moved camp from the bluff to the lowlands Bellin Place.

Thursday, February 12: Sheldon gets no better. He is going to Minnesota for the benefit of his health. We are beginning to live again. Our shanty was finished so that we moved into it last night. The boys are all building log huts. The Potomac has been all alive with transports for the last two days. The Ninth Army Corps is taking passage down the river for Fortress Monroe, they say.

Tuesday, February 17th: Nothing of any importance has occurred since my last letter. We are lying in camp doing nothing except to make ourselves comfortable and living on the bounty of Uncle Samuel. Yet I am busy enough. Our company books and accounts have not been attended to for two months now, and I have at last got to work on them. I am now half done with my job, and shall finish in a day or two if nothing happens.

We have been having the finest April days imaginable, birds singing, sun shining, almost too warm, until this morning when on getting up we found everything covered with snow. It has been snowing steadily all day, but a kind of wet sugar snow that will not last long.

Thursday, February 26: Mr. Pinch from Hornellsville arrived on a visit to James. We took him in at our H'd Quarters.

It is rainy cold and cheerless still. I suppose it will continue to rain until April. The most unpleasant part of a Virginia winter comes in the spring. Our rain is occasionally changed to snow which fell more than seven inches deep here two or three nights ago. Weighed myself yesterday and found that I weighed 154 lbs. (I am well enough so far as I know), which is twenty pounds more than I ever weighed at Rochester (University). But through the regiment, the fell destroyer is beginning to make sad havoc again. Men are very sick and dying at a fearfully rapid rate with us now. The hardship of our last march and the exposure and privations which our men have suffered since then, are having their effect at last. The cloud of sorrow and gloom which darkened our stay at Maryland Heights last October seems to be enveloping us once more. The hospital will not hold all who are sent to it, and the dead cart standing behind it has almost constantly an occupant waiting for burial. So it was as I write and I suppose that even now a member of our company, James Fuller, is dying in the hospital, and he will make one more. Poor fellow! Grief driven, he came into the army to drown his sorrow for the death of his wife, leaving his two little children in the care of distant relatives. Can they dream that their father is slowly sinking away, this dismal day, so far from them? A few more hours and they will be orphans. This is but one of the daily incidents of our life here.

We are being surrounded by troops. The 11th Army Corps (Sigel's) is moving down the creek — and a large cavalry force has lately camped near us. The 6th & 8th NY Cavalry are encamped but a mile or two from us.

Saturday, February 28: Went to Aquia Landing with Mr. Wood to procure a coffin for James Fuller, who died yesterday. Thus avoided the muster and inspection of the regiment. The funeral was held in the afternoon and he was buried on the bank of the Aquia.

D. M. October 14. 1685.

These were the characters cut in an old tomb-stone near where Fuller was buried. We were told that it marked the grave of a Dr. Mills; and we found that he was buried in the center of an ancient cemetery; of which no trace remains save the one stone, and the cedar trees that grew above it. It's the cemetery of the old town of Stafford Court House. (The present town, four miles away, looks old enough!) Just above, on the bluff and overgrown now by a dense forest, are the traces of that old town. The foundations of the different homes can be traced out in the woods.

Sunday, March 1st: A fine beautiful day. Religious services were held. It seemed good and like old times to have them once more. In the afternoon the Major told me he secured the notice of the promotion of Orderly Corporal John Orr and myself to be 2nd Lieut. Was very glad to hear it of course. The notice was read at Dress Parade and the boys of our company were kind enough to give me their good cheers as they broke ranks in the company street.

Tuesday, March 3rd: Was detailed as officer of the guard today. It seems to me they are rather fast in putting me on duty as officer so quick. Also, a lonely dismal watch I have to keep tonight. Not ten feet from me is the dead cart, in which lies all that is mortal of two poor fellows who have received their long furlough from soldier duty. And in the hospital, a few feet farther one more has just died while another they tell me cannot live till morning, and many are very, very sick. These are gloomy times.

Thursday, March 5th: Attended today a double funeral. George Kompton, of Company C, and one from Co. H, were buried together. It was a solemn occasion. God is afflicting us sorely now. In the afternoon I saw a deserter drummed out of the camp of the 134th NY near us, sitting all day long on the bleak hillside. closely pinioned, scantily clad and bare head from which his hair had been closely shaved. Even the blanket that was thrown to him, hardly kept him from freezing. After the evening parade, the regiment being drawn up in line, he was brought out, his hands tightly tied behind him, his shaved head bare, a rope around his neck, and by which he was lead, and the regimental drum corps playing the Rogue's March. In this condition he was marched along in front of the whole regiment, and I was informed finally given a good dunking in the bay. Rather tough!

Friday, March 6th: Received a visit from LeRoy Goff of the 86th N.Y. Enoch Babcock returned today, having been absent since Antietam. Saturday, March 7th: Capt. Sill went away with LeRoy this morning. Is going after his sword. Left me in command of the company. Have enough to do. Rorko was taken much worse and sent to Hospital. He cannot live many hours. Wrote to his father. Drawing and distributing clothing.

Sunday, March 8: A box came today for James Fuller, the contents of which I sold for about $25.00 which will go to his little orphan children. "Brother Fletcher," Chaplain of the 134th NY, and a graduate of Madison University made me a call and looked at my *Examiners*. Busy, busy all day.

Monday, March 9th: Uncle Wood went home this morning on a twenty days' leave. The old man was tickled enough. Knickerbacker died today, in his own tent, and very unexpectedly. I had to take the company out on Battalion Drill. Got mixed up. Tired, sick, and mad. But at Dress Parade I got my little commission. Capt. returned.

Wednesday, March 11th: On guard. Received a lot of old January letters. Plimpton sends me a splendid ring, the work of his leisure hours in Hospital.

Thursday, March 12th: There came today, in a letter from Father, the sad, sad news of the death of Rutha Lee. My good friend. Can it be possible that she is dead, she so young, so promising, so true, so pure, so loved admired by all... And today George Coon died and Henry Rorko followed him an hour later.

Alas what times. Henry's father from the 141st NY reached here before he died.

Friday, March 13th: Taken sick today. Was officer of the Police, though feeling not very well. Couldn't stand it. Came in and gave up sick. In due time found I was down with a raging fever.

Saturday, March 14th: Sick. Sick. Sick.

Sunday, March 16th: Getting no better fast.

Tuesday, March 17th: Still very sick. Have a raging bilious fever, which is however, very fortunate as it is not by any means as dangerous as the low typhoid fever that has been prevailing so horribly in camp. Uncle Allen has written home about me.

Wednesday, March 18th: Made out to write a letter home (to Father) as I am beginning to get round in the land of the living once more. I find upon trying that my hand is a little nervous and unsteady, but I guess I can go it. Well, I have been sick, and am better. When I was first taken down I didn't know but I was ticketed to go the same road with the dozen or more of poor boys whom death has lately taken from among us. But I soon discovered that mine was not the low malignant camp fever that was raging here. But my old spring fever that I used to have at home, with hot flushed cheeks and high pulse instead of the yellow sallow face that they have here. The surgeons have been very kind and faithful in their calls, and Uncle Allen has made a perfect slave of himself in taking care of me, and I couldn't help getting along well, so much for earthly agencies, while to God above I have another burden of thanks and gratitude to give, that He has spared my life through one more season of dying and disease.

Thursday, March 19th: Still better. Went outdoors and back.

(To Father) Morning: Almost well. My tongue is all cleaned up. Settling up accounts in the camp, and getting ready for a new start.

Saturday. March 21st: A good letter from Carrie. Answered it immediately.

The sickness in the regiment is very gradually decreasing. There are no more in our own company who are at all dangerously ill. But it was a sad, sad time when so many were sick. Co. K lost four in two weeks time, first James Fuller of Canisteo, then Louis Knickerbacker from the eastern part of the county, and then, within an hour or two of each other Henry Rorko of Greenwood and Geo. Coon of Hornellsville died. Henry's father, a Lieut. in the 141st NYV was here and took his boy's body home. You remember Geo. Coon who used to work in Pardee's store, poor fellow! He thought from the first of his sickness that he would not get well, that he would die. I went up to see him when he died. He was not in his senses. An hour or two later Henry Rorko died. It was that same day that I heard of Rutha Lee's death.

Sunday, March 22nd: Arrival of my Father, After your box came, (for which many thanks) I had the Capt. write acknowledging its receipt. How carefully they are fitting us out for the spring's work, feeding us up to the best possible condition, distributing clothing and bountifully supplying all deficiencies in arms and ammunition, furnishing new and improved ammunition, reorganizing. The army is in tip top order, and instead of being demoralized, was never, I think, in such good condition as now.

Evening: I was going to write you a good long letter tonight, but Father has come to see me, heard I was so sick, you know, and I now have to visit with him. Nothing could have astonished me more than his arrival and such a lot of good things he brought!

(To Carrie) I am glad you spoke to Mrs R. as you did. She is entirely too much secesh for me. I would not go into her house. You may tell her first that I can come home any time that I please. An officer who wishes to resign, in this army at least, can do so and his resignation will at once be accepted. But tell her that I do not want to come back. That I came here to help put down the Rebellion, and mean to stay here until that is done, if God spares my life until this question is settled and settled right, even should it take years, it is useless to think of anything else for me but a soldier's life, for I mean to see the thing out!

Monday, March 23rd: Showing Father the sights, the camp, the landing, the pontoon train, the graves of our soldiers etc.

Wednesday, March 25th: Father tried to leave today, but the boat for Aquia would not take passengers. Had another inspection by Major Buckingham. I passed off well.

Thursday, March 26th: Father left today, after waiting a long time and being left by two boats, he hired a boy to row him over to the other landing, where he just succeeded in reaching a departing freight boat. I was too much worn out to dare to go on with him.—As his boat left another came in having Gen. Carl Schurz on board. In the evening I felt tired and half sick, and a little lonesome also.

Friday, March 27th: Splendid day. Brigade drill in the afternoon with the 134th NY. Formed three Battalions with Col. Costen as Brigade Commander. Visit from John Prentiss of the 23rd.

Sunday, March 28: Capt. Miles, having received the officers of the regiment met at Col. Diven's tent to give him a farewell expression of respect, and of sorrow at his loss. Appropriate resolutions were adopted, a few remarks made, and we all gave him a farewell handshake. He was very much affected, as indeed we all were. Rain, rain, rain all day long. Funeral of Mervandervil who was with me when I was last on guard. This is the 6th death we have had since we came to Aquia.

Sunday, March 29: Stafford C.H. to be mustered in as Lieut. Had a very muddy four miles walk to get there. Col. Ross is no longer mustering officers, and no succession has been appointed. Saw John D. Win, Elsie Williams' friend, a few moments. On my way back visited the boys in the NY [6th] Cavalry. Uncle Wood has returned from his sick furlough.

Wednesday, April 1st: Three generals in camp today! Evening report, that Colby is Lt. Col. and Cap. Fox Major. Took command of Co. D in Battalion drill today, and did first rate. Chaplain brought from Father a splendid outfit: sword, belt, sash, strap, hat, pistol, & etc.

(To Father) I am overwhelmed at your generosity in purchasing such an outfit for me. It has just arrived all safe in the care of the Chaplain. The sword is a beauty and is the admiration of all who see it. I do not think there is a finer one in the whole line, and so with everything. Such fine accouterments put to shame my old uniform clothes. But the Chaplain has sold me a nice uniform coat somewhat worn but which has been cleaned up to look almost new, for $15.00, and Major Colby has a fine new pair of pants that he will sell me. He wants a different color now that he is a field officer. Both coat and pants fit one exactly.

You remember the spot where Geo. Coon was buried? A half dozen more graves have been added to the number already, but there are more dangerously ill among us now. I noticed today that a fatigue-party were constructing a good fence around our little cemetery, and setting up headstones at the graves.

Friday, April 3rd: Capt. Sill went down to White House Landing today on special

Capt. Chas. T. Fox Co. C. 107th Reg, New York Volunteers.

duty, and I am left in command of the company. Out on Battalion Drill with my new accouterments on. Very gay and festive.

Saturday, April 4: Mr. Pardee of Hornellsville arrived today, and of course we have been having a great visit with him. Learn that Father arrived home alright.

Evening: Went over to the Chaplain's tent and had a good sing.

Sunday, April 5th: Snow on the ground nearly six inches deep. Went down to White House Landing in a row boat with Pardee and Howard. Saw the Captain, and then had a tough row back to camp. If I am to have no chance to write to you hereafter, you must blame our Major. For he has sent off my Captain to command forage depot four miles down the bay and thus the company is left entirely in my charge (Lieut. Howard being Quarter Master). Now the taste of commanding a company in actual service is no slight one, and I have all I can do to keep the machine running properly. There is a rumor that on account of our sanitary condition our regiment is to be detached for permanent duty at the Landing where the Captain now is, all stuff!

Snow and storm, but I have enough to do indoors. Gen. Hooker has ordered an extra muster of the whole army for the 10th inst. and I have a set of muster rolls to make out of course. When I was Orderly I had to do almost all the writing. Now that I am Lieut. I have to do quite all. It would be the same if I were Captain. My commission, I find, dates back to Jan 18, the date of my entrance on my 24th year.

Thursday, April 9th: Gens. Slocum, Williams, Ruger, Jackson, and Knipe reviewed us today, and made a general visit. They kept us waiting on the Parade Ground a long time while they went on a pleasant sail over the bay to Edringtons. They had a splendid dinner at Col. Diven's and went off apparently quite pleased with our situation here.

Friday, April 10th: Grand Review of the 12th Corps at Stafford Court House by President Lincoln and family. Gen. Hooker, etc. Big thing. But Col. Dura disgraced himself and his regiment by having them right shoulder shift and double quick before they had passed the review stand. I'm disgusted.

(To Luther) Messrs. Goff and Pardee are here today. They start for the north tomorrow. I have not written because I have been so busy, busy, busy. We had our grand review today. Think of marching four miles, to Almond, say, of standing around under arms all day, marching in review, etc., and then of marching home again, all for the fun of the thing! I don't see it. I am clear tired out tonight. Had rather travel twenty miles a day on an ordinary march. Met Ben Dewitt at the Review.

Saturday, April 11th: Muster Day. Muster in order to find how many conscripts will be needed to fill up our ranks. Let 'em come! Death has got his hand on us for certain now. The small pox and the spotted fever have shown themselves among us.

Sunday, April 12th: Splendid weather this. We will have to march soon if it continues. Everybody is expecting it, and the feeling is general that this is our last Sabbath in this camp.

Tuesday, April 14th: A day of troubles. Marcy has been appointed Orderly Serg't over Wells. And I cannot wonder that Dave feels deeply hurt. March tomorrow morning. Everything to be ready for a start at day light.

Wednesday, April 15th: No march, for with the day there comes a storm of unusual severity which does not cease, and there are now no prospects of a march. A dull day. Miserably merry doing anything to pass away the time.

Thursday, April 16th: No march yet. Living all in confusion, having sent off everything but what I need to march with. Things do not go right. The attack on Charleston is a failure. Our own movement is delayed.

Saturday, April 18: To Aquia with Capt. Sill. A long pull back to the White House, and at last to bed for the first time in six months. Went down to see Capt. Sill who commands at the 12th Corp. Landing and with him to his boarding place, a Mrs. Kipps, who is a regular secesh, with all her interesting family, of one son who is in the Rebel Army, and two daughters who sing "The Bonnie Blue Flag," and talk secesh generally.* And they say that Miss Anna will smoke. The yard is full of flowers, from which I picked one or two, and came away. At the office where Capt. Sill reports for orders I became acquainted with Clay Hammond of Boonsboro, Md., a boy who was detailed from the 1st Md. Cavalry as clerk for Capt. Steiner. Their hospitality there supplied me with whiskey, two cakes of hardtac, handfull of cardamon seeds, and a tooth pick. I had use for them all. Then the Captain, Lefty Bronson, and I got a boat and took a ride. First straight across the bay, and then down to the house which was once the home of the Pirate Semmes. It is now fitly used as a Rest House and is now full of small pox patients. Gathered some "relics" and again embarked, made then for the Prison Ship, out in the river. It is full of secesh soldiers, Rebel citizens and Yankee Deserters. I heard an old violin going between decks, and it seemed to be leading a break-down dance. Next we started out toward the Maryland side of the river, but were speedily overhauled by a Provo Guard boat. Luckily for us we happened to be acquainted with the officer in it (21st NY Buffalo Vols.), and they let us run. It was a long pull even to the center of the river, but we kept on until we came to a gun boat. The Lieut. commanding invited us

---

*"Bonnie Blue Flag" was the second most popular patriotic song of the Confederacy, after "Dixie." Lyrics by English-born Harry McCarthy, set to an old Irish tune, "The Irish Jaunting Car" in 1861.

on board, and we had a fine visit. He showed us all over the boat, and we were charmed with all we saw. I would by far prefer the Navy to the Army were I to enlist again. Last and best of all was the sleep I had that night in a bed, a positive luxury.

Sunday, April 19: A rapid walk up the shore of the bay in the morning brought me to camp just in time for a fatiguing Battalion Drill, which was followed by a regimental inspection, rather an extra bill of fare for Sunday. Sleepy and tired, but the day was a fine one. Religious services in the afternoon. A good sermon by the Chaplain. It really seemed like church at home.

Tuesday, April 21st: Went up to Gen. Williams' H'd. Quarters at Stafford C.H. with Reynolds, Knox, Middleton, and Koloon, to get mustered. We were unsuccessful as usual. Got some pie at an Army bakery, some mail at the Stafford Co. Clerk's Office, some flowers at another place (where a house once was), some waterfat at Mrs. Morton's, where the four young ladies dwell, and got very tired ere I got home.

Wednesday, April 22nd: Brigade Drill at the C.H. We did poorly, through the Col.'s stupidity, and came back very much chagrined.

Thursday, April 23rd: A rainy day. It has fairly poured all day. Long to write, but managed to grind out only one poor letter. Little Katie Johnson is dead. How dark the days must be for Fanny now. God bless and comfort her!

Friday, April 24th: Our Company went on guard today, and I acted as "officer of the day," the first time I have officiated in that capacity. I bear my honor meekly!

Saturday, April 25: Took an evening walk with Lefty Bronson, and Drake, down to White House Landing.

Sunday, April 26: To Stafford C.H. Va.

A beautiful day. We had good church services and enjoyed the delicious quiet of a beautiful Sabbath day. But the evening brought orders to march, which set us all as usual to packing up and writing home.

(To Father) All is confusion and bustle with us here. We have orders to march at daylight. As the Capt. is still away, I have to attend to the getting ready of the company, and to making up the Company and Mess property. Nevertheless I have stopped short in the business, have come into Howard's tent, for my own is all down and packed, and will try to write you a few lines. I have got me a skeleton knapsack, and shall get a summer blouse, to save my uniform. The paymaster has been paying off our Brigade for a day or two. He has paid all but us, and now we expect we must say goodbye pay master for the present. It comes rather tough, for we ought to have some pay in starting on a march like the one we now look forward to. You remember the great stacks of grain that we saw down at the Landing. Well, the whole landing is deserted, not a tent or a wagon is left nor do any more boats stop there. All is deserted and desolate. Howard drew some grain the other day and some of the sacks were marked "Peter P. Horick, Hornellsville" Rather queer that they should get down here to us! Well, I must go to work packing up again. I am well and in good spirits. We are well prepared for what is before us, and let it come! At sunset we were on the move. Joined the Brigade at Stafford C. H. Were paid off in the night, and all ready for another push against the Rebellion.

Hooker's Campaign of the Spring of 1863

Monday, April 27th: Stafford C. H. [Court House] to Hartwood Ch. [Church], Va.

Once more on the march! How inspiring! The roads are good, the sights and scenes are interesting, and all are in the best of spirits. This is the joy and the interest of a soldier life. Co. K was paid off about four o'clock in the morning. Capt. Sill got in with his detachment from White House in time to be paid, and now has charge of the company again. We found a fine camping ground at Hartwood, in the woods near the site of the old church. Got into camp early, and were all ready for our night's rest before dark. Away over toward the Rappahannock we could see great camps, where the 5th Corps were encamping for the night. Visited the Hartwood church and picked some flowers from the neglected graveyard behind it.

Tuesday, April 28: To Kellys Ford, Va.

From Hartwood we marched to Grove Ch. where we made a halt for dinner. Gen. Hooker passed us here and received a cheerful salute from our command. Here too we met the 6th NY Cavalry boys.

P.M.: Marched to Kellys Ford. From the precautions adopted we seemed to be nearing the enemy. Drums were silenced and large fires prohibited. We could dispense with the music, but the fires seemed necessary for our cooking, and Col. Diven's personal efforts were brought into requisition, in the way of kicking over fires, etc., to enforce the order. This morning he seemed to think his personal efforts necessary to get the regiment awake and ready to march. He went around to the pup tents and shook out the

Fight at Kelly's Ford, *sketch by A. R. Waud, Harper's Weekly*, December 5, 1863.

laggards who had not obeyed the first summons of the reveille "Get up! Battalion! Get up and cook your coffee."

Wednesday, April 29: To Germanna Mills, Va.

It seems that the 11th Corp has been ahead of us, for this morning we passed through their camps and took the lead. They were encamped just south of the Ford (which however was crossed by Pontoons). When we passed the 107 Ohio there was considerable yelling by the boys as they saw the numbers on each other's caps. Pushed ahead through the 11th Corp skirmish line, but saw no enemy excepting two or three detachments of prisoners. Our Brigade was in the advance, 3rd Wisconsin, 2 Mass., 27 Indiana, 13th New Jersey, 107 NY.

Had a long march through a splendid region, fine roads and grand old trees. Occasionally on nearing the woods, the column would be halted, a regiment or two deployed to advance, and the rest of the troops passed, ready for action. But the skirmishes would find nothing and the column would string out again. The Cavalry ahead of us were sufficient to drive back the small Rebel in our front. But they came to a standstill at the Rapidan, near which we arrived about two o'clock. They found Rebels enough there to give them a sharp fight. But the infantry went down, the advance of our Brigade, and soon stopped the fun, taking the whole Rebel force prisoners. Our regiment was drawn up in double column and with gun loaded were waiting to be led into the Bloody Fray. The first Brigade was passed at our right. The 134 NY just beside us, the officers of which were cutting off their shoulder straps that they might not be too prominent marks. Then a column of prisoners came in, about two hundred in all, ragged, dirty, and sassy. The order came to advance, and we marched down to the Ford to find the Battle all over. Crossed by deep wading.

Thursday, April 30th: Got up at three. Stood around in the rain till 8 or 9, then made a rapid march down the plank road toward Fredericksburg. Got within 8 miles of it and encamped, detached to support Battery. Cheers and music. We have done a big thing.

May 1st: Advanced on the road to Fredericksburg to cover a movement of Gen. Mead on Bunk Ford. Came back, and then went back to get knapsack. Slight skirmish. Back to camp and had a fight. 27th Ind. ahead of us. Capt. Rutter was struck by a shell. Poor fellow, a sharp fight along the line. Slept on our arms.

Saturday, May 2nd: Capt. Rutter is dead. Poor fellow. What a terrible thing is man! Started off on a wild goose chase through the bushes. Returned to find the Rebels had turned our flank. Great confusion in our own entrenchments. Formed at last a new line. But little sleep that night.

Maj. Gen. George G. Meade Commanding, Army of the Potomac (Wenderoth & Taylor, Late Broadbent Co.).

Sunday May 3rd: Went into action in the morning, the Rebs attacking us where we lay. Did well. Used up our ammunition before retiring. Eugene Howe and Theodore Morris left dead in the field. Capt. Sill wounded, and Will Hammond, Geo. and Charles Norton, and Jim Pinch.

Evening: Went over to the extreme left.

Monday May 4th: Taking position behind a row of batteries where no Rebels could drive us out. Just before the 107th is the old Doubleday's Battery that fought in Sumpter with Major Anderson.

Tuesday, May 5th: A day of quiet but a night of deepest anxiety. We supposed the whole Army was crossing, and we were to be left to cover the retreat, to fight and then either die or be gobbled. The darkest hour of my life. I could only trust in God and God was gracious unto me.

Wednesday, May 6th: After sitting up all night, crossed the Rappahannock in the morning. The whole Army, in safety. Met Truman Mason of University of Rochester on the Pontoon, and we went over together. A terrible march to Stafford Court House, through mud, creeks, rain, taken in by some Good Samaritans of the 9th NY Cavalry.

Thursday, May 7th: (Sick and writing letters for comfort and consolation). Six years ago today Lorenzo Doro preached here.

Friday, May 8: Still sick but around. No chance for me to try to give up as I am Lt. Commander. My old school friend Dexter with Will Mason of the 23rd NYV made me a visit.

Saturday, May 9th: The First Division was reviewed today. I was not able to go out with my company. Gen. Slocum told them that they had not disgraced their star. That they had made it indeed a badge of honor. He promised us rest.

Sunday, May 10th: Little Alden is married. The Captain is in Seminary Hospital doing well. It was a painful task to write to Mrs. Howe and Mrs. Morris of the death of their sons.

Monday, May 11th: Col. Diven and Adjutant Fanton have resigned. The Col. made us a noble speech at Dress Parade. He says that Col. Colby of the 23rd will succeed him. Good.

Tuesday, May 12: Col. Diven left us today, after going around and bidding each one goodbye. The adjutant also left having secured me for his correspondent. Very hot today. Beautiful music in the evening from our Brigade band.

Wednesday, May 13th: Surgeon has resigned. So they go. Well, so long as the Lord spares my health, I trust he will give me the pluck to stay. I am messing with the Adj't, and live high. I am not very well or strong. Our last movement was tough on me.

Thursday, May 14: Nin writes that she has experienced a change of heart. Blessed news may she be faithful to the end. God grant that all around her may feel the same gracious influences. Would I could hear this from home too! Nin is also much grieved by my talk of her faults, and by my fancied neglect.

Friday, May 15th: Am getting rested up and will be able to march soon again. God gave me strength and courage to do my duty. I often think longingly of home and friends, but it must not be. I must see the thing out or be worn out in the attempt.

Saturday, May 16th: Refreshing to get such good letters. Cooper gives the names of several who have been converted, among them Miss Fredenbury. He says that Densmore and Ben are also anxious for their souls. Regimental inspiration by Lt. Snow.

Sunday, May 17th: Truly a day of rest. These are beautiful days, and we are all feeling their good influence. Listened to a sermon by the Chaplain of the 27th. Ind.

Tuesday, May 19: Capt. is going home with his crutches on a 30-day leave of absence. Pinch was in the hands of the Rebels who treated him kindly for fifteen days.

6. Hooker's Campaign of the Spring of 1863

Wednesday, May 20th: Done gone sick, got a bad diarrhea somehow, which is taking the strength right out of me. Rec'd per Chaplain a splendid meerschaum from Capt.

Thursday, May 21: Feeling a little better. Very warm today, very warm.

May 22: Sick after drill, severe headache, very warm still.

May 23: Oppressively warm. Went over to Brigade Drill, but arrived before the rest of the company. Capt. is home and doing well.

May 25: Sick with Remittent Fever.

May 26: Getting no better.

May 27: Sick, sick, sick.

May 28: Sick

May 29: Sick

May 30: Sick but I roused of strength enough to write home. This was enough for one day.

June 1: Received vignettes from Honey and Hartman, Rochester U., Russell as a student, now how different!

Tuesday, June 2: Sick as ever very weak.

June 3: Moved to Hospital. Better bed. More regular care taken of me.

June 4: Fever about broken up but I take more medicine than ever.

June 5: Pitched camp again. A long exhausting day for me.

June 6: Glad to hear from my friends but am too sick to answer them.

Monday, June 8: Changing camp. As the Hospital unit was taken down I came back to the adjutant's tent.

June 9th: Take no medicine today for the first time, after taking so much.

Wednesday, June 10th: Visit from Col. Van.Valkenburgh. Wish I could be in Rochester today. Senior examinations, etc.

Thursday, June 11th: My fever has left on me a disease of the groin, which hurts me when I rise up or sit down, or try to walk, or to turnover in bed. Kam Brigade will have an accession. Orders have come again to march. Everything is unsettled, but God ruleth.

Saturday, June 13: Orders to march early in the morning. Merely to move the camp back so as to draw in the picket lines. Fell back about two miles. Pitched camp. The 107 in Gen. Stein's old quarters. Suddenly the whole Brigade was ordered off toward Dumfries. The sick waited long at the Carlen House for the ambulances. Took us to Aquia. Reached there at midnight, with troops moving north all the time.

Sunday, June 14th: In the morning they came to clean out the whole hospital. So they took us to the Landing and loaded us on boats (I on the Hero). By a rare chance got a bunk. Boat unloaded at Alexandria. I saw Mt. Vernon and Fort Washington on the way. Capt. Bennet and I came on to Washington. Went to Markhams. Got something to eat and went to bed.

June 15th: Saw Gen. Knipe stopping at Markhams. Early went up with Capt. Bennet to Seminary Hospital Georgetown. Was admitted and put in ward 14, bed No 74. Was delighted to find in a room near me my old friend and brother ψγ Ira Clark.

June 16th: My groin trouble is pretty bad. I walk with great difficulty.

June 18: Another warm day warmer than yesterday, but so hot! And my disease has been getting worse so that I cannot leave my bed to get a draft of air. But in the afternoon, how welcome! There came up a thunder shower, and after that we were more comfortable.

Sunday, June 21: A little more like Sunday than when in camp, though I had to keep my bed as on other days. But I could hear the church bells ring, the first I have heard since the 14 of last September at Frederick City when we marched to the Bloody South Mountain field. How good they sounded!

Monday, June 22: There are rumors of our going to Philadelphia. They have been taking all our names including Ira Clark, Capt. Bennett and I, in anticipation of a big battle in front, from which they expect many wounded to whom we must give place.

Tuesday, June 23: We will not go to Philadelphia until a battle occurs. Dr. Peters talks discouragingly about a leave of absence.

June 24: Down to the city and didn't get my pay but I did get an awful lame leg. Rejoiced to hear from home. Reports again that we go to Philadelphia tomorrow. Is the great battle at hand?

June 25: Went down to the city after my pay again. Found Major McConnell and got my 205 dollars in greenbacks. At one o'clock we were all packed up and waiting to go to Philadelphia. After waiting two or three hours we were sent back to our rooms. Won't go till tomorrow.

Ira C. Clark, Adj., 140th Reg. New York Volunteers

Friday, June 26: Morning: Ambulances did actually come. Took us to the depot. Put us on the train. Saw Capt. Dann and wife Jolly load. Baltimore, Wilmington, and at last Philadelphia. Supper at the citizen hospital, fine ride to Comaco Woods. In room with Ira Clark and two other Monroe Co. boys.

June 27: Officers Hospital Comaco's Woods is a splendid place in a grove that was once an English lady's country seat. We live like Lords here. Went down to the Chestnut Street theatre with Ira Clark in the evening and heard Camille poorly played.

Sunday, June 28: A beautiful day, quiet as a Sabbath in the country. Could not go down to the city to church as the street cars do not run on Sunday. Our Hospital Chaplain recently appointed will not go on duty til tomorrow.

Monday, June 29: Made a raid into the city with Ira Clark. Made a lot of purchases. Got an immense dinner and returned. Had a visit from four good Methodist ladies who are interested in the soldiers.

Tuesday, June 30: Was detailed with six or eight others to go down to the city and report to Lt. Col. Frink for light duty. Was placed in charge of a company whose Capt. was away. After taking dinner and thinking it all over I concluded that Comaco's Woods was a better place than corner of Broad and Cherry St. and resigned.

July 1st: Made another raid into the city with Ira Clark. Bot me a pair of shoes and paid a visit to Independence Hall where the Declaration of Independence was signed.

Thursday, July 2: Downtown with Ira Clark. Visited the Navy Yard and Ninth Fairmount Water Works, after having taken the biggest dinner at the Continental that I ever attempted to devour.

July 3rd: Concluded not to go downtown but after waiting till afternoon could stand it no longer, and made another raid into the Quaker city. Got my pay for May and June.

July 4th: To the city. Around with Lt. Horlove, then to West Philadelphia Hospital and saw Will Hammond. Back to the Continental where I met Major Fox. With him the rest of the day. Fairmount in the afternoon.

July 5th: A rainy day. Reading and sleeping. In the afternoon went over to the Monument Cemetery just opposite the Hospital.

July 6th: Got a certificate of disability today from Dr. Kamak (Finding out that I was a $\psi\gamma$ in the operation) and sent it up. Have reason to hope for a twenty-day leave.

Tuesday, July 7th: In addition to the glorious news from the brave Army of the Potomac, we hear that Vicksburg is taken! Glorious.

Wednesday, July 8th: Gladdened by the arrival of Capt. Sill. He will stay with us here instead of reporting at Washington. Rainy day.

Thursday, July 9: Another rainy day. To Fairmount with Capt. Rained so we came back to the same car. Jolly load, ran off the track twice.

Friday, July 10th: Around with Capt. all day. Tried Fairmount Park again and had a splendid afternoon stroll. Came home and found to my great joy a leave of absence for twenty days waiting for me.

Started for home at 10. P.M.

Reached Elmira at noon of the 11th of July, Saturday. Saw Rob and other friends and took the four o'clock train for home, where I arrived before dark finding the dear ones all there and well. Thank God. Home again!!

During Tuttle's hospitalization and home leave, his unit moved Saturday June 13th from Stafford Court House, Va., to Dumfries, to Fairfax Court House and northward through Palisville and Frederick, Md., to arrive at Littlestown, Pa., near Gettysburg Wednesday July 1st. Following the battle of Gettysburg, they returned via Littlestown Sunday 5th, and continued southward through Monocacy, Md. the 8th to Robersville the 9th, Bakersville the 10th, and on to near Bealeton, Va. where Tuttle rejoined them on the Rappahannock August 13, 1863. — Editor

One Year of Service Is Passed

The Story Begins Anew with the Return to the Army After the Twenty Days Furlough

July 1863

Arrived in Philadelphia at about 7 o'clock in the morning, and soon reached Comaco's Woods. Capt. Sill, Capt. Bennett, and Ira Clark all doing well. Found two letters from Nin (Alas) asking for a picture, which I sent. Tired out.

P.M.: Called at Mrs. Heilmans.

Friday, July 31st: Getting rested up a little but slept all the forenoon — Afternoon went downtown with Capt. Sill. Sent some music to Preima. Made quite a long call at Mrs. Heilmans again. Writing in the evening.

August 1st: Running around with Capt. Sat for some photographs,* made purchases, etc., preparatory for speedy return to the Army. Doctor says he will send us back next week. Chestnut Street Theatre in the evening.

August 9: Spent the day quietly, at the hospital. All ready to rejoin my regiment.

In the evening took a ride with my new found friend Charlie McKan. We had a long talk, all about our visits home, of our loves and our resolves to lead a better life.

---

*See photograph on title page

Monday, August 10th: Philadelphia to Washington

We leave: Horton, Blain, Kaesin, Dutton, and I go in a party together. Kaesin and Horton I like. Through delays at Philadelphia and Baltimore did not reach Washington till evening.

Found Mrs. Baker at the Penn Hotel. Theatre in the evening.

August 11: Spent the day in Washington, the dirtiest, dustiest, filthiest place I ever saw. Intolerably hot, as it has been for some days. Nothing like it. Sleep out doors o'nights. Visited the capitol, and went to Georgetown to see Lieut. Quirk.

Wednesday, August 12: Washington, Alexandria, Warrenton, and Bealeton, where we five separated to go to our different Corps. Saw John Smith at Alexandria, and Litton Wilburn came down with us on the train. Started for camp with Capt. Balcom of the 3rd. I stopped at Corp H'd Quarters. He went on.

Thursday, August 13: Rainy morning but I walked on to my regiment, on the Rappahannock, a mile down Kellys Ford. Col. Crane and everybody seemed glad to see me. I was glad to see everybody. Found the Co. and Regiment in much better condition than I had expected. Tired and lame.

Friday, August 14: Do not report for duty yet, as I want to rest a day or two so writing letters, found a batch waiting for me. Lt. Van Valkenburgh is and has been in command of Co. K.

Sunday, August 16th: Reported for duty, but Van still stays with us. Attended church and prayer meeting in the evening. Confessed my sins before men. Lt. Van ordered to H'd Quarters as AATG.

August 17: Went on duty and appeared at inspection in command of Co. K. The event of the day was the receipt of a letter from Preima. Such a good letter! Ah, I have had the blues for some days, but I am all right now. Answered it in the evening.

August 18: Things look as if we were soon going to move. I am trying to find my Savior once more. "Nearer, my God, to Thee."

Lt. Ed. P. Van Valkenburgh Co. A, 107th Reg, New York Volunteers

August 19: I wonder why the Capt. delays?

August 20: All quiet on the Rappahannock.

August 21: Brigade drill in the afternoon (of the 13th, 107th, 150th). The 2nd, 3rd, and 27th have gone off on some mission. Tired me out. Am not strong yet. No letter from home yet. Howard returned today. Seems good to see the boy once more. He is looking pretty thin though. He brought my letter from home and a splendid picture of Carrie.

August 22: Terribly warm these days are.

August 23: The Chaplain gave us a good sermon today.

Monday, August 24: Began work on the muster rolls.

August 25: Went on picket for the first time in my service, along the Rappahannock. Call from Charlie Baker. He says the Capt. is at Pleasant Mt. (better be here attending to his business!)

Beautiful night, tho cold, and our tour of picketing was most pleasant. Carrie never wrote me a longer letter. Carrie writes that Emmet is dead. Sad!

August 28: Sat up in Howard's tent till very late in the evening, talking with him and the Col. Burned out the Q.M.'s candle, then the Adjutant's, then the Col's, and then I went and got mine. It was half past two when we went to bed.

August 29: The Capt. has not come, and another week has rolled by. My muster rolls are now nearly all made out, and Company waiting. Read and so much writing occupy my time.

August 30: Another quiet Sabbath with interesting services at church in the afternoon. "Watch ye stand fast in the faith, quit you like men, be strong."

August 31: Muster day: Muster Rolls are in and a great worry is off my mind. What a glad surprise was Preima's letter! And such a good letter.

Scare in the evening, under arms all night. Sat up and wrote to Preima. "And ye shall know the truth, and the truth shall make you free. All things are possible to him that believeth."

September 3: "Lord, I believe. Help thou my unbelief."

September 4: Built me a new house. Three Rebels came over and gave themselves up to our pickets today with their horses and arms and accouterments complete.

September 5: Went on picket. No Rebs came to give themselves but they showed themselves waved hats, etc.

September 6: Came in from picket dirty and sleepy. Lt. Benedict, the new Adj., has come. Good church in the afternoon, good attendance, good sermon. Evening Cap. Bennett arrived. Says Capt. Sill is at Bealeton.

September 7: Today the Capt. arrived bringing with him T. R. Trembly, of Dansville formerly, now *New York Herald* reporter. I feel better now that my "Pa" has come.

September 8: The Chaplain has resigned, and expecting the acceptance of his resignation, he this evening preached his farewell sermon.

September 9: No letter from anybody. The Capt. and I are going to work at Ordnance and clothing accounts. Brigade Review. Big thing on the double quick. Great joy in camp. The Sutler had arrived.

September 10: Division Review. Went off well. Carrie writes me that she expects to be married next month, is aware of my disappointment, has been much troubled by it but cannot change her determination. Farewell sermon of the Chaplain. He is gone!

September 11th: Lt. Col. Colby has resigned. Now there will be another epidemic of "Major on the brain."

September 12: Cannot see why I do not hear from home or from Preima, and the long silence of Louise is a puzzle to me too.

September 13: The rainy season is coming on. Had one or two heavy showers already. Our Cavalry crossed this morning and took the Rebs just on the other side…still driving them. We have heard firing all day.

September 14: Lt. Orr has just heard that Prof. Ford has married his sister-in-law.

September 15: In the evening Col. Colby and Major Fox arrived in camp. The Col. was discharged for inability against his wish. The Major was unable to walk without crutches. Not feeling at all well, sick headache. Something new for me.

September 16: Kellys Ford to Stevensburg.

Started early from camp but did not cross the ford till nine. Hot march, though full of delays. Van let me ride his horse, which saved me. Reached Stevensburg at five. Magnificent view of country. Poor I was sent out on picket.

September 17: A day of painful waiting. Expecting all the time to get into a fight, but the night came and no fight yet. Toward night a little artillery firing added to that of the musketry skirmishing. Rain. Expecting a hard fight on the morrow.

September 18: All quiet. No fight. A heavy rain.

P.M.: Saw a 3rd Mass. deserter shot. Sad sight. Nin has had a long talk with her mother who advises that our correspondence be stopped. Yet it is left to me to desist.

September 19: Quiet enough until night when there was a sharp engagement on our left and we had quite a scare. Have caught cold and am sick. Strange indeed that I hear nothing from Preima.

September 20th: Changed camp to a better spot near Corp H'd. Quarters. Laid out a good camp. Good letter from Preima. Her delay explained. Happy again, tho almost sick. Beautiful evening sing in the adjutant's tent closing with "Praise Him from whom etc."

September 21: Fixing up camp, building a house. Charlie Baker (cousin) came over to see us. Worked all day, and at evening received orders to put up eight day's rations. Everybody disgusted, yet we may not march immediately. I have a very bad cold.

September 22: Well, we did not march today after all. Went over to see friends with the first Brigade. Found that Mc — of R. U. lost a leg at Chancellorsville. He was in Co. H 20th Conn.

September 24: In the afternoon, we were suddenly ordered to dig out. Marched to Stevensburg, and then to Brandy Station. Met Robert Niven on the way. Everybody puzzled by the movement. But it seems to be agreed that we are going to leave the Army of the Potomac.

September 25: At Brandy Station all day: turning over everything except private baggage, and taking that up for transportation. Some say we are going to Tennessee, some to Texas. Witnessed the shooting of another deserter.

Evening: Col. told us we are going to Tenn., and under Gen. Hooker.

September 26: Made an early morning march to Bealeton via Rappahannock. Waited all day at Bealeton but no cars came until evening, though the paymaster came and we got our little greenbacks.

September 27: Bealeton, Alexandria, Washington, Relay House.

At One P.M. embarked for our journey. At Alexandria met some of the 107th boys, some 141st NY boys, and took dinner with John Smith.

Everybody drunk in Washington or soon after. My car a pandemonium. Passed Relay House about midnight.

September 28: Harpers Ferry to Cumberland, Md.

At day light we were moving through Maryland, passed through Harpers Ferry into Virginia again, and took refreshments at Martinsburg. Passed through the Kingwood tunnel ⅛ mile long. Reached Cumberland at evening, and saw more pretty girls waving handkerchiefs than usual.

Tuesday, September 29: Grafton to Belaire, Ohio.

At Grafton looked for Johnson and his wife. He was away, and though she was in town I could not find her. Through other tunnels and wild scenery reaching Benwood about midnight. Crossed a pontoon to Belaire, and off on the cars again.

Wednesday, September 30: Zanesville, Columbus, Zenia, & Dayton.

Took breakfast at Z at 10. AM. Saw Col. Brockwell of Rochester there. Staid sometime at Columbus.

Passed through Zenia and Dayton in the evening, where ministering girls attended us. Miss Sallie Eshiren of Dayton has my grateful remembrances.

October 1st: Richmond and Indianapolis, Ind.

Reached Indianapolis in the forenoon and staid several hours. Took

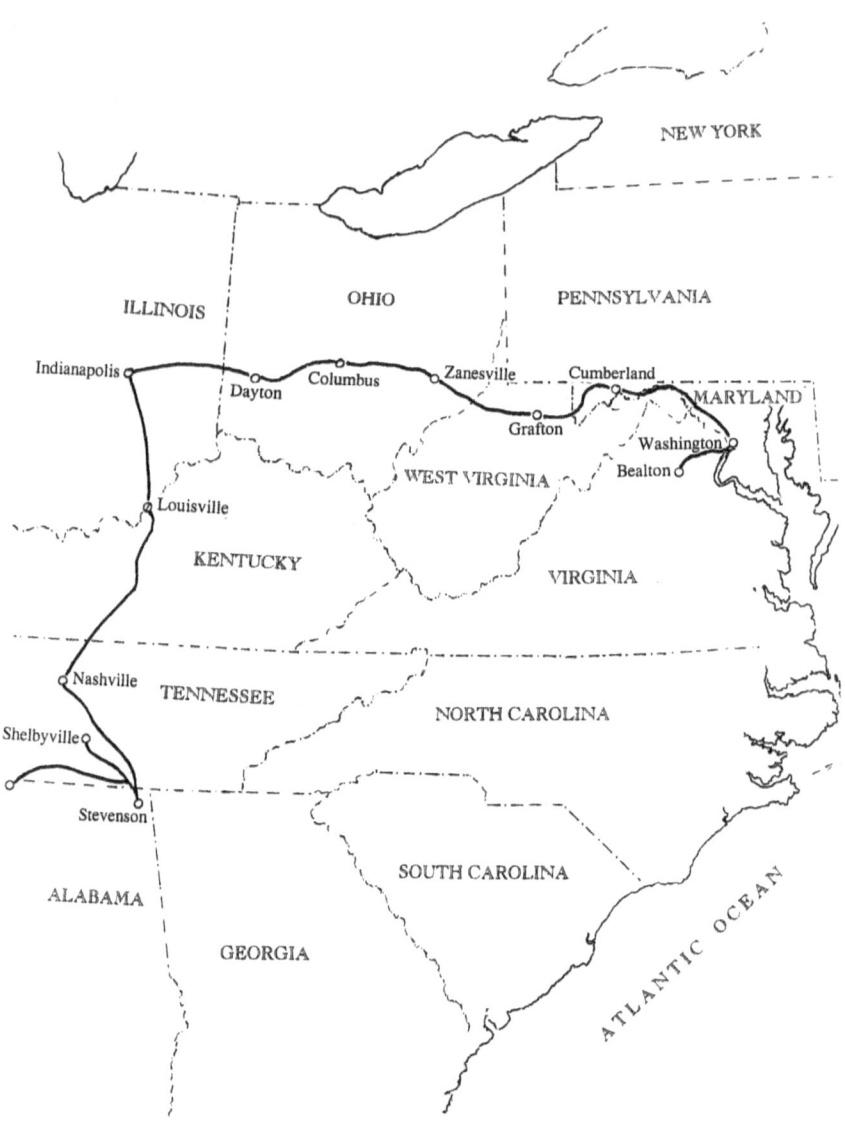

Rail Route, Virginia to Tennessee

refreshments at Soldiers Home — pretty girls to wait on us. And started away in the afternoon.

Friday, October 2nd: Louisville, Ky. to Nashville, Tenn.

Found ourselves at Jeffersonville, Ind in the morning. Crossed the Ohio and marched through Louisville. Took refreshments and then the L&N RR. Crossed Kentucky by day and reached Nashville by midnight.

Top: Murfreesboro, Tennessee, *sketch by F. Beard, Harper's Weekly,* January 31, 1863. *Bottom:* Decherd, Tennessee, *sketch by Hübner, Harper's Weekly,* September 20, 1862.

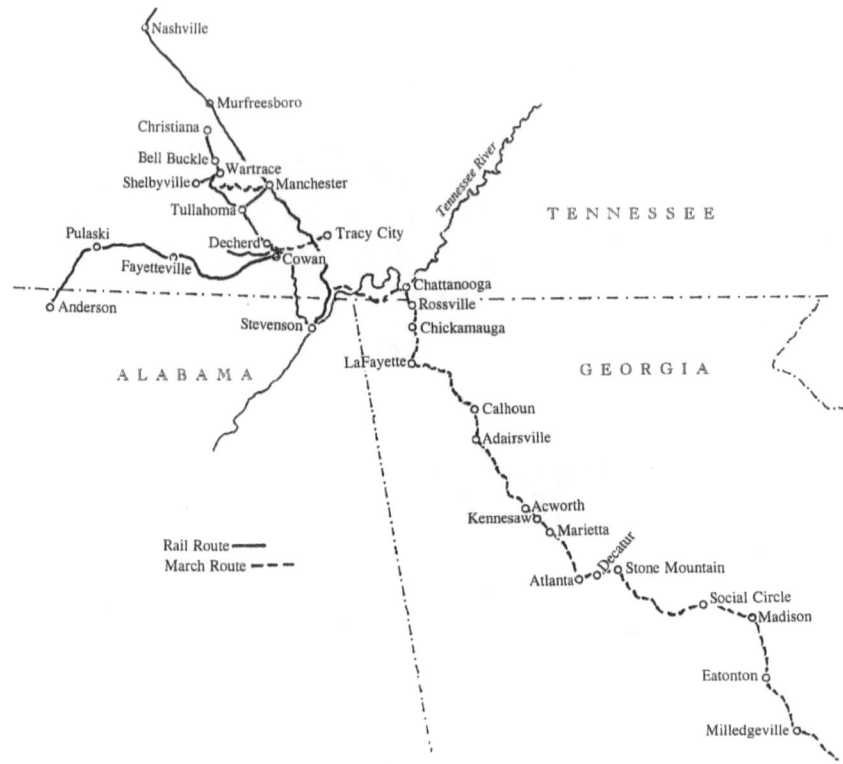

Tennessee–Georgia Campaign

Saturday, October 3: Murfreesboro to Tullahoma, Tenn.

Going through Tenn. Murfreesboro looked finely by moonlight. Reached by nightfall and crossed the Cumberland Mountains in the night to Stevenson, Ala.

Sunday, October 4th: Debarked at 1 AM and found ourselves "way down in Alabama." Wrote a letter to Charlie Wood, and started a letter to Preima when orders came to embark again, and we were taken back over the mountains to Decherd. This looks as if old Rosi didn't need us much.

October 5: Decherd, Tenn. The regiment is together again having been separated since leaving Belaire, O. Laid out a new camp and settled down to the strange conviction that the 12th Corp is to guard the railroad instead of going to the front.

Tuesday, October 6th: Waiting around for Forest's guerrillas. They are at work on the railroad. At near midnight, through darkness, and driving rain and dust we embarked on the cars, en route for the enemy. Cars awfully crowded, no comfort, no sleep.

Wednesday, October 7: Tullahoma & Bell Buckle, Tenn.

Passed Tullahoma at day break, at Goose Creek bridge (or some other). Debarked, and marched first to Wartrace and then to Bell Buckle. It rained and we were wet and tired, but got into a good camping place, and had a bully supper, and then a good sleep.

Thursday, October 8th: Bell Buckle to Fosterville & Christiana.

Marching down toward Nashville keeping near the track. Passed some of the most beautiful groves of hardwood that I ever saw. This is indeed a much finer country than Virginia. See nothing of the Rebs.

Friday, October 9: At Christiana still. Communication open with the North at last. In the evening, Co. I came in bringing six recruits for Co. K. Baker, Bonney, the Goffs, Nickelson, and Wells.

Bought some sugar (5¢ a lb) of a pretty girl whom I showed how to do it up.

October 10th: A long and hard march, Christiana to Normandy, and a little farther, full twenty-five miles by the road. Marched till some time after dark, till many fell out, and everybody nearly bushed, till most were swearing and all were thoroughly exasperated.

Sunday, October 11th: Normandy to Elk River Bridge.

Rec'd letters, one from R.T., from C.S.T., one from Preima, and Enos and Cooper and Torrey. Another long march, not so bad as on the day before, but more fell out. Received our mail at Tullahoma and our baggage at Estille Springs, near which we camped.

Monday, October 12: Sent letters to Carrie and Preima. A paper informs me of the marriage of "Sister Em," one sister less to Mr. A. P. Main of Madison. Wis. Carrie will be married on her next birthday, this day week, so they goes. Capt. and I took dinner with Mrs. Mason, who allowed she was for the Union, though Tennessee born. Prospects of a permanent encampment.

October 13: Rain, rain, all day long. Men all out of rations, obliged to forage or share. Capt. Sill went up to Tullahoma to procure supplies.

Wednesday, October 14: Continued to rain all night last night and all day today. Heavy spell of weather! Carrie declares the great surprise manifested by our folks at hearing from us at Indianapolis. Nell writes a regular girl letter, but is very cordial — and she is one of Preima's friends.

October 15: No let up yet of the rain, day or night. Everybody is decidedly uncomfortable. I reckon this will raise the Tennessee so as to multiply old Rosi's communication. Let it rain. No mail yet. What is the matter?

Friday, October 16: A fair day at last. Detailed to take charge of a fatigue party, worked on fortifications across the river.

Hired a servant boy. Mak Rolls — age — size — hair wooly, complexion dark, height —, at five dollars a month, etc. I'll give him six.

Saturday, October 17: Getting ready to build. Got brick from the ruins of the cotton factory over the R.R. And in the afternoon the Capt. went out with a party and a team of the engineers and got some lumber, some strippings for beds and a couple of sheep. Went up to the Springs.

October 18: A resting day. Tomorrow we will begin on our house as most of the materials are collected. No religion services. With no Chaplain we lost our religious life seemingly. Finished a letter to Preima. No mail yet.

Monday, October 19: Commenced on our house and got it inclosed and roofed. Slept in a dry, elevated from the floor bed for the first time in many weeks. Carrie is eighteen years old today, and today I expect was married to Dr. J. W. Robinson. I wish God's blessing on them.

October 20: Built a chimney on our house. Putting in a fireplace neat enough for any parlor. In the evening had the satisfaction of sitting by our own hearth, and penning these lines by our own firelight.

October 21: Rainy day but we worked a little on the inside of our house. Put in a glass and a bunk.

Thursday, October 22: Finished our chimney and made a table and took our ease — I was almost sick.....with.....

Left: Maj. Gen. George H. Thomas (Commanding, Department of Cumberland). **Right:** Gen. Ulysses S. Grant (Franklin & Co., Opticians).

Gen. Rosecrans is relieved, Gen. Thomas succeeding him, while Gen. Grant commands the United Armies of the Mississippi, the Tennessee, and the Cumberland.

Friday, October 23: Elk River Bridge to Decherd.

Pack up (*horribile dictu!*) and leave our new house!! But off we started. The Capt. remaining behind to finish the packing up, which they did not give us time to do. Rain, rain, rain, all day long and far into the night. Drew six days rations at Decherd.

Saturday, October 24th: Decherd to Tantalon.

A hard march though not so very long. But it took us over the Cumberland mountains. The Capt. came up, but is not well, and was about bushed at night. My boy Mak pleases me much.

October 25: Tantalon to Anderson, Ala.

The Capt. was not at all well, and got on the cars in the morning for Bridgeport, our supposed destination, but got off at Anderson. Marched to Anderson on the railroad track when we were surprised by being put into camp. "Down in Alabama" again.

Prayer Meeting.

October 26: Anderson to Cowan, Tenn.

Tuesday, October 27: Cowan to Tullahoma.

October 28: Tullahoma to Wartrace.

October 29: Wartrace to Shelbyville. Letters to R.T. & C.M.B.

Shelbyville, the only Union town in Tennessee, *sketch by H. R. Hübner, Harper's Weekly*, October 18, 1863.

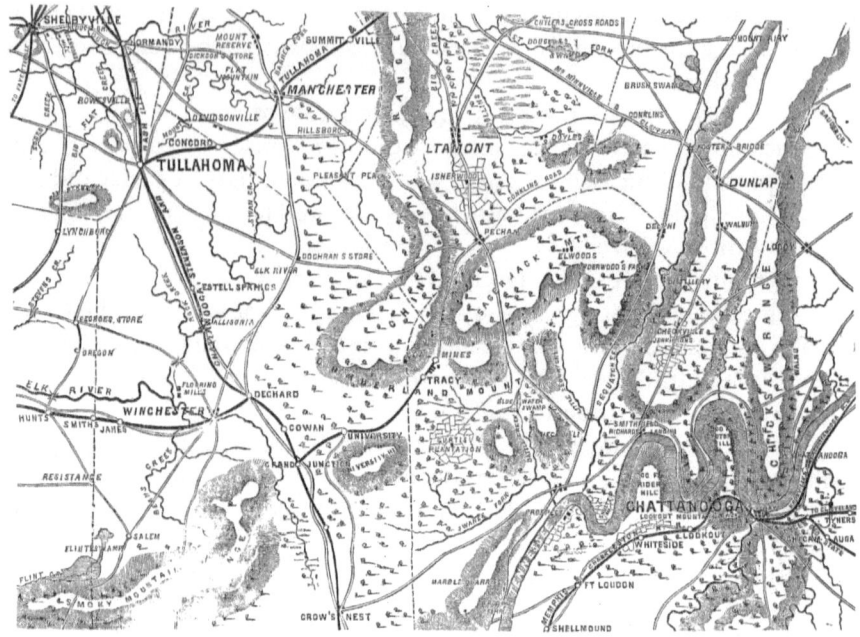

Tennessee, Shelbyville to Chattanooga, *Harper's Weekly*, September 5, 1863.

Friday, October 30: Rainy Day.

Saturday, October 31: Took board at Dr. Blackmore's.

November 1: Busy on Muster Rolls and reports.

November 2: Letters from Charlie Wood, Carrie, and Preima.

Capt. started for the regiment. News has come that Fox is Lt. Col. and Baldwin Major. Charlie gives good news from old ψγ. Carrie sends my Badge. How good it looks! and gives me the arrangements of the approaching marriage. Preima is glad to hear from me at last.

November 3: Capt. returned from Regt.

November 4: Letters from R.T. and Preima.

Father writes Carrie was duly married to Dr. Joe last Thursday 22nd inst. and they are away on their Bridal tour. So you see "there is one Tuttle less." Preima describes the wedding too, but thought all day of me.

Father is getting better of the lameness brought on by his fall.

November 5: Mrs. Blackmore is exercised greatly because her cook left her after living with her twenty-two years. "So much the poorer am I today on account of the Rebellion."

Feeling not very well. Wrote a letter Preima in the evening and listened to the band of the 33d Ind.

November 6th: Fine warm day. Sent letter to Preima. Splendid weather we have been having for some days now. Took a walk with Capt. to the Female Seminary and a beautiful place it must have been sometime.

November 7th: Am beginning to have some excellent drills. Was out on skirmish yesterday and on bayonet exercise today.

Sunday, November 8: A letter received from Preima.

November 9th: Visit of Col. Crane, Col. Hawley, & Lt. Flood. Cold day.

November 10: Skirmish drill.

November 11: Letter from Carrie. Now CSR.

November 12: Letter sent to Preima.

November 13: Letter written to R.T.

November 14th: Letter to Joe.

November 16: Rumors of a coming raid. Went out to Mr. Goslings in the evening with Will Caldwell. Was much pleased with the young ladies, Miss Saira [Sarah] & Miss Josephine who entertained us there.

November 17: Went to Wartrace by handcar, found the 107th at Wartrace Bridge in a fine camp, and had a tip top visit with the boys. Took a ride with Doc Pendergast up to see Van "Brig" etc. A classic sing in the evening.

November 18: Returned to Shelbyville on the train, bringing Charlie Fox with me. In the evening we were taken by Will Caldwell up to his Uncle Tom's and spent the evening with the Misses Bosworth.

November 19: Working on Ordnance and clothing. Letter from R.T. and Sheldon. Sent to Preima. Call at Mr. Goslings. Ordnance & clothing.

November 20: Letter from Preima. Wrote to Sheldon. Ordnance and clothing.

November 23: Wrote to Carrie.

November 24: Col. Slunderant and Capt. Beeman, Commissary Officers, are boarding at Dr. Blackmore's. Mr. Drabell is going to the hotel to board.

November 25: Wrote to R.T. Went over to Wartrace with Cap. Sill and Lieut. Swan and got our pay, and the pays of our companies. Missed the train and had to walk back. Paid off the boys in the evening.

Thursday, November 26: Thanksgiving Day. By order of old Abe. Went

Dr. P. Pendergast 1st Asst. Surgeon 107th Reg., New York Volunteers

to church in the morning, and heard a stiff Union sermon by an Army Chaplain. Drank a little too much egg-nog with Clay.

P.M.: Lon, Fox, and Doc Pendergast came over

November 27: Letter from Preima. Running round with the fellows. In the evening we four went up to the Goslings again. Pleasant evening entertainment. Many of the 107th boys over here and many of our boys drunk. Confound the whiskey!

November 28: The 107 delegation went back.

Sunday, November 29: Waked up and found it snowing a regular winter. Morning went to church and heard Mr. Marks.

November 30: Rumors of a coming Cavalry raid. One thousand Rebs at Salem. Getting ready for them.

December 1st: Sent Carrie some sprays of mistletoe. Took tea at Mr. Goslings. The Misses Bosworths were there, Will Caldwell and I with the 10th Maine officers. Pleasant time of course.

December 2: Eugene Thacher has arrived. The rest of the Elmira delegation came with him, and Ed Wellan comes back as 1st. Lieut. Glory! Delos also has come to Co. K. Eugene brings letters etc. from home, a roast turkey with...

Thursday, December 3: Made our Ordnance reports in the afternoon. Took a sleep in the afternoon. Woke up looking so blue that I took a walk with Will Caldwell to wear it off. A quiet evening spent in letter writing.

December 4: Sent letters to Nell R. and Preima. Beautiful weather this, a splendid rich mellow day this, all day long. Hunting up a new boarding place. Mrs. Konningham was not at home. Went up with Will Caldwell and played Euchre with the Misses Bosworths.

December 5: Wrote to R.T.

December 6: Went to church in the morning, heard Brother Marks—poor sermon. In the afternoon heard the Chaplain of the 17th Ind. at the Presbyterian Church, a good sermon. Sang in the choir. A still Sabbath-like day. Visit in the evening from Capt. Bachman, 107 NY. and Lt. Beers of the 18 Ill. Pioneer Corp.

December 7: Running around a little with Capt. Bachman. He wanted rather to be taken up to see the Misses Gosling. Preferred to remain and entertain Capt. Mitchell and Will.

December 8: Wrote to R.T. Rainy day. Bouton of Lockport has come to the Doctor's to board.

December 9: Rec'd from R.T. and Sheldon. Still rainy. Evening: Went up to Tom Caldwell's with Will and passed the evening as comfortably as could be expected.

December 10th: Capt. Sill appointed Provost Marshall here.

Shule here. Went to Miss W's with Will. Found there Col. Galbraith and lady, Capt. Norris, Mr. Win, and Miss Edith G. Some fine music. Mrs W. sings some like Preima.

December 11th: Wrote to R.T. Capt. Norris went to rejoin his regt. today and Col. Galbraith went too, to report to Gen. Thomas. Capt. Sill commands post.

Evening at Tom Caldwell's. The Misses Gosling were there with Capt. Sill, Hammond, Bouton, Will, and I. Music. Good time.

December 12: A letter from Preima and Charlie Wood.

Sunday, December 13th: Rainy day. Took dinner with Capt. Phrunson at the house of Mr. Cooper, Ed Cooper and several others. The nicest dinner I ever sat down to. Appointed inspector of letters.

Monday, December 14: Capt. Bachman has come to take command of this detachment.

Tuesday, December 15: Howard and Van Valkenburgh and Shepherd over from the regiment. Howard brought over some clothing which I had a great time in distributing. Howard tells me of my recommendation to Topo. Eng. on Ruger's Staff.

December 16th: Howard and Col. went home today. Just about sick. My head ached and ached as if it would split open. Went to bed really sick.

Thursday, December 17: Writing letters, almost well. Got an order from Gen. Ruger to report to him in person and without delay. That Topographical Engineer thing.

Evening party at Mr. Fletcher's. Everybody there. Miss F. told my fortune.

December 18: Shelbyville to Wartrace.

In obedience to Gen. Ruger's orders started for his H'd. Quarters but found no train at Wartrace. Staid in camp overnight.

December 19: Wartrace to Tullahoma.

After waiting nearly all day got to Tullahoma on a freight train. Col. Hanley went down on same train. Was welcomed at Brigade H'd. Quarters. Was examined by the Gen. and passed.

December 20: Tullahoma to Wartrace. Wrote to R.T.—R.M.T., Lt. & AAT. E.

December 21: Wartrace to Shelbyville. Wrote to Carrie and Preima. Col. Fox and others came over with me. Van came too, to take command of Co. K. Took tea at Col. S. with Capt. Sill, the Misses Gosling with Fox & Howard.

December 22: Beautiful day and beautiful evening. I never enjoyed the weather better in my life. Around with Howard all day and in the evening went up with him to see the Misses Bosworth. Found Capt. Sill and Clay there. Had a good time.

December 23: Shelbyville to Tullahoma.

Lt. Ed. P. Graves, A.A.Q.M. 3rd Brig, 1st Div., 12th Army Corps

Reported to duty at Brigade H'd Quarters. Found to be a pleasant acquaintance, as I knew I would. Visited with Capt. Bennett and wrote letters. I did hate to leave Shelbyville.

December 24: Was invited to Gen — Ball at Decherd, at which the Lt. Graves and Dekert went down, but I concluded to remain. Had a good time all alone in the evening writing letters.

December 25: Wrote to Preima. A dull Christmas at home all day reading & writing letters.

Saturday, December 26: The Capt. writes that Aunt Jane is with him at Shelbyville, and wants me to come over — next week the Bosworth girls say. Good my Lord! News from the regt. is that the two companies at camp have been poisoned by a Thanksgiving turkey.

December 27: Tullahoma to Shelbyville. Met Col. Crane on the train at Wartrace. Met the 107 boys now there. Met the Brigade Band who had been over to Shelbyville and had a loud time. At Shelbyville went to Tom Caldwell's. Saw Capt. and Aunt Jane and the young ladies.

December 28: Grand party vesperé at T.H.Caldwell's. Many there. Good time. Supper Euchre dance etc. The Misses Gosling, the Misses Galbraith, Miss Molly Burk, Mrs. Mamie Fletcher, Col. Fox, Van, Bachman, Beeman, the 10th MC, etc.

Thursday, December 31st:

Good bye 1863. Eventful year, which God for me has crowned with his goodness.

Visiting with Capt. etc. through the day. Went up to see Aunt Jane in the afternoon and staid to tea. Walked over town through the darkest night I ever saw. The wind blowing a storm, and flurries of snow coming now and then — cold as blazes. Yet I went up to see the Misses Gosling. Miss Laura was sick. Chatted a while with Josie and came away.

With Ely, Hammond, and the boys of Co. K. To bed. This ended the year.

Shelbyville, Bedford County, Tennessee

From Army Note Book   **January 1, 1864**   Day by Day

Shelbyville, Bedford County, Tenn.

January 1: A cold blustering day. Thermometer down to zero, and winds blowing direct from the North Pole. Very cold. Intended to have gone back to Tullahoma today but the Shelbyville express was no go in such a cold snap. Came back. Took breakfast with Capt. Steiner, and then spent most of the day with Capt. Sill & wife playing Euchre etc. At four went up to dinner at Tom Caldwell's with them. Staid there a part of the evening. Played Euchre with Miss Helen.

January 2: Made one more unsuccessful attempt to get away from Shelbyville. RR still froze up.

Visiting with Aunt Jane as before and went up to supper with them. At the Caldwell's a good share of the evening. So I missed Howard and Binney who went up to the Goslings and desired me to accompany them. Letter from Preima. When I told Aunt Jane of which, she said Preima was "a bright girl and a good friend of hers."

"My Home"
"She often comes to meet me. Will she come
"And stand just in the corner of the lane?
"She is my Home! Oh will she come again
"And make me by her coming, nearer home?"

Sunday, January 3: Shelbyville to Tullahoma

Got out of Shelbyville at last. Left Lt. Binns there. Capt. Beeman and Steiner came over also. Met Mr. Caldwell at Wartrace. To Tullahoma with Capt. Beeman. Found that Gen. Ruger had gone home on leave of absence. Maj. Parks and Lt. Dekert went with him. At Brigade H'd Quarters found Capt. Horn of the 150th in Capt. Parks place. Looks like Uncle Frank.

January 4: Col. Crane is here with the 145 regiment NYV. It is to be broken up. Five companies go into the 107th, three into the 150th, and two into the 123rd. The officers of all to be mustered out. The Col. will send two more companies to Shelbyville. Gen. Slocum will leave Capt. Sill there yet. He is doing well there. The people seem to like him, so all is lovely yet. Ball in the evening at the hotel.

Got my two dollars' worth in a very few minutes and came home to have a little visit with Col. Crane. Adj't Henderson of the 145 came in and had a little talk.

January 5: Very cold year. Entirely too cold for comfort. Read *Sady Audley's Secret* till after midnight; shivering with cold all the time, and went to bed to sleep, cold as blazes till morning.

January 6: Got up with an awful cold. Made me feel like a fool. The temperature has moderated not a bit all day. Could do nothing but sit by the fire and doze. A letter from the Capt. with the good news that Col. Galbraith has been put in command of three regiments of Cavalry. He goes to East Tennessee. Capt. Ruger says that a detachment of the 2nd Mass. is to relieve the 107th boys at Shelbyville. Not so lovely, but I don't quite see it.

Janaury 7: My cold is positively getting no better. The weather ditto. Received no letters and so got mad and wrote a couple in the evening. Pikwik came over for a little visit.

January 8: This Staff life is a superlatively lazy one. The work amounts (at times) to little or nothing. Absolutely nothing for me just now, and servants, orderlies, and clerks do all there is to be done. Eating, sleeping, and reading constitute my sole employments. We rise at eight or nine to find boots blacked, clothes brushed, fire built, and breakfast ready, and as the day begins, so it progresses. This is a wreckless life too. He is not at home here who cannot swear like a trooper and risk money at cards, and drink unceasingly.

January 9: I did get a letter from Preima today, written just after she heard of my appointment on this Staff: "God hath sent me a Happy New Year in the good fortune sent you. Your sweet mother is not happier and prouder in her boy than I in my love."

January 10: A letter from Carrie at last. It must be that some of her letters have been lost.

January 11: Tullahoma to Shelbyville, Tenn.

January 12: Today I am twenty-four years old.

January 13: Today was noted by the arrival of a lot of Staff officers.

January 14: Staff officers all drunk. In the evening there was a party at Tom Caldwell's to which I took Binni, the only sober man in the party.

January 15: Got an awful cold in the head, just about sick. Wherefore cannot bum around with the fellows. Good thing.

Janaury 16: Started in the morning for home. The staff had had a grand drunk. Peers had had his ankle sprained, Bennet his nose peeled — and they all were about played out. We went in three ambulances overland to Wartrace.

January 17: Returned to Tullahoma. Found all as usual. Did what little business there was on hand for me, and recruited preparatory to returning to Shelbyville.

January 18: Tullahoma to Wartrace.

Went down in the night. Found Howard up, but got right on the Shelbyville train. The train didn't go, however, and I slept at the post Q.M's until morning.

January 19: Morning: Went from Wartrace to Shelbyville.

In the evening had a superlatively good time at Tom Caldwell's, but I found that playing Euchre with Miss Fanny did not pay. Mosly is gone! Capt. Beardly has been fooled completely. Everybody is indignant, yet half glad of it for they have predicted this very thing and Capt. B. laughed at them for it.

January 20: Evening at Mr. Gosling's with Will Caldwell. Had a very sociable time, but nothing particularly interesting. Lon Howard in town, but did not go with me.

January 21: Running around with Howard. We bought a fine coon. Ely, Hammond, Howard, and I went up to Tom Caldwell's in a hack and had a regular time. I feel at home there.

Eve: Called with Will Caldwell to see the Misses Mathews. Was very much pleased with them, in spite of their secesh politics. They are true ladies. Howard went home in the afternoon taking the coon with him.

January 22: Big thing. Some secesh women are going South, and I was detailed to go to their houses to examine

Arthur S. Fitch 1st Lt. 107th Reg., New York Volunteers (A. P. Hart, photographer).

their baggage. Took Arthur Fitch with me. Was a little modest with Miss Wallace, too easy, whereby I won her admiration. At Miss Witthorn's I met Miss Maggie Cunningham, a bright eyed girl, and at Dr.——I took quite a shine to Miss Agnes. Met more secesh women today than I wish to meet again soon, though some of them are nice people sure enough. Big thing.

Evening at Miss Amy Thompson's with Will Caldwell, etc. Met there also the Misses Galbraith and Miss Weisner, Miss Edith took a fancy to my handwrite...

January 23: Took a morning walk with Aunt Jane up to Mr. Caldwell's. On my return met Ed Fay who had been waiting for me, and who blew me up for running round to see the girls so much.

Returned to Wartrace in the afternoon having had the most pleasant visit I ever had there or perhaps anywhere. The weather was fine, and every evening I was out and had a good time.

January 24: Wartrace to Tullahoma. Balmy days. Firing near.

January 25: Shelbyville

January 26: Ride. Letter from Carrie.

January 27: Arrival of whiskey at H'd Quarters.

January 28: Ride. Grand Pow Wow

January 29: Ride. Return of General.

January 30: Ride to cave and cascade. Good time. Col. Crane going home.

January 31: Rest of Staff gone to Normandy. Carrie's letter. Nin's letter.

February 1: Fine weather yet.

February 2: Capt. Knight arrived.

February 3: Letter from Capt. From Preima.

February 4: Ride to RR Bridge. Inspection. First Topog duties.

February 5: Letter from Sheldon and Barton.

February 6: Letter from Crandall & Carrie.

February 7: Graves gone to Mulberry.

February 8: Inspection of 27th Ind. Forts etc.

February 9: Letter from Preima. More about tobacco.

February 10: Arrival of 3rd Wis. No inspection.

February 14: How are you religiously. Negro meeting.

February 15: James Stillman, Sam Benjamin

February 16: "Wm" Gone to Nashville A.A.A.C. Clothes arrived. Will Caldwell.

February 17: Pay of Major Stone. Hooker on the move.

February 18: Capt. Rugen returned. Tullahoma to Wartrace.

February 19: Wartrace to Shelbyville.

February 20: At Tom Caldwell's, Howard & Thorne.

Capt. Platt M. Thorne, A.A.I.G. 2nd Reg., 1st Div., 20th Army Corps

February 21: Abed all day. Awful cold & fever. (being at Tom's couldn't been the best thing)

February 22: Getting better. Fine weather. Evening at Tom Caldwell's.

February 23: Shelbyville to Wartrace. Gen. Schurz.

February 24: Wartrace to Tullahoma.

February 25: Fine weather. Ride. ADC Religious discussions.

February 26: Seriously began on CC & GS reports.

February 27: A quiet Sabbath until evening. Letters and Dictionary.

February 28: Letters from Preima, Father, Capt. Sill, and Matt Hale. On the march.

March 1st: Our H'd Quarters have been thronged all day with 2nd Mass. and 3rd Wis. veterans. I must confess that a better acquaintance with the officers of the 2nd has not improved my opinion of them to any extent. Parson Quint I like.

March 2: Finished a long letter to Preima closing it with a word of warning, that she must not consider me perfection itself. Who would wish to be disbursing officer? Graves woke us up in the night to ask us if we had his money. $2,000 — he had lost it, and we could tell him nothing about it.

March 3: Mr. Graves has found his money. It fell out of his pocket in Binni's room, and was picked up this morning by the "dark" who was honest enough to take nothing from it. Good for Graves. Writing letters nearly all day. Drew my pay from Major Stone for the month of January. He remembered me on the former pay roll of Co K.

March 4: Our H'd Quarters were enlivened by the presence of a lady, Mrs. Bartlet, who took tea with us. She is a lively pleasant lady, and has a retinue of officers around her wherever she goes. Mrs. Pattison called on us yesterday too—a pert little woman, but very pleasant I should guess.

Lost a good part of my sleep and all my patience by a lot of drunken officers. When an officer gets drunk and at a late hour of the night goes into another's quarters, and tears round, it is, to say the least, in very bad taste.

March 5: Had a call from Mason. He has got a leave of absence, and is going home tomorrow night. How I wish I could go with him. Dr. Anderson helped him to get his leave with a letter to Gen. Slocum in his behalf.

March 6: A beautiful day. Wrote a letter or two.

He was drafted, as was also the newly installed Chaplain of the 150th New York regiment in our Brigade. It's a very nice thing to be drafted as Chaplain, very different from shouldering a musket.

Is not life at Head Quarters a lot like life at court. I should think it was, very like. Of course I know but little of life at court, and scarcely more of life at H'd Q'rs. For this little Brigade Head Quarters does not amount to anything, and I can only judge from what I have heard. There is the same gaiety at Army Head Quarters, as at court, the same high living, extravagance, pageantry and show, the same vanity and pride, ambition and selfishness shown.

Gen. Hooker's Head Quarters on the Potomac a year ago, were a scene of magnificent dissipation. And at Head Quarters generally, where favors are to be sought and influence willed, throng courtiers as ambitious and designing and as unscrupulous in their small way, as can be found at any court. All this when in camp. But when an active campaign is entered upon, the scene changes very much. Earnest business is on hand, and the recklessness of camp life is for the time laid aside. Fine clothes are packed up, "blue and gold" give place to clothes of plainer hue and texture, and all start out as true campaigners, prepared for rain and storm and mud. I do not say that campaigning renders men any more high-minded, or temperate or honorable, except that they are too busy and find too little chance for the exercise of their failings then.

I met Smith B. a few days ago. He is a clerk in the same office with Jim Stillman, and brought me late news from him. They are in the office of Capt. Craig, Quarter Master of the 2d Calvary Division of this Department. A clerk in government employ has a far better place than an officer. Their wages are greater than mine, their expenses less. They share none of the dangers, and very few of the hardships of the soldier, and they are free men as no soldier or officer can claim to be.

On the same train with Smith was Major General Schurz with an aid-de-camp, going home on leave of absence. The train was delayed a long time at Wartrace, and I had the pleasure of taking tea with the man of two stars. Well, he is a very ordinary appearing Dutchman, a man of a high order of genius, but as a general not above the average. He is a fine orator, I think I never heard a more eloquent or interesting speech than I have heard him make on politics, or a more finished lecture on literature. And he used the purest English, free not only from any idiom of his native tongue but even from the slightest trace of the German accent. He is a fine scholar, but a radical republican in politics. He was a Rebel against his own government in Europe.

Nearly every General and general Staff officer manages to get at least one each year. Gen. Thomas has issued orders promising to grant furloughs, to the extent of five percent of all the forces in his Department. Each applicant is required to give the reason why he desires leave to go home. Ed Van Valkenburgh, brother of the former Colonel, 1st. Lieut. in our regiment, and at present commanding the company I belong to, sends up an application for leave of absence for the following purpose, "to consummate a matrimonial arrangement with the girl I left behind me" and will get his leave. I've no doubt.

March 7: I am disgusted with _____. He is all selfishness, sensuality and impudence. At table he wants the whole side of the table, helps himself, and goes to eating without thinking of the courtesies due to anybody, even the General. It is a great trial to me, to have him around, to sit near him at table, or to try to do any business when he is in the room. Sat up very late playing "California Jack" with the General & William.

Tullahoma, Tenn., March 8th, 1854:

Mr. Graves has returned from a short visit from Nashville. Visited the detachment at Poormano Creek Bridge. The Gen. has taken another inspection fit, and is going to visit the various posts under his command. He expresses some apprehension of a trend now that our cavalry have been unsuccessful in Mississippi.

Here is a sheet of rebel note paper, destined, though never intended, for a Yankee's use. It was "confiscated" at Shelbyville, but is worth but little except as a curiosity. As Capt. Sill says, one might as well try to write on a blanket as on this paper, unless he can write very softly. Once we had a rebel prisoner in our hands—a Lieut. from Forrest's Body Guard, and we allowed him to come into our quarters (at Shelbyville) and write a letter. He had nearly finished his letter, when he discovered some of this shoddy paper, tore up the fine commercial note on which he was writing, and wrote his letter on its rebel substitute. If it was any satisfaction to the poor captive, I was willing to let him take his choice.

I have been out on a long ride today inspecting defenses along the line of the road. I shall go on a longer trip tomorrow, if nothing happens to prevent. The General has an idea that the Rebs may attempt a raid on this Rail Road ere long, and he wants to be prepared for them. The failure of our recent Cavalry operations in Northern Mississippi, with certain other indications nearer us have roused the General's apprehensions. It would be a queer thing if we had a fight so far back from the front as this. The defensive works on the line are under the charge of the Brigade Topographical Engineers, so just now I have a plenty to do to see that every Redoubt and Stockade and Earthwork is thoroughly defensible. If the Rebs are really coming, I wish they would hurry along, and have the thing over with. I don't wish to be riding along the line all Summer, stirring up delinquent and negligent Post commanders. But it is pleasant rambling through this country, barring a little mud, which is inevitable here. But the air is pure and bracing, this is the highest point on the road from Nashville to Chattanooga, and a stroll through the woods and over hill and vale is a nice thing at any time. Spring flowers beginning to show themselves now. A young lady from the country brought in a fine bouquet for Capt. Knight our Brigade C.S.

March 9: Inspection of Fort in the morning and then went with the General and Capt. Horn to Normandy and Duck River. Inspected defenses at the latter place, and returned to Normandy to dinner. Took dinner with Col. Bartlett & lady. Inspected defenses at Normandy and then home, forming a part of the escort for Mrs. Bartlett, Green, and others going to Tullahoma in an ambulance to attend the Grand Military Ball. My horse kicked Capt. Bliven, hurting him seriously. Was very tired. Did not go to the Ball, but to sleep under the rain on the roof.

March 10: Tired out. Did little but lie still on my bed all day. My head ached a little too hard even for me to try to read. Nearly every night now, as the sun goes down, the storm comes up. "It rains & the wind is never weary." I go to sleep under the music of the pattering rain drops on the roof above me.

March 11: A letter from the Capt. All as usual at Shelbyville, and one from Preima.

Am reading Charlie Rud's *Hard Cash*, and am quite absorbed in it. I cannot fix my mind on anything more solid than novels now. I am half of a mind that I am ruined as a scholar. I will never more be good for anything that requires any thought. (It will be better maybe when I leave Shelbyville and Tom and Will Caldwell.) Large artillery force going on to the front.

March 12: Letters from Charlie, Luin, Stillman. Charlie wants me to become "Army Correspondent" for the *Rochester Democrat*, which is to pass into new hands soon and of which he is to be the Editor. I hardly think I can do it. Received my Topographic Engineering instruments and materials at last. Now I can and must do something. Took a survey of the Fort and a preliminary survey of the town with Binnie and Pinehorn.

March 16: Went to Shelbyville Dance.
March 17: Shelbyville — Wartrace — Tullahoma
March 20th: Sick
March 21: Letters. Bad news.
March 22: James Stillman mail all about Nin & Sizpec (Not Preima)
March 23: Topog. labors. Gen. returned.
March 24: Topogging all day.
March 25, 1864: Tullahoma, Tenn.

8. Shelbyville, Bedford County, Tennessee

I was too tired to write the letter I began last night, for I had been out all day long in the wind surveying, and had come in cold and hungry, and tired. The cold and hunger were easily disposed of, but I could not so quickly get rested. James Stillman has been here to visit me, and we have had a good visit together. We have not seen each other since I left college, until now, so we had a good deal to say. He tells me that H. P. Brown, an old Alfred friend, is dead. He was in the Army of the Potomac, I have heard; another soldier "mustered out."

We are going to march soon, I suppose, and that, to the front. Gen. Slocum has today received orders to build block houses along the line of the Rail Road, to leave a few troops to guard them, and to proceed with the rest to the front. And we are sure enough that the First Division will not be left behind, when Gen. Slocum goes anywhere. So here we go, in a few days, if no different orders come. It would have been very pleasant, here in Middle Tennessee, but if we are wanted down in Georgia I shall be glad to go there. When we get on the march I shall have to act as Aid-de-Camp, and will probably be regularly detailed as such. The General said today that I would soon be relieved of my duty as Engineer. That would return me to my regiment, unless he intends to make me Aid-de-Camp. When at Shelbyville the other day I saw a *Hornellsville Tribune* that Deacon Thacher had sent to Eugene, and in it I read about the Santaria Fair.

I am going to Chattanooga tonight. (Providence permitting! One can make no calculations on the Nashville and Chattanooga R.R.) I shall return tomorrow night I hope.

March 26: 1 A.M. fine. To Chattanooga & return.

Sunday, March 27: I went to Chattanooga and have returned. A long and tiresome ride over an execrable road, but a great deal that is of interest to see along the route and when one gets there. The Tennessee River furnishes many fine views and the mountain scenery is grand. Lookout Mountain, its crest snow-covered, and the Tennessee winding around its base, looked magnificent as the sun rose above it yesterday morning. I passed Shell Mound without thinking that the 141st N.Y. was stationed there. But I suppose that Miles has not yet returned, and I know but few others in the regiment. In this far country one is rejoyced to see the face of even the slightest acquaintance.

My anxieties are relieved a little that Father is better. It is only when I think of possible calamity or trouble at home that I realize how completely the soldier is fettered and deprived of his liberty no matter what takes place at home. I can only wait for the good or bad tiding that shall come to me.

Beautiful weather we are having again. Here so near the mountains the season is not so advanced as in the valleys, and in the lowlands of Middle Tennessee, but with singing birds and balmy breezes and the awfulist sunshine, it seems like summer again already.

March 28: Started on survey. Pinhorn killed. Storm.
March 29: Surveying. Cold day. Tompson Creek and Rogers Mill.
March 30: Tompson Creek to Shelby.
March 31: Bad weather. No visiting. Working.
April 3: Church. 46th Pa. Ride to Tom Caldwell's!
April 4: Maps. Another examination. Dance, good too.
April 7: Surveying up the river. Tired. The Bosworths at Joe Thompsons.
April 8: Out to see the secesh with Doc't.
April 9: Ride to Ors Mountain. Didn't go to Mrs. Weisners. Walk with Lindsey to Caldwells.
April 10th '64: Shelbyville, Tenn.

We have been out on Topographical Survey of the country between this place and Tullahoma, then we were making our maps; and now we are waiting for orders. You already know of Shelbyville and what a pleasant place it is, and that I have done my best to enjoy its advantages during my stay here. In the day time I am generally out surveying somewhere through the country. Evenings are mostly devoted to visiting with my friends here. This is the latest season that they ever had, almost, but spring has fairly come at last, and through the country the view is fine. The peach trees all in blossom contrast their bright pink finely with the holly and the southern popular, whose bright green is most rich and beautiful. This is a magnificent country, fertile and well cultivated, and before the war was most prosperous, in spite of slavery and its depreciating tendencies. Should this become a free state, I could not wish a more pleasant place for my home than Middle Tennessee, The Genesee valley in our state is somewhat like it.

It is very pleasant visiting with my friends here. There is a good society here (among the ladies, the men have all gone to war) and I take much pleasure in making calls. John Lindsey and I generally go together. But the Secesh and the Union people of the place form two distinct circles who never meet together. Once in a while I go to see some Rebel ladies. They sing their Rebel songs for me, but are very pleasant and sociable, and yet they have an abiding faith in the complete success of the Confederacy, and the complete defeat and overthrow of us Yankees. Poor girls, they admit that unless the Southern Army does return here, they will all be old maids, and they really seemed quite mournful on the subject, despite their faith in the success of their cause.

You will hear of the consolidation of the 11th and 12th Corps in this Department, relieving Gen. Slocum from his command and placing us under Gen. Hooker as Corps commander. We do not like it at all. We are very reluctant to lose Slocum, but like good soldiers we must make no complaints, and must do the best we can under the circumstances.

We will very soon go to the front now. I have no doubt as Gen. Hooker is very anxious to make for himself a name. The Corps will have to be entirely reorganized and will have a new number, the "20th" I believe. This may make some changes in our Division, and perhaps in the Brigade. I may be in my old place in my regiment before long, but I rather guess I shall remain where I am.

Have you flowers in bloom at the North? A lady gave me a fine bouquet the other day, and in the woods I see a great many beautiful flowers and trees that I never saw before.

Miss Josie Goslyn went away. P.M. at Tom Caldwell's.

April 11: Heavy field day. Howard came over today, and Col. Fox, and Van. Steiner goes tomorrow and is turning all his stores to the Division Q.M. He is going to Vicksburg. Lindsey, Howard, Binnie, and I planned a ride with some girls, but as sufficient horses could not be procured I withdrew, and let my horse go with the others. The Misses Bosworth and Miss Weisner went with them. Visited with the Capt. Called on Mrs. Warren. Took tea with Jo Tompson. Romped with the little girls. Buggy ride, to Tom Caldwell's, and then to Mr. Goslings to hear good music. Unsuccessful attempt to see Laura.

April 12: Howard to be post Q.M. here. Calls with Lon, and lastly at Tom Caldwell's.

April 13: Ride in the forenoon with Fay and Backman.

April 14: Orders to proceed Sunday — Farewell call at Tom Caldwell's! Practice firing of the 14th NJ Battery; and skirmish with the Chicamaugians. Call on Miss Laura, (with Ken. Officers). Call at the Galbraiths.

April 15: Started on Second Topographical survey, en route for Manchester. Went from Shelbyville to Shafners Ford. Was sorry indeed to leave Shelbyville. Took leave of the town, expecting not soon to see it again. Went to my work. Took dinner at noon with Doc Caldwell, and what with — what with good dinner, good smoke, and the Dr's jolly company, we had quite a good time. He went with us til we stopped at night.

The Duck River "is mighty crooked!" (Is this a double pun?)

April 16th: From Shafners Ford to Three Fork Mills.

Start. Easy work. At two, stopped work for the day. Went over to Major Williams. Dr. Caldwell was to be there, but failed to connect. Found D. Cobble of Shelbyville there, who gave us a mint julip, then dinner, and a smoke. Camped near Hoosters. Storm.

April 17: Surveyed from Three Fork Mills to Duck River Bridge, Camp of the 13th Jersey where we halted to lay over for the Sabbath. Met Whittlesy, Graves, and Binnie with O.M. Smith of the 150th inspecting teams, etc. Graves has been appointed Capt and HQM, which sets Howard and I up a peg.— Went to Tullahoma with two Orderlies. Took dinner, saw the folks, and rode back through the rain. Got a letter from Fuller there, and was glad to see him so much improved. The Gen. thought our surveying a humbug, and said we will all be marching soon.

April 18th: Duck River Bridge to Normandy, Tenn. and stopped for the day, to allow our escort to draw clothing. Plotted our work up to date and am confirmed in my opinion that the Duck River is highly crooked. At Dress Parade found by an order that we belong to the 2nd Brigade, 1st Div., 20th Army Corps. Evening, visited with O. M. Smith and other officers of the 150th, and wrote a short letter to Preima.

Proceed in the morning toward Manchester. In three or four days we expect to finish up our work.

April 19: Normandy to Krompton's Creek.

A hard day's work along a most crooked river, across the streams and up and down the mountain sides, getting seven or eight miles from Normandy by the road, and nearly twice as far by the river. We have had no accident happen to us thus far, and I hope we will finish our survey without anything of the kind. Another day, if we are not delayed, will see us at the end of our work. The Lord speed us!

April 20: Krompton Creek to Manchester.

April 21: Manchester to Tullahoma.

April 22: At work in the evening. Trial plot.

April 23: Review at Decherd.

April 24: Working on maps.

April 26, 1864: Tullahoma, Tenn.

Whenever orders came to march or to go into battle, it was the practice of Capt. Sill to sit down immediately and write to his wife; as our marching orders have come at last let me imitate his example, and ere we bid adieu to Tullahoma and Middle Tennessee, send a letter home. "March to the front," says the order to Gen. Williams, "as soon as your division is relieved by that of Gen. Rosseau." One by one the regiments of our Division are rendezvousing here, as they are relieved by other troops, and soon we will all be moving together, for Lookout Valley or Chattanooga. This is our third attempt to reach "the front" in this department. Twice already have we crossed and re-crossed the Cumberland Mountains, and I am afraid, now, that ere we reach to Main Army, some Rebel raid may call us back, as Wheeler's raid did last fall. We little thought when we left Virginia, just seven months ago, that we should wait so long before getting into a fight. We supposed we were a forlorn hope, hastening the relief of Rosecrans, we have found ourselves located for more than a half-year in a pleasant land among fine people, and doing the easiest soldiering we have seen in the service. We may have earnest work before us now, however, but what ever may come I think that all are glad to be on the move once more, excepting perhaps, the troops at Shelbyville.

8. Shelbyville, Bedford County, Tennessee

We finished our survey three or four days ago, and have been engaged on our maps since. We finished them today, and now we are all ready to march. It was very pleasant out on the survey through the woods and green fields, and by the riverside all day, and camping out under the clear moonlit sky at night. Wild flowers were scattered around in great profusion, very much the same as are found at home, wild violets, "bluebells," wild lilies, red and white, and many others whose names I never knew. In my last, I sent you a flower gathered by Capt. Bennett by the side of Duck River. Does it not look like a duck?

But I never fully realized what a terrible scourge this war is, as when out in the country, I visited the homes of the people, saw their destitution, and heard them tell the story of their sufferings. Tennessee is paying dearly for its disloyalty. Manchester was once a most flourishing manufacturing town, its broad streets, and neatly planted houses, and decorated yards, all reminded me of some northern town of intelligence and enterprise. I think I never saw a finer sight than Manchester by moonlight. But all was so silent as a city of the dead, the whiteness of whose marble in the moonlight, and whose pervading stillness were reproduced exactly in that "deserted village." Strolling through its deserted streets I met scarcely a person anywhere, found few occupied houses, and not a store or place of business of any kind open in town. All trade in that section is forbidden, people have to go many miles for food even; and goods they do not get at all, using the remnants of the days of their former prosperity.

I am occupying a pleasant room, in the summer residence of Judge Catron, a member of the Supreme Court of the United States, and thoroughly loyal to the government throughout. Of course his property was confiscated by C.S.A., and this house was used for Army Head Quarters by Polk and afterward by Bragg. Then Rosecrans moved in, and all last winter Gen. Slocum and Staff stopped here. When the 12th Corps was consolidated the Corps Staff was broken up. Two or three yet remain here, and Capt. Bennett and I occupy the room that Gen. Slocum had. Its lofty ceiling, its satin-gilt papered walls and its balcony windows remind one of anything but a soldier's life. From "our" front steps this evening I watched the sunset over the vast plain that stretches away to the west of Tullahoma, starting from the foot of the little elevation upon which this place stands. Here is an immense herd of cattle, guarded by a cordon of sentinels around them, and beyond, the camps of our newly arrived regiments, and of troops passing through to the front. Bands of music are playing continually, and the whole scene is most enlivening. A Wisconsin Band has been discoursing for us that beautiful air, *Tale of Beauty*, nothing more appropriate than those words, "Shades of night, close not over us."

April 27: We march tomorrow at nine o'clock, so says Gen. Williams, and we all have to do as he says. Today we are all packing up, and it is a world of trouble, come to get at really. We have been lying still so long that we have accumulated a great amount of property which we must now leave behind; as only a limited amount of baggage is allowed in an active campaign. I am "all ready"; now I'll use the rest of my time in writing. It seems a long time since I have heard from home. We get one more mail, (tonight) before we start, after which I do not know when we can get our letters. I hope I shall not be disappointed tonight.

We had an Army Review the other day of the 1st Brigade of our Division at Decherd, fifteen miles from here. Gen. Ruger and Staff were invited, and I was so foolish as to go. The ride there and back was bad enough, especially for our horses, but that of the review was execrable. Then followed a grand dinner at which were present a number of Rebel ladies from Winchester. The Generals present were toasted and speeches made, etc. Whenever "the old flag" was mentioned, or the restoration of the Union, our Rebel guests held their hands over their ears and refused to listen to Union talk. After dinner, however, they were more pleasant, and gave us some very fine music there being a very good piano in the house. Upon invitation, they gave us *The Bonnie Blue Flag*, and other Rebel songs. But it was refreshing after they went away, to hear a Union lady sing *The Star Spangled Banner, Red, White, and Blue*, etc. The festivities of the day were closed by a bacchanalian revel! on the part of some of the officers, and then we all started for home. A ride of fifteen miles after dark is not the most pleasant thing imaginable, nor the least dangerous, at the speed we came.

By the event of the consolidation of our Corp, the 141st New York, Miles Hawley's regiment, has been placed in our Division (in the 1st Brigade, which I saw reviewed). They are now at the front, but will join us when we get down there. That will bring the 107th and the 141st very near together, and I shall see Miles and the others very often. But our own Brigade, I am very proud of it, and I do not believe there is a better one in the Army. It has made a glorious history already, and will get more honor if ever given any chance.

Just remember these six regiments; 2d Mass. Col. Cogswell, 3d Wis. Col. Hawley, 13 N.J. Col. Carman, 27 Ind. Col. Colgrove, 107 N.Y. Col. Crane, and 150th N.Y. Col. Ketchum, for they constitute the Brigade I like to brag on; the 2nd Brigade, 1st Div., 20th Army Corps. And tomorrow they start for the front. When we get there you'll hear again, perhaps sooner, life and health permitting.

April 28: Tullahoma to Decherd.
April 29: Decherd to University Place.

On the March

Marion County, Tenn., April 30, 1864:

You will excuse my writing in pencil, for we are "on the march," and at such a time it is hard to find ink, but, on the march one sees so much that is of interest, so much that is beautiful, and sometimes grand, that we are always wishing those at home could be with us to share our enjoyment. It is a positive enjoyment, a luxury almost, to travel through this country now, that is as I am traveling, on horseback, and walking could not even destroy the pleasure. We have been two days in crossing the Cumberland Mountains, on the southern slope of which we are now encamped, not ten miles from Bridgeport. We are not yet in sight of the Tennessee River, however, and over the mountains we saw so many beautiful sights, and sometimes such magnificent views, that I often wished I were a poet or a painter, that I might be able to describe them fitly.

On the march we go very slow, of course, so as not to tire the men, and stop often to rest. After a round of chatting for the first, we grow silent, and each one rides on communing with himself. Thus it is that most have recourse to smoking for company, but I have company enough with my own thoughts.

Last night we camped on the mountain top. Away up there so many thousand feet above the sea, is "University Place," a little nest among the mountains, as pleasant to the tired traveler as an oasis in the desert. There is a noble spring there; water is very hard to find on the mountain, and near it was once a little settlement, clustered around a former school for orphans. Nearby is the corner stone of what was to have been the Great University of the South. Here the talent and the wealth of the South met together a few years since, and voted to start a Southern College, pledging themselves to contribute liberally for its endowment, and to send all their children thither instead of letting them go north. Here they laid a corner stone and made some great speeches and partook of a grand dinner. The corner stone remains as it was (excepting a few pieces have been chipped off by curiosity hunters) and the University of the South has progressed no further. The large shed or slab pavilion under which the banquet was served is also standing, but all the other buildings at University Place have been burned. From here a fine carriage road runs along the mountain top, ten miles and back on which at different places are the summer residences of Bishop, Polk, Elliot, and French, and of other worthies who were interested in the school at the "Place." From these residences you can get some of the most magnificent views the eye ever beheld. The whole of Middle Tennessee lies spread out before you with its mingled light and shade of cleared land and wood, dotted with villages here and there, and the view only limited by the shorelines of your own vision. Oh! If I could only describe to you the magnificent beauty of the scene, grand in its extent, and gorgeous in the rich fresh lines of springtime, but words fail me! We all wondered how they came to locate a university in such a place, so difficult of access as the summit of the Cumberlands, but we found nearby a little railroad that came up the mountainside, connecting with the Nashville and Chattanooga R.R., and running up to some coal mines beyond. University Place, where a little town has grown up called "Tracy City."

By means of this railroad our mountain perch has communication with the world beneath it, but such a railroad! I never saw such heavy grades and such sharp curves. And there we camped, much nearer the Rebel General Polk's residence than he can approach just at present. University Place to Battle Creek

May 1st: Battle Creek, Bridgeport, Shell Mound

May 2: Shell Mound, Nikajack Cave

May 3: Whiteside, Wanhatchee, Chattanooga

Chattanooga, Tenn., May 3, 1864:

We were in "Sweeden's Cove" when I wrote you last. The next day we marched to Shell Mound by way of Bridgeport where we crossed the Tennessee. It was a very long day's march and we did not get into camp until very late. These long marches are very tiresome, but as long as I make them on horseback, I cannot complain. I was speaking of the many hours on the march when none are talking, but all busy with our own thoughts. I expect I have nearly worn out a song to which I have taken a great fancy, and the first stanza, all I know of which I am continually trying to sing. *Lorena.* It is a great favorite with the Rebels. I could find none but Rebel girls who sang it in Shelbyville. But I have always liked it, both the music and the words.

Nick-a-Jack Cave, Shell Mound, Tennessee, abandoned Rebel saltpeter works in foreground, *Harper's Weekly*, February 6, 1864.

> This first stanza goes thus:
> "The years creep slowly by, Lorena,
> The snow is on the grass again;
> The sun's low down the sky, Lorena,
> The frost gleams where the flowers have been.
> But the heart beats just as warmly now
> As when the summer days were nigh
> Oh, the sun can never dip so low
> A down affection's cloudless sky!"*

With these eight lines I have beguiled away many hours of my marching. Before leaving Shell Mound, we went over into the celebrated Nikajack Cave. It is quite a large one, running back seven or eight miles into the

---

*"Lorena" was the most popular sentimental song of the Civil War. The original poem by Henry De Lafayette Webster (1824–1896) was called "Bertha," but when Joseph Philbrick Webster (1819–1875, no relation) set it to music in 1857, he chose the three-syllable name, "Lorena." The song was said to have been banned by at least one Civil War general as it appeared responsible for homesickness and desertions.

mountain. Of course we couldn't go in but a little ways. Two of our Corps went in there last fall and have not come out yet.

From Shell Mound we marched yesterday to "Helna," a coal mine settlement near "Whiteside," along the very bank of the grand old Tennessee River, with the rock ledges hanging over our heads hundreds of feet above, and the railroad cut in along the very face of these ledges so that the trains seemed to be almost flying in the air, then up among the mountain losing sight of the river until we get to Chattanooga. At Whiteside we pass under the immense railroad bridge reminding one very much of that at Portage, but the timbers are so slight it seems made of kindling wood.

The march today, to this point, has been one of great interest to me. I cannot better describe this approach to Chattanooga than to use B. F. Taylor's words, "A glorious region for painter and poet, whatever plowman may make of it. At last, threading a needle's eye of a tunnel, we begin to get into broader ground, and the Tennessee bears us company. We wind around the angle of the mountain wall of Lookout. Camps glittering on the hills everywhere, in the morning sun, *tumuli* of red earth, with sentinels pacing to and fro, regiments checkering the low grounds, engines backing and filling, great store-houses, show new in their fresh planed wood; forts dumb but not dead; the whole landscape alive with crowds and caravans, and there in the middle of it all, like a rusty hatchet buried in the live oak that grew around it, lies Chattanooga."

Logan's Corps on Bald Hill shelling the railroad at Resaca, Georgia May 14, 1864, *sketch by Theodore R. Davis, Harper's Weekly*, June 18, 1864.

I have told you before of the great liking I have for B. F. Taylor's letters. I'll enclose a specimen of them. For the faithfulness of his pictures I can vouch, having seen the original today, and its beauty you can appreciate yourself.

We are encamped tonight under the very foot of Lookout Mountain, from whose crest are gleaming and dancing the signal lights mentioned by our poet correspondent. How majestic is the mountain tonight, as it rears its head so far above us in bold relief against the sky.

Around us are twinkling the camp fires of our Division whose three Brigades are now together for the first time. A splendid Division is ours, and very soon too, may its fighting qualities be put to the test. When we reached here tonight we were not a little surprised at being ordered immediately to the front. Tomorrow morning we start out for Ringgold, or thereabouts, where we shall probably see our Gray-back friends once more, whom we have not met since last September. Things begin to look rather dusty, as the boys say, in the front already; and you need not be surprised if you hear of a hard fight near here before many days go by.

Just one year ago today our regiment saw a little harder fighting than I ever desire to see again, the Sunday fight at Chancellorsville. I little thought then that a year would roll by without my seeing another fight. That thing could hardy happen again. I only hope that the fight which we expect so soon now, and into which we will again be led by Gen. Hooker, may not be another Chancellorsville. *Spero melior* is my motto henceforth.

As we were coming into Chattanooga today down the slope of Lookout Mountain we met Gen. D. E. Sickles and Staff. He is much liked in his old Corps, the 3d, but I am glad he was not placed in command of the Potomac Army, as was once rumored. It's late and we must be on the march tomorrow.

May 4: Rossville, "Chickamauga," Gordon's Mill

May 5: Gordon's Mill, Pea Vine Creek, Pleasant Grove Ch.

Maj. Gen. Daniel E. Sickles (Brady's National Photographic Portrait Galleries).

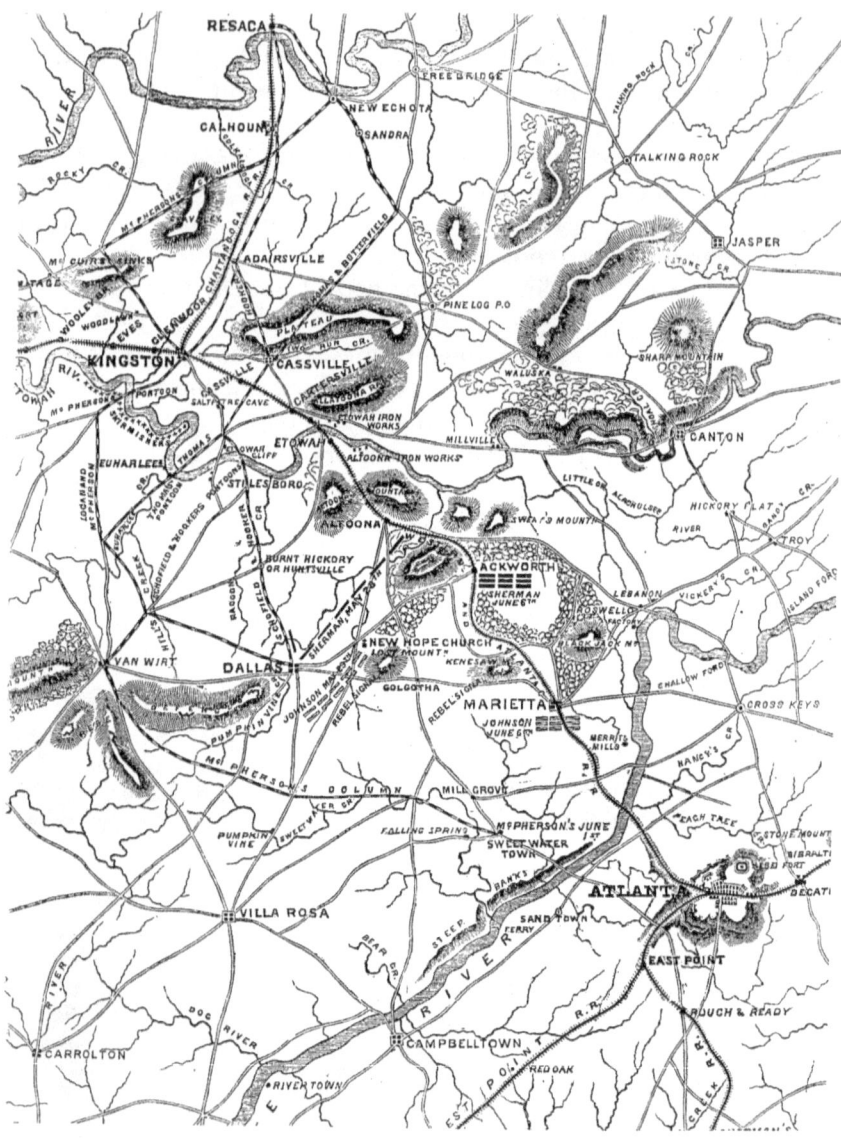

North Georgia, Resaca to Atlanta, *Harper's Weekly*, July 2, 1864

May 6: At Pleasant Grove Church. Reducing baggage.
May 7: Over Taylor's Ridge, Anderson's P.O. All quiet.
May 8: My first Sunday in Georgia. All quiet.
May 9: Geary's wounded. Gen. Hooker, 107 come!!!
May 10: To Snake Creek Gap by a hard night march.

May 12: Snake Creek Gap. Getting into position.
May 13: Ditto only more so.
May 14: 1st Div. engaged P.M. Saved a battery.
May 15: Into the fight at last, and did well.
May 16: Near Resaca to Field's Mills.
May 17: Bryant's Ford to near Calhoun.

After the Battle

Near Calhoun, Ga., Tuesday, May 17, 1864.

It was just before the battle, on Sunday morning, that I received your last letter and the stanzas inclosed, for all of which I thank you. So, now when the battle is over, and all are writing to their friends to let them know of their safety, I with the rest hasten to write. I dropped a line to Father this morning, this evening I hope to be able to write a letter. We have been on the march all day and we will probably be called out to march at three o'clock tomorrow.

I do not care to tell you all about the battle. I could not find words to fully describe it, nor have I any desire to live those scenes over again. The long suspense of waiting to go in, the excitement of getting into position, the shot and shell and bullets, the attacks we made, the charges we repulsed, the desperate attempt the Rebs made to flank us and the glorious repulse we gave them, the horrible part of the scene, the dead and wounded, the thousand incidents of the fight, it would fill volumes if I should try to tell you, But if I shall ever see you, can tell you something of it, for none of it can ever be forgotten. You will read of the battles before Resaca, in due time, and if the account is at all complete, you will read of the doings of the 20th Corps. Mr. Theodore R. Davis of *Harper's Weekly* took sketches of our part of the field, and you may thus see just where we were engaged.

The loss in our Regiment was but small as it was not in the hottest of the fight. One man was killed in "Co. K." I thank the God of Battles that he preserved me through all the dangers which surrounded me. As I rode back to the Field Hospital of our Division, and saw there the wounded and dying in such great numbers, as I saw several of my friends, some of the best men I ever knew, mangled and almost dead, I could not but wonder that I was not also injured, and I had to "thank God" for his mercy to me. But we are not through fighting yet, a hard campaign is evidently before us, and my time may come next.

After waiting some time yesterday morning for a renewal of the fight, we were surprised at receiving orders to march. There were no Rebels to be seen in our front. On we came, through the battlefield, over the Rebel works, and so by the rear of their position, "On to Atlanta." But we have not gotten to Atlanta yet, and it will be a hard journey from here to there too. A battlefield is a hard-looking place, after the fight is over. The dead were lying around everywhere, (the wounded had been cared for), about as many Yankees as Rebels.

Through Resaca, and we had crossed the last of the mountains. We are now in a most beautiful country, of wide cultivated fields and orchards, fine roads, etc. Such a country as is the Genesee Valley or the valley about Elmira. All day today we have been marching through a garden country, the air is sweet with the perfume of flowers, and everything is in the full bloom of summer. The battle and its horrors left behind, all is jollily and good spirits in the army. Our march is like a pleasure excursion. Tonight the bands are playing beautifully — A's letter was given to me by Capt. Brigham. Our regiment never joined the Brigade until we had arrived in front of Resaca, having been left behind at Shelbyville to guard the train. They came up soon enough to get into the fight, however.

I begin to like Gen. Hooker much better than I did. I think he is more careful and trustworthy than when I was under his command in Virginia. By the way, Generals are very plenty here now-a-days. Sunday morning just before we went into the fight I saw Generals Thomas, Hooker, Howard, Schofield, Sickles, Stanley, and Butterfield, with as many more Brigadiers, all in a group together discussing the prospect of the battle. Here was Sickles with but one leg, talking to Howard, with but one arm. Gen. Thomas was a little apart, with Gen. Hooker comparing notes and looking over a map. It was arranged that Hooker's Corps should make the grand attack, passing through and thus relieving the 4th Corps, Gen. Howard's. Gen. Howard was going to take Gen. Sickles with him, and go up on a high point to see the battle, his Corps being in reserve. Gen. Schofield was to keep his Corps (the 23d) in support of ours, (and ere the day was over we had occasion to ask a little of his support). Soon they all separated, ere long we heard the roar of cannon and musketry, made by the 2d and 3d Divisions of our Corps, and next our Division went in. I think there is nothing so grand as an army moving out to battle, colors gaily flying, officers galloping to and fro, artillery thundering over the field, and the long column of glistening muskets rushing forward. You have often read descriptions of such scenes, but no description can equal the reality.

I am told that all our mail is detained at Nashville, but now that the battle is over I trust they will allow our letters to go on. But I am safe and well, thus far, and I trust in god for the future.

May 18: Near Calhoun to near Adamsville.
May 19: Near Adamsville to near Cassville, light work.
May 20: Disgraceful conduct of our troops in Cassville.
May 21: Moved down into the town. Flowers, music, etc.
May 22: Sick. A "2d" going home. A day of rest.
May 23: Cassville to Euhartee. across the Etowah.
May 24: Etowah to Burnt Hickory. Through the mountains.
May 25: Fight near Dallas. Hot time for 1st Div.
May 26: Resting, Eugene Thacher buried, letters. Duties A.A.A.G.
May 27: Battle opened at 5:40 AM., a skirmish all day.
May 28: Skirmish firing all day and night long.
May 29: Ditto, ditto. Rec'd letters. Sent letters. Night fight.

Near Dallas, Ga., Sunday May 29, 1864

Sunday it is, but what a Sabbath! I look up through the still green foliage of the trees, through the warm quiet sunlight, to the clean calm sky above, and think of the quiet sabbaths I have enjoyed in days gone by, of going to church along the peaceful streets, and listening in quiet composure to the words of life spoken in the house of God. And now, the booming of cannon around me, with the popping of muskets and the whiz of bullets makes the contrast seem horrible, terrible, yet we are not having a battle now, only a continual skirmish along the lines, which may however at any moment blaze up into a struggle of the fiercest character. This is the fourth day now since we met the enemy on this ground, and had the hard hand fight in which our regiment suffered so severely. Four days and nights, not a moment of which time we have been free from the eating anxiety and expectation of a fierce battle opening. The high tension of mind is terrible and one almost wishes the contest to come quickly, that it may the sooner be ended. In God's own time come the scourges as well as the blessings of life: in his own time (I pray it may be soon) shall come the end of these days of blood and bitter sorrow.

Poor Eugene Thacher — what a blow to his friends will be the news of his death! A braver soldier never died for his country, and he was a true soldier of the cross beside. He has gone to his rest, to his exceeding great reward. God grant that we may all be as well prepared to answer our Master's call as was he! Let me die the death of the righteous, and such a death was Eugene's.

I do not think I have grown fearful or melancholy, but I really do not expect to survive this war, perhaps this campaign. It seems a miracle to me that I passed through the terrible fight of last Wednesday unhurt, and as I see my friends taken around me, one here, and one there, it seems almost a certainty that my time will come sooner or later. Yet this may be a morbid sentiment, that I ought to allow the thought of. I trust in God that he will preserve my soul, I pray, if consistent with his will, He will preserve my life also till these troubles be over past.

You may well believe *The World* when it says Joe Hooker fights, and he keeps close to his men when they fight; however thick and fast the death shots fall around him. Fighting — yes there is plenty of it to be done, and I would not shrink from it. The most I could give, my life, is not too much to lay on my country's altar. Pray for me that I may do my duty fearlessly and faithfully.

I am very busy now. Our Adjutant General was wounded in the action of the 25th and I am doing his work, and there is more work to be done in this Department than in all the others. Do not think me despondent or hopeless, do not be depressed because I tell you of what may happen.

May 30: Skirmish firing all day, all day & night. Nothing new.

May 31: Skirmishing as usual. Country roads to the left.

June 1: Moving to the left.

June 2: In rescue — Topog. — heavy rain.

June 3: Surveying a little.

June 4: Surveying a little. Changed position at eve.

June 5: To Allatoona Church. Survey.

June 6: Allatoona Church to Kemps Mill.

June 7: All very quiet by mutual agreement. The skirmishers in our front do not fire. An immense mail came today, but nothing for me but an old letter from Carrie (May 3) Too Bad. A letter from Aunt Jane to Uncle Allen says that Father is failing very fast, that he has not recovered his strength. He stoops very much, he is losing his sight, and memory too. Mother is worrying very much about him, and Aunt Jane thinks, with reason.

June 8: No move. A good disappointment. A letter from Preima.

June 9: The expected move did not come off today. Very, busy as A.A.A.G. Do it all under protest, but have to do it nevertheless.

H'd Qr's 2d Brig 1st Div. 20th Corps
Near Acworth, Ga., June 9, 1864.

It was just after a battle, and a most fatal one for my regiment, that I wrote you last. But a day or two afterwards a mail was captured, and perhaps my letter went South instead of North. If so, I am not so sorry as I might be, for it was a sad, gloomy letter that could have given you no pleasure. I write what is in my thoughts, and dark thoughts come to me very often.

Annoyances trouble me, hardships do weary, privations wear upon me, and dangers make me fearful. I am not one of those who "know no fear." I do not grow despairing because of annoyances, nor do I complain of hardships and privations, and so I also count the perils of my position are things which are to be met with an unswerving purpose that shall not permit them to interfere in the least with the full discharge of my duty as a soldier fighting for my country. But in spite of all this, the haunting dread will sometimes come back to me, the question, "What if I have seen my home for the last time? What if I shall find a resting place in this strange land, like so many, many around me?"

Contrary to the expectation that has haunted us almost hourly, we have not been in a fight since our bloody encounter of the 25th ult. Other portions of the army have been engaged here and there, but there has been no general engagement, and none in which our Division has participated. It hardly seems possible that the two armies can confront each other here much longer without there being a collision. Our picket lines are very close here, and everywhere I suppose. We have been very much annoyed throughout this campaign by the constant popping of guns all day, and all night long on the skirmish line. It does no good whatever and keeps the whole army in a constant fever of restlessness. We have done away with that in the front of our lines, however, there being a mutual agreement not to shoot at each other. The pickets can just as well discharge their duty, that of observation. But this truce to firing has made the confronting pickets communicative. They meet each other half way, talk over common place matters in the most friendly manner, exchange coffee, sugar, tobacco, and newspapers also, and have further agreed that when either party gets orders to fire, the other side shall be duly warned so that no confidence shall be betrayed. Think of it! Chatting friend-like together, and then when they have done playing at friends, going back to shooting at each other. After that warning is given woe to the careless skirmisher who exposes too much of his head or arm to the opposite sharp-shooter's aim. But now the officer as well as the private walks fearlessly down to the very line and his enemy in friendly conversation.

We used to do this on the Potomac, and it is said by our Western friends here that we make a play of war, and don't fight. It has been said, but few in this army will now say that Hooker's Corps "don't fight." If we may believe the statements of Rebel prisoners, and the pickets in front of us, they on their side have no poor appreciation of the fighting qualities of Joe Hooker's men. They are never anxious to attack the men who wear stars on their caps. The star is our Corps badge. They say Hooker's men "fight hard." Some of them respect us, as one true soldier always respects another, while others meditate a huge revenge. Two Rebs told one of our men the other day that they were going to whip the Yankees in this campaign, and as for Joe Hooker, he and every man man who fought under him should be dead before the end of the summer. They have a "job on hand" if they annihilate the 20th Corps in one summer.

So much for army gossip. I wrote to Lydia about Eugene's death but inclosed the note in a letter to Mr Waldo, and now I hear that he is not at home. I trust that my note not be lost. I have not much time to write. I have not time to perform the legitimate duties of my office, or offices, for I am now trying to fill two. I have ceased keeping a journal, and almost ceased writing letters. I do not like the position of A.A.A.G. There is too much to do. And my duties as Adjutant General have for the time swallowed up the time that should be devoted to my business as Topographical Engineer.

It is very warm here now, in the daytime, though cool at night, and we begin to realize that we are in a southern clime. The insects alone are sufficient to teach us that. Spiders, ants, gnats, and moths of all kinds are not noticed. They roam over us at will, wood ticks we take care to get rid of, "swifts" we avoid, and scorpions we have a genuine fear of. Every day we find them, however, in our blankets or papers.

June 10: The expected move again.

June 11: Moved a little to the left. Got within shell range. Letters. Moved to near Pine Hill and a cannonading ensued in which Gen. Polk was killed.

June 12: Rain, wet day. Wrote to Mother. Expected attack at eve. Rain all night.

June 13: Wet morning. Wet all day. Wrote home.

June 14: Surveying all day. Letters. Sick.

June 15: Pine Hill to Dixon's House.

June 16: Dixon's House out in the woods. Skirmish lively.

June 17: Topog. Eng. all day.

June 18: A rainy day. Surveying some in the afternoon.

June 19: Advanced to Moses Creek. Surveying. Darby's stand.

June 20: To Dallas and Marietta Road, to Alkinson.

June 21: Alkinson's Plantation.

June 22: To Ridge East of Alkinson. Charge of Hooker's Corp repulsed, a fight in which I did not participate.

June 23: Relieved of duty as A.A.A.G. Letters rec'd.

Near Mariettta, Ga., June 23d, 1864

I have just been over at the 1st Brigade H'd Qr's, just across the road talking to Capt. Mason. He is, like me the A.A.A.G. of his Brigade, and he was a fellow student with me at Rochester. Four years ago we called into each other's rooms and chatted over college honors, society politics, awards of "honors" etc. as now we come into each other's tents and discuss the merits of the fight we had yesterday, the chances of the fight we expect tomorrow, or any other of the many topics on which the soldier whiles away his time. Three years ago he and I went to Elmira together to witness the presentation of their colors to the 13th New York Volunteers, the first regiment sent out from Rochester and of which Professor Quimby, the most loved and honored teacher in our college, was Colonel. We saw those colors presented, the regiment being drawn up in a hollow square, and we said amen to the words of praise and encouragement that were spoken to those men as they took those colors and promised to stand by them always. They did stand by them, bore them through many a hard-fought field, and returned with them, when their two years of service was ended, more than a year ago. I little thought then that I should see that regiment in such a place as the Antietam battlefield, that when they were filing down by "Burnside's Bridge" I should be trudging by them, with gun on my shoulder, and knapsack on my back, one of Uncle Sam's "Boys in Blue," like the rest of them, all these things, and lots of college news besides, we talked over together this morning, until I came away at last, and left him to finish his letter to his "Dear and Ever Beloved Wife." (He obtained a leave of absence last Spring and went home and got married.)

For a wonder I recall three letters today, one from a good brother studying Theology at Union Theological Seminary, one from my father, and one from Binghamton post marked "June 14." Blessed am I among Blue Coats! My father says he cannot write very often, that Carrie is away, but I must write very often, as it is more important that they should hear from me, than I should hear from them! My father seems to have no idea of the value a letter from home has, to the soldier. Yet, I can appreciate his anxiety to hear from us here, and I am thankful that I can say, thus far, that all is well with us.

This has been an awful campaign, we are on the move constantly, continually skirmishing with the enemy, taking new positions and forming new lines every day, in hourly expectation of a great battle, which however does not come yet. The weather has been very unfavorable, too, a constant succession of furious rain storms that has kept us thoroughly drenched, until we have come to believe ourselves almost amphibious. In the meantime letter writing has been very impracticable, but Father shall have the news, as he wishes.

We had a battle yesterday, not a very extensive one, as battles are estimated in this war, but a very sharp one while it lasted. Stevenson's (Rebel) Division of Hood's Corps attacked William's (Yankee) Division, of Hooker's

Corps, attempting to take one of our batteries, and to break our lines. But they were most severely repulsed, and went back whence they came, leaving a great many dead and wounded on the field. Last night they got most of their wounded away, our men allowing them to bring wagons up for the purpose, almost to our skirmish line, yet we have many of their wounded in our hands, and many of their dead were buried by our men today. Our loss was very slight, hardly more than a hundred killed and wounded in our whole Division. But when ever the 20th Corps gets into a fight, some New York home has cause to mourn. There are a great many New York troops in it, constituting fully one third of its effective force. In our Division both of the Batteries and seven out of the seventeen regiments are from New York. So it is with the 2d and 3d Divisions. Many a soldier's grave have I seen, with "N.Y.V" on the headboard. So many, it saddened me deeply to think of all the homes, so far away that shall wait in vain for the return of their brave defenders. Mr. Theodore R. Davis, the artist correspondent of *Harper's Weekly* was out on the field today, taking a sketch of the scene of our fight. I expect to see it in the papers in due time.

I am a little disgusted with the newspaper correspondents, the accounts they give are too highly colored and are not at all reliable. There may be exceptions to this, but I have seen none, and today I became especially disgusted at a *Herald* correspondent who was exhibiting a piece of a rib of Gen. Polk, who was killed by a shell from one of our batteries some days since. The shell as it struck him tore him nearly to pieces, and our correspondent, finding where he was killed obtained this piece of bone as a memento. He must have a refined taste!

You have heard of people shedding tears at the sight of the stars and stripes? Well, I have seen an instance of that, myself lately. While Geary's Division was advancing down the "Sandtown Road" with colors unfurled, they passed a house where a lady, sitting on the porch with her children around her, was weeping for joy at the sight of "the dear old flag." She had not seen the Stars and Stripes before, since the war began, she said, and they looked "beautiful."

June 24: A day of genuine rest. I began this letter last night. I am trying to finish it this morning. To be free from interruption, I have come out in the woods, for it is not raining today and I can sit in the open air as I write. In the woods here all is still, or seems so. Close behind me the skirmishers are popping away (a bullet just came over and struck a tree in front of me a few feet), but one gets used to that after a several weeks' day and night acquaintance with it, and the sound blends not inharmoniously with that of the moving branches above and of the buzzing of flies around me. A delightful breeze is stirring through the wood, and the sun comes dancing through the leaves so softly, one can almost dream of the arcadian quiet

Writing home. From *Harper's Weekly*, July 20, 1861.

and happiness here, only that down in the beautiful valley below us, around the house we see so prettily situated there, and through the orchard beyond it, are to be seen every second or two, the white puff of smoke, where our skirmishers are firing. And in the edge of the woods, just beyond is another line of white puffs, showing us where the Rebel Sharpshooters are. And away to the left too, I hear the occasional booming of cannon, so my picture is not completely arcadian after all. Never mind, we are resting, if our skirmishers and the army at our left are not, and we may not have another fight in two or three days, therefore let us enjoy our quiet and repose. Ah! Now, the bugle is sounding. So, Good morning.

June 25: Hot weather. Moved in early to rear of Gen. Geary.

June 27: Topog., warm, fight.

Near Marietta, Ga., June 29th '64.

Our Brigade has changed position since I wrote last from "Near Marietta," but no fighting, nothing to speak of, and we have not reached Marietta yet. It is very warm, the weather we are having, warm enough for discomfort here in the woods where we have our Head Quarters, but out in the trenches where I would be if with my regiment, the sun on the sand is blinding, blistering. So warm is the day, — but look out for the nights, chilly and cold they are, and when it rains the chill and cold "strike in." So it may not seem to those who live in houses in a civilized way, but so it is with us who live in the woods and burrow in earth works, rain or shine, for days, and weeks and months.

(One of my classmates recently wrote to me, that when I got back from "the war" he should consider me "a hero." If he could only read the querulous accounts I send home of our condition, he would change his opinion very quick.)

Didn't you once ask me if the holly I saw was evergreen, and if it was not the "Christ" holly we read of? It is I think, it is green always, the leaves glossy as if varnished, and it has a little red berry. I saw a "passion flower" the other day. General Knipe had it; and again I rode by where several were growing, but it was during an engagement, and I could not stop then. Gen. Knipe is a great admirer of flowers. When we crossed the Etowah, near Enhartee, we had to stop two or three hours while a pontoon bridge was laid, and at a fine large house near the river all the Generals and their Staff were gathered. I have rarely seen a yard where so many fine flowers were kept, as there. And more beautiful than all else was an exquisite yellow rose that Gen. Knipe found. He confiscated it for his wife. And those passion flowers are beautiful, are they not? We were in a land of flowers and cultivated fields and grand old plantation houses, from Resaca to Enhartee, then nothing but woods and hills until we came here. Now we are in the "open country" once more. Out of the woods, into the fields. I am glad of the change.

What would I do if it were not for music? Our bands are right up with us, they go down to the lines, in the very rifle pits, and play for the brave boys there, and the enemy does not shell them. Perhaps the Rebs enjoy music as much as we. We never heard one of their bands, but once. At Raccoon Ford on the Rapidan, in Virginia, a Rebel Band came out, one September evening, and rehearsed for our benefit. A band is now playing at Gen. Hooker's Head Quarters, a few rods from here, the best band in this army; the only one that excels our own Brigade Band, the band of the 33d Mass. And I am listening so occupied with the music, that I scarcely know if I am writing sense. Last night as I rode down the line I heard our Band playing *Her Bright Smile Haunts me Still.** More beautiful than when I heard it in a serenade at Shelbyville, more beautiful than when I heard it sung there, that song itself haunts me ever. I returned to the army from my furlough, that song ever in my head, it unconsciously became the chief souvenir I brought with me, of my visit home; just as John Lindsay did little else, for sometime after his return to service, but sing *"No one to love none to caress."*

Regimental gossip, doesn't interest you. Changes are ever taking place, and more now than ever before. By death, by wounds, by discharges and transfers, our ranks are thinning out; how many will be left when our three years are up? Among the officers from our "Thirty-seven" will there be left "eleven"? Since we started from Middle Tennessee two months ago what changes. Two are dead, two have resigned, several have been wounded, and one has been transferred. The latter is Lieut. Graves. He is now a Capt., and a QM in U.S. Vol's., and today Col. Crane told me he had recommended for Quarter Master vice Graves, and for 1st Lieut. of Co. K, vice Howard. What difference does it make whether I am 1st or 2d Lieut.? I don't know. Lieut. Col. Fox, wounded at Resaca, has resigned. Major Baldwin will be Lieut. Col., and an effort is being made that Capt. Sill shall become Major Sill. But regimental politics are even more uncertain, than party politics at home. You know my autograph book? Col. Fox wrote his name in it for me, a plain "William J. Fox, 107th Regt. N.Y. Volo." with no hint of his rank, but with this device and motto above a captain's shoulder strip, and an Orderly Sergeant's Chevron, with the thought, "Perchance hereafter it will be pleasant to remember these days." (I translate liberally), the days when he was a captain and I was an orderly, the days when our regiment was new in the service, and all was hope and pride and bright anticipation of the future. But wasn't it a neat idea putting his name in so?

June 30: Letters rec'd and sent. Can it be that year is half gone already? I can scarcely believe it, and yet the days are very long.

---

* "Her Bright Smile Haunts Me Still" was a popular ballad from the mid–1800s with a nautical theme. Lyrics by W. T. Wrighton, music by S. C. Carpenter.

10. After the Battle

July 1: Away go the Third Wisconsin men who did not reenlist, and in come some new recruits for the 2nd Mass.

July 2nd: Eve: Serenaded Gen. Hooker.

Orders to move.

July 3rd: Moved into Marietta. This morning the C.S.A. was a minus quantity in our front, and we therefore made one more onward movement.

July 4: Moving into position through the upper waters of Nikajack Creek. Heard the *Star Spangled Banner* played by all the bands, and celebrated the 4th as best I could.

July 5: Another falling back from strong works by the Rebels. Another advance by the Yanks. Over the Sandtown road, over the Nikajack Creek, over a ridge, up another ridge, two miles from the Chattahoochee. The spires and houses of Atlanta visible in the distance.

July 6th: Moved to the left, a hot hard days march. The day closed with so much grumbling that I no longer discredited the report that our Army swore terribly in Flanders.

July 9: Surveyed with Wallace to the left as far as Ruff Station. Visit with Capt. Norris of the 98 Ohio.

July 10: Surveyed with Wallace back to Mrs. Henderson's on route of July 5th.

Vining's Station, Ga., July 11, 1864.

It fares well with me. Though I have plenty to do, it is pleasant work, and one in the prosecution of which I see and hear much that is of interest. Vining's Station is the first station north of the Chattahoochee River, and indeed the first one north of Atlanta, on the railroad to Chattanooga.

View of the public square, Marietta, Georgia, *sketch by Theodore R. Davis, Harper's Weekly,* August 13, 1864.

Turner's Mill on Nickajack Creek, Georgia *sketch by T. R. Davis,* Harper's Weekly, *August 13, 1864.*

South and West of it along the river, Sherman's army is camped. The Rebels hold the South side of the river. And across it whistle the bullets of the opposing lines. Away to the right Gen. Schofield is reported across the river and approaching Atlanta. I reckon he won't approach very far. From the ridge held by our Corps Atlanta is in plain sight, only about eight miles away. Its church spires, its brick blocks, its white dwellings, the tall chimneys of its factories, and its very streets are plainly discernable. Close in front of us the Rebel forts and lines of works guard all approaches to the river. Then stretches away an expanse of mingled wood and field, hill and plain, reaching beyond Atlanta to Stone Mountain, blue and hazy in the dim distance.

"The heart of the Southern Confederacy," Atlanta has been styled. Verily, as our curious eyes peer away South, over the Chattahoochee and beyond Atlanta, it seems as if we have reached the heart of Georgia at last. And we are resting. Blessed be the Giver of Rest! After sixty days of continual skirmishing or fighting we are at last allowed a short breathing spell. Not that the army is really doing nothing, but with a river in our front a new series of movements must be begun before we advance much. Clear as mud?

Just now our Brigade Band is playing *Marching Along.* Oh! Yes. We go marching along pretty soon; but until all is ready, what a blessing for the worn out troops is this rest! In the meantime I have only the more to do. When the army is resting we "Topogs" are busiest. When the army moves we have only to survey the roads followed by our respective commands.

July 3d saw us enter Marietta, a once beautiful place, it reminds me of Canandaigua more than any place I have seen, or perhaps Batavia. A wealthy place with fine public buildings and a profusion of elegant and stately residences, lining all its principal streets. The business part of the town is neat and of substantial appearance, nor is it too large to disturb the aristocratic ease and dignity of the entire place. Had I the means to live at ease, I could chose no more pleasant and congenial home than Marietta, before the war. But Marietta now. What a solitude, for the people nearly all fled at our approach, but not a desolation, for our troops passed through those almost deserted streets doing no injury to the place. There were a few people left, of the "common folks," and I saw one or two of the more elegant mansions occupied still. Straight through the town our columns passed, the men keeping their ranks in the center of the streets, bands playing and the glorious Stars and Stripes unfurled in every regiment, and our men would cheer as they marched along. How the people watched us, a little enmity, a little fear, a little resignation, and a great deal of curiosity in their looks. They did not like to see the Yankee invaders in their streets, and yet, very evidently they were agreeably disappointed at the appearance and conduct of the vandals. It was Sunday, and at one church an aged pastor was preaching to the congregation of five. Faithful men, they were literally leaving all to follow their Savior, for they knew not in what condition they would find their homes on their return.

"Tis the middle watch of a midsummer night." I have been waiting until all is still, so that I can write undisturbed, and how fast the memories of the past come back to me at such a time as this. Almost a year ago now our Corps was guarding the Rappahannock in Virginia as now it guards the Chattahoochee in Georgia, and when I returned to duty, from Hospital, I found it guarding ford and ferry and picketing the river's bank, as now it is doing. And it was just a year ago, I believe, that I arrived home with more gratitude in my heart than I ever supposed for one small heart to contain. It seemed like a return from the dead, almost, to see my home after such an absence, not long, but from the nature of the business which kept me away seeming to separate us by an immense distance. And now, the thirteen months that remain of my term of service are not of themselves so long, but the chances of a soldier's life, and his surrendered liberty, his going and coming not his own will, but at the direction of others, these make the time seem very long, and the distance from home very great.

I am glad you are having such pleasant visits, and finding such good friends. We go visiting here too. The other day I took a ride over to Jeff C.

Davis' Division of the 14th Corps, to pay a visit to my old friend Capt. Norris. Ten months ago I knew him in Shelbyville, Tenn. The last time I saw him was at the house of a Judge Wisener there, (whose daughter is such a fine musician) and now we had a good visit, discussing "old times," the good Union people of Shelbyville, etc. So we go visiting here, take dinner or supper with each other, have a good talk, and then take a ride along the lines, or perhaps climb some signal tree from which we get a view of the surrounding country. Just now, to show a friend a fine view of Atlanta, is equivalent to giving him a dish of strawberries and cream at home.

I got a letter from Luin today. He is proud to announce that he is just now in command of his regiment, the Col. being in command of a Brigade, and the Lt. Col. being absent on some expedition. He had not heard of Eugene's death. Fort Smith, Arkansas. If I were there I should think myself out of the world certainly. So does he, and he wishes he was in Grant's or Sherman's army.

July 11: Had a survey to the river.

July 13: Surveyed roads leading from River Ridge Road to River. Letters Rec'd. Ordnance returns. Have I got to make them out at last! They're "after me."

Oliver Mumford is dead! Killed near Petersburgh. How long, Oh Lord! My dear Mother has met with an accident. Fell down the cellar stairs. Oh, to be at home with the folks. They need Carrie and I, and Preima writes a mournfully loving letter from Owego. Almost sick, from working in the heat of the day, and sad. Truly when our hearts are wandering the Lord calls us back in His own way.

July 16: In my survey today I was at a house of where there was a sick, sick girl, just on the lines. I wonder how they dare run the risk of the conflict that may rage right around them.

Sunday 11 A.M., July 17th: A real Sabbath day. Cannonading is going on at the left, but all is quiet on our front. The men are sitting around in their cleanly kept camps; writing, some of them; — and in many places religious services were being held. Going along our corps line, today, is like going through a quiet country village on the Sabbath day, all is as still. All are in their best clothes, doing no work, and at different places preaching is heard, as in passing by the different churches of the place.

July 18: Moved across the Chattahoochee. Randall's Plantation to near Buckhead.

July 19: At night, moved up to Peach Tree Creek.

July 20: A hard fight and repulse of the Rebel attack.

July 21: Col. Loges died last night. Major Baldwin's case is hopeless. Col. Colgrove will lose an arm, and probably his life, and Col. McNell has lost his right arm, and Col. Bowman has lost both legs. The fight yesterday was unusually hard on officers. Went to 14th Corp Hospital to see Maj. Baldwin.

P.M.: Surveyed with Capt. McDowell.

Third Anniversary of Bull Run.

July 22: Early in the morning found that the Rebels had left our front and we advanced to the town of Atlanta. Found the enemy strongly entrenched in the outskirts of the town. We pushed up as close as possible to their works and entrenched ourselves. We are fighting in the very suburbs of the town, thundering at the gates of Atlanta. But I'll not undertake to say when we will get through those gates.

July 23: Busy surveying around our position, and the roads near our lines. They had a hard fight over on our left yesterday. Gen. McPherson was killed.

July 24: A splendid quiet Sabbath day, quiet as far as nature can make it so, but disturbed by the unholy work of war stuff. I was going to have a quiet day of rest, and was sitting down to write to Preima, when an order came to hurry back to the battle fields of Wednesday. It took me all day to survey the piece and make the plot.

In the evening a sharp attack was made by our Division. The flying shells made a fine sight at night, as Knight & I watched from the Hill.

July 25: Fell in with a ψγ, Capt. Seely of Gen. Baird's Staff from the B. It was a pleasant visit. Doing no work today. Feeling sick. Letter from Cousin Elsie Williams.

July 26: Received a letter from Lydia Thacher thanking me for the letter I did for Eugene. Selestia and Louise are mentioned. They have been with her. Selestia is now in Almond.

Doing no work just now. Not much to do until we get into Atlanta.

Near Atlanta, Ga., July 26th, 1864.

This morning I found in my Engineer's Note Book that little scrap about "A Child's Faith." Having left it on the table, the General found it when he sat down to breakfast and was very much amused at the child's idea. Last evening we were talking about children's prayers, and each his story to tell, of some little friend.

We are living in a cellar now, or rather in a cave under a hill. For shot and shell are constantly coming over from the enemy's works in front of us, and we have to put up protections. I can begin to realize the cave-life of the Vicksburg people, during the siege of that place. We are close up to the enemy works, and they are in the very suburbs of the city.

Up by our "Head Quarters" runs a main road straight into the city. Our Brigade is in position on the left of the road, and on the right is the brigade commanded by Col. Wood of Dansville. Our line runs along the crest of a little ridge, on which our batteries have been entrenched and from which they shell the town. Up the road is a fine house, the suburban residence of some first family, and from which the enemy's skirmishers annoy ours. We'll shell that house and fire it yet, if they do not stop. Just between our Brigade and Col. Wood's, where the road crosses the crest, is Dilger's Battery of 2016 Parrots, which shells the city every night, sending a fiery message every ten or fifteen minutes, through the whole night. Artillery firing in the night is an interesting sight to see. First the bright flash of the guns, lighting up the smoky atmosphere around, and then you can see the fiery trail of the shell away over into the city, until it bursts with an angry flash most pleasant to view at the greatest distance. You have to listen a long (time) before the report of the explosion comes back to you, deep and heavy in the distance.

Last night I saw a bright light over the city, a fire caused by our own shell I guess. And back, with a vengeance, come their shells and solid shot, the latter at our battery, to dismount it. When our men see the flash of the Rebel guns, they dive down behind their earth-works. Presently the visitor comes, sometimes falling before us, sometimes going quite beyond us, and sometimes exploding close by us. When shell explodes just over you, don't mind it, but when it explodes just in front of you, look out! Poor Captain Orton, of the 3d Wis. Vet, Vol's, in our Brigade was killed yesterday by a shell, as he was writing, in his tent.

We had a sharp bloody fight on the 20th. The enemy massed a very heavy force and made a fierce attack on our line, just as we had crossed the "Peach Tree Creek." The brunt of the attack was received by Hooker's 20th Corps, and of course the Potomac boys did nobly. The enemy could not break them, but on the contrary, was smashed back with great slaughter. But our loss was very heavy. The proportion of killed was very great; and unusually large too was the proportion of officers killed and wounded. Oh it was a bloody fight. The loss in our Division was over six hundred. We are consoled, in a military point of view, by the reflection that we hurt them very much more than they did us. The 3d Div. of our Corp buried almost 600 Rebels in their front, and as I rode over the field I saw several of their dead yet unburied.

I've said enough about war. As I write I am sitting in a house, in one room of which is the office of the Top'l Eng'rs 1st Div., 20th A.C. In the rest of the house the family is still living. Wilson Evans lives here, and he has a daughter who looks like Bertha Doty, who dislikes Yanks, and who "dips." I saw her with snuff bottle in one hand and brush in the other, scouring her teeth with snuff and energetically spitting at a fireplace a few feet distant. Yet as I listen to the women's voices in the other room and listen to their singing as they are busied with their household duties, as I hear the clatter of crockery and sniff the savory smell of approaching dinner, I am reminded of other days and other scenes, of peaceful times, and homes undisturbed by war's alarms. Oh! Should I be permitted to enjoy the comforts of home ever, think you not I will appreciate them? All the morning the hymn with a tune I used to like so well (Hendon) has been running in my head.

> "To thy pastures fair and large
> Heavenly Shepherd had thy charge."
> And today seems like a Sabbath, quiet and still, spite of the shells.

July 27: Gen. Howard takes command of the Army of the Tenn. Gen. Hooker (and reports Gen. Logan) asks to be relieved (and makes thereby a great mistake). Gen. Williams succeeds to the command of the Corps temporarily — and Gen. Kneip to the command of the Division, and perhaps Col. Corman to the command of this Brigade, for Gen. Ruger will leave this command I fear. There will be great mourning throughout our Corps at the departure of Gen. Hooker. His name was a tower of strength to us, a kind of terror to our enemies; and he had gained the (respect) of us all, spite of our former attachment to Gen. Slocum, spite of our old time dislike to himself, and the consequent changes.

July 28: Went over with the rest to bid good bye to Gen. Hooker. Shook hand with him, and listened to his leave-taking. Rather sad to say goodbye, but I do not think he did rightly in leaving at this time. I do not think he did well in making the announcement of Gen. Howard to a higher position the reason of his action. He should not let personal feelings interfere with the discharge of his duties to his country.

July 29: I received my commission from the Gen'l as 1st Lieut. in Co. K 107 NYV.

July 30: Sick.

July 31: Rainy day. Was mustered in as 1st. Lieut.

August 1st: Sick.

Maj. Gen. John A. Logan 15th Corps (Brady's National Portrait Gallery).

August 2nd: Getting no better.

Before Atlanta, Ga., Aug. 2d, 1864.

Night before last I received yours the 22d July, from Belmont. Still visiting? Never yet saw I the place where I could enjoy a visit of more than two days' duration, but I am interested in the accounts you give of the home circles you have visited. I have heard of all the "Macs" you mentioned, yet never saw but one. It was at Bealeton Station Va., when our Corps was about to start for the West. We were loaded onto freight cars, forty in a car, somewhat as cattle are loaded, and Col. D.C. was directing and overseeing the operation. A commissioned officer was placed in charge of each car, and I remember, as he came along by my car, he was particularly careful to inquire if I had the full number in my "load." That was the only time I ever saw him. I am told that he is with this army, or behind it rebuilding bridges and repairing the Rail Road as we advance, and Lon Howard told me that he met several men at Marietta the other day direct from Hornellsville and the Erie Road.

Hornellsville! How precious seems everything that comes from there, even to the envelope postmarked with that familiar name. Often, when looking over Brigade mail, I see letters from home and vicinity, I experience a thrill of glad reassurance, that I am not so far "out of the world" after all as I might be. And I confess I was startled, as if catching a glimpse of some dear old friend, when I saw a letter, the other day postmarked "Alfred Centre." It had been a very long time since I had seen that name in print, and you cannot imagine how many memories that postmark excited.

August 3: Still sick. Enervated. Used up.

August 4th: A little better.

August 6: Capt. Sill has received his commission as Major.

August 7: Capt. Sill mustered in as Major.

August 9: Went up to drink some wine with Major Sill in honor of the promotion.

August: How swiftly flies the time. Our Spring Campaign has lengthened out into a summer Campaign, nor am I sure that it will stop at all before the winter. 'Twas in April we started, and May, June and July have been an uninterrupted campaign actively prosecuted, as our magnificent army has steadily pushed its way southward. Truly this is the Battle Summer. And I am tired of wondering, where will it end? or when? Soon will the Summer be merged into the fall campaign, and winter itself, so far south as this would not, alone, be sufficient to stop the tide of war. We have been hoping for a rest when we shall have taken Atlanta. But Atlanta is not yet taken, and God only knows whether it will be taken soon, or late, or ever. And if we take it, what then? Not much rest, I fear. So, swiftly goes the time, and as our boys say, "it all counts in the three years." Do you know, my regiment has but about a year yet to serve.

10. After the Battle

August 13th 1865 is the close of our term of service as a regiment. But I was mustered in (as 1st. Lieut.) the other day, for three years from July 29, 1864, "unless sooner discharged." One must not accept promotion, in the service, if he expects ever to see the expiration of his term of service, at least so long as the war lasts. Yet how anxious are all to be promoted, accepting these conditions.

It was a praiseworthy act, when Capt. Wickes, the mustering officer for this Division, went to the Hospital to muster in a man who had been dangerously wounded in the fight of the 20th ult. Dangerously wounded, not expected to live, yet while he lived he would have more privileges as an officer than as a sergeant, and if he died his widow would receive a much larger pension. He had received his commission before the fight, and now it did him a world of good to secure his muster in. With what interest did all the inmates of the Hospital listen to him as he took the oath of allegiance, and swore to fight for the integrity of the country, and the enforcement of its laws. And when he had been mustered, torn and mangled with wounds as they were, they crowded around him, some having to crawl, to congratulate him.

As the 3d Division of our Corps was marching the other day, I went through the ranks of the 19th Michigan Reg't looking for "our mutual friend," Capt. Charles A. Thompson, Jr. But I did not find him. He is at home, sick. His 1st. Lieut. thought he would not return to the service. His health had been broken down when he was in Libby Prison. The whole regiment was captured at Franklin, Tenn., some months ago I believe. They were very soon exchanged, but even a short stay in "Hotel de Libby" is not healthful, I reckon.

Gen. Hooker has left us, left because it had become evident that there was "no open door to him for advancement in this army." It is no doubt true that he has had to struggle against prejudice, envy and jealousy ever since he came West, that he has not been allowed to do all that he could have wished, that he has not secured due credit for what he and his command have done. But it was hard to take leave of him, to take him by the hand, as many of us did, and tell him how much we regretted his departure. The Generals and their Staffs, and the different regimental commanders, of the Corps, met together to bid the General good-bye. He said but a few words, halting and disconnected, but full of feeling and manifesting, as no finely worded discourse ever could, how much he loved his Corps, how much, he knew, they loved him. Col. Selfridge of the 46th Pa. gave a toast, "Gen. Hooker, no man more feared by his enemies, no man more loved by his friends," which brought the tears to the General's eyes, "I know it," he said, "I know I have the trust of friends. I know I have the confidence of all this Corps, and never since I have been in the service have I been with any troops that I loved so as I love the 20th Corps." He was the idol of the Corps, and a terror to the enemy. Prisoners were always talking about Joe Hooker, and Hooker's men, about as our boys need to regard "Stonewall Jackson."

General Williams temporarily commands the Corps. We hear that Gen. Slocum is to be assigned to this command. I hope so.

The day is fair, it is a still summer's afternoon, the sun is not too warm, and a cool breath of air fans my forehead, as I sit half a dream, for I am not well (exactly), and off duty for the day I can be as lazy as I wish.

August 10: Got under a fire of shell.

August 11: Took a ride with the General over into the 16th Corp line. Got under another fire of shells. They were further to the right.

August 12: Went up on the hill with the band. It was a beautiful moonlit evening. As soon as the music began the skirmishing stopped. One piece they played was *Auld Lang Syne*. The Battery at our right commenced shelling the city. It was a fine sight; the camp fires of our army, the shells bursting over the city, far away, and the bright moonlight over all. Came back and played Whist with the General.

August 13, 1864

The anniversary of my muster into service two years ago.

I "swore in for three years," or during the war unless sooner discharged. It seems a wonder that I have lived through two years of service, yet now that I have done it, I have hope for the one that remains. "Hither to, the Lord hath helped me." Shall I not trust in him for the future? Wrote to Preima and sister Carrie.

Before Atlanta, Ga., 13th Aug. 1864.

Injurious as may be the practice of sleeping in the day time, I must never the less own that I did take a long nap this afternoon. The noteworthy circumstance was that my sleep was filled with dreams, not a bit of which I could recollect when I awoke. "Golden Dreams," how many they are, sleeping around the camp fires, on the picket bivouac, or on the battle-field, walking, as the long march is made, and walking on in silence and thought, or when the sentinel treads his lonely beat, or he often goes the rounds of the picket lines in the silence of the night. Dreaming ever, and of what? Almost always of home, of the glad return to old friends, and scenes which is to follow all this peril and hardship, which is to compensate for all we are now deprived of, which is to make substantial the honors gained in the field. I used to see coarse prints, colored pictures of "The Soldier's Return," "The Soldier's Dream," etc., where some dashing English Sergeant or French Grenadier is pictured as being met on the door by his beloved, with a welcome evidently much more affectionate than dignified. And I have read poetry picturing similar scenes. I can realize the sentiment of all this now, and I can tell you there is a deal of romance in these same visions of happier scenes that come to gladden the soldier and fill his heart with bright hopes. War and its havocs are always considered. The company that came out a hundred strong is to go back with but ten or a dozen, but the fond dreamer is always one of the fortunate survivors, and he trustingly dreams of the return home after years of service, with a little band of heroes, proud of their record in the field, grateful for the privilege of at last meeting their loved ones, and remembering with tender regret the comrades left sleeping their last sleep beneath southern skies. The picture is always bright, for the dreamer, never does it place him as one of those left behind, when the rest shall return. Never does death in the field of battle, or in the hospital find a welcome place in his vision. Alas! Then how many are disappointed. Yet strange as it may seem, few seem to be disappointed or surprised when they are called to be on the field. It may be different in hospital, but death on the battle-field when it really must come seems to be accepted as a matter of course, as no more than ought to have been expected, with the most patient resignation. "I guess I'm done for now. I can't live long.," said Eugene Thacher, calmly, as he was carried to the rear at Dallas. "I rather guess they've brought me down at last.," said Capt. Orton, when an exploding shell mutilated him most terribly the other day. "I would like to live to join my regiment," said Henry Howland of the 107th, mortally wounded when we first came here. "I would like to be permitted to fight the Rebels a little longer, but if I must die now, I know I cannot die in a better cause."

Over twenty, more than one fifth of the one hundred men of Co. K who enlisted in the service two years ago are now dead. As we are now an "old Regiment" and will thus have harder fighting to do, we will probably lose as many in the year to come, as in the two years past. Is it not an interesting speculation, who is to fall and who is to survive? But brightly as ever the soldier dreams of a happy return for some of us, and each one pictures himself as one of the survivors.

This 13th of August is an interesting anniversary with me. It was just two years ago that I took the oath of enlistment "for three years or during the war, unless sooner discharged," into the service of the United States. That was an event never to be forgotten by me. It was a fearful risk I felt to absolutely give up my liberty and life to the entire control of others for so long a time, fearful because it was a matter of extreme doubt whether my health would be sufficient for the life of one who had to carry a gun and knapsack. And it was just one year ago today, that having been absent from duty through the Gettysburg Campaign, I rejoined my regiment and reported for duty. I have told you of my journey from Philadelphia, through Baltimore, Washington, Alexandria, Warrenton Junction and Bealeton Station to Kellys

Ford on the Rappahannock, where I found my regiment. I had been off duty so long, now sick, and then visiting at home, that I was all unfit to go to soldiering immediately. I seemed like a new recruit, and always dated the beginning of my second term of service from Aug. 13, 1863. Should I live to see Aug 13, 1865, the expiration of our regimental term of service, what then? Ah! What may not happen before that time!

When I awoke this afternoon it was to view the last of a most beautiful sunset scene, to watch the quiet coming of the twilight that followed. Quiet and calm and soothing as a Sabbath evening were the evening shades that settled down upon us, until at last the moon as serene and tranquil came up, and now we are having a magnificent moonlit evening. Moonlight and sunshine are among the luxuries that we take with us even into the military service. We have not left every God thing behind us.

Every night our band goes up to serenade the troops in the trenches. They take position on the crest of a little ridge, behind our lines, and for which their music is plainly heard in all directions. Just as quick as the music begins, the skirmish firing stops on both sides. "Rebs as well as Yanks" call for their favorites and interchange comments on the music. Our lines are so close that we can easily talk with the enemy in their works. Last night I went up to the lines with the Band. One of the pieces was a beautiful arrangement of *Auld Lang Syne*. Did it cause the hostile troops to dream of the old times when our country was at peace, and Columbia was indeed a "happy land"? If so, the dream was roughly dispelled by a Battery of twenty pound Parrotts just at our right, which sent shell after shell whizzing over the Rebel works away back to the center of the city were they exploded with a lurid flash, and a dull heavy report that came back to us after listening many minutes. So we reminded them of the past, so of the present. Let them decide which they like best. But the mail boy is waiting for my letter. Quickly let it go, and may I find you well and happy.

August 14: A mild pleasant day, real Sabbath like and still.

Eve: Went over to Dept. H'd Q'rs with Knight, Binney, Fay and the Band. Made a lot of new friends, Capt. Stone, Lt. Duffried, Capt. Kellogg.

August 18: The rebels thought we were leaving and opened a heavy cannonade on us early in the morning. Nobody hurt. They soon found that we were here.

August 19: We retaliated on the Rebs by a heavy cannonade this morning, the heaviest artillery fire we have had this campaign. Those who saw it said it was a magnificent spectacle.

August 21: A new Capt. has been commissioned in our regiment. His name is Reed and he used to be in the 145th. He has been assigned to the temporary command of Co. K. Col. Crane has promised to let the matter stand, leaving me the choice yet to return to my regt. and take promotion. All right.

August 22: Engaged in digging a ditch along the RR track and inside the corporation line of Atlanta.

A letter from Will Caldwell. He has lots to say about the Shelby Williams. Major Sill got a letter also from Mr. Caldwell. Went up to Corp H'd Quarters with Thorne, Knight, Binni, Williams, and the Band. The 33d Mass. band was there also, and several from Thomas' Staff. Loud time.

August 23: Letters from Father and Preima. Good. Took a ride with the General to Gen. Sherman and Gen. Howard's H'd Quarters. Coming back we found that some of the Staff had gone up to Department H'd Quarters with the Band.

August 24: Didn't get any pay, as I hoped. Met Capt. Banbridge, who was formerly on Gen. Slocum's Staff.

August 25: Rode over to the train, across the river with Binni. Saw a paymaster and have hopes of getting my pay. At eight o'clock P.M. our troops withdrew from their trenches and retired to the road leading back to the river. There we massed to wait until the 4th Corps should pass us in their movement to the fight. At midnight, but a part of Kimball's Division had passed. But all was quiet on the Reb lines.

Chattahoochee River, Ga., 30th Aug. 1864.

I sent you a paper the other day because I could not then write. There was a letter in it from our friend F. B. Taylor. Does it not spoil the beauty of his picture a little, to know that he was expelled from this army by Gen. Sherman, for revealing too much in his letters? Of Arlington, which he describes, saw but little when in Virginia. It was after dark, one night about two years ago, when we marched by on our way to Antietam, but the glimpse I then had of the place was sufficient to assure me of its beauty.

The 20th Corps has made a retrograde movement, and is now resting quietly along the Chattahoochee, guarding the different ferries contiguous to what the boys call our Cracker Line, the Rail Road. In the meantime the rest of the army is making another "flank movement," the effect of which is yet to be ascertained. How grateful is the rest! We work very hard, but it is fatigue duty, not fighting, digging, not skirmishing. We have not the constant anxiety of an expected conflict, and at night when our work is done, we lie down with probable assurance of a good night's rest before us. True we are but eight miles from Atlanta, and we meet Rebel Cavalry every day, but we are ready for any assault that may come, and in the meantime, we rest.

Today we sent out a reconnaissance toward Atlanta. Result, one or two men shot. No satisfactory knowledge gained as to the size of the force in our front. It is a fine road from here to Atlanta, one of the oldest in Northern Georgia, yet nearly half of it is through woods, so slow is Southern enterprise. There were some fine residences along it though before the war.

One especially I noticed, the house not so elegant as many I have seen, but having a general comfortable look as if it had been a happy home for somebody; nor was there a large plantation around it, but in front was a large flower garden that must have received great care and attention so nicely was it laid out and so carefully kept. But the house had been sacked and the fences all torn up, hardly a flower was left. I picked a rose which withered before I reached camp with it. Shall I send it to you? I was going to visit that flower garden again, but the Rebs now hold that road.

Do I express an unmistakable scorn for Best Society? Perhaps I do. And you wish to know why. I use those terms in their common acceptation, not in their literal meaning, and I only object to the name "Best Society" being applied to a class, which are no better, as regards honest worth, purity, honor and integrity, than those who move in much lower circles. In England one might expect to find the most honor and purity, as well as the most refinement among the wealthy alone, they have a clearly defined "Best Society." But it is not so with us. There is no one class who can rightfully arrogate that name in our land. And I confess to a feeling of scorn when I find out, in my occasional glimpses of Southern Life, how shallow and unreal are the claims of the better classes here to the name of Better Society. Such society may have been their "Best," but I can not call it good. Better society could be found in any industrial town of the North, I think.

Given a goodly heritage at the start from labor as a necessity, with time and energies and abundant means at one's complete disposal one might, by living purely in the sight of God, and loving his neighbors as himself, be enabled to merit a place among our Best Society. The poor may be good and pure, but culture and refinement, good breeding and accomplishments add to the charm of good society, are a necessary part of it, in fact, and these are not in the reach of all.

Gen. William Tecumseh Sherman (K. & H. T. Anthony).

12

Entered Atlanta

Friday, September 2, 1864

Atlanta, Ga., Sunday Evening Sept. 4th, 1864. The papers will tell you of the occupation of the "gate city" by the 20th Corps, of the great destruction of property effected by the retiring Rebels, of the welcome we received from the Union people who awaited our coming, of the beauty of the city, of the destruction caused by our shells during the "siege," and of a thousand other things curious and interesting which I cannot now describe to you, much as I would be pleased could I do it.

How much there is in an ordinary conversation, that becomes tedious when we attempt to detail it on paper. Should I be spared to return to my home, I shall have many stories of our campaigns to tell, that I may perhaps become as disagreeably garrulous as a regular "old soldier."

But I'll tell you of what I've seen today. I attended church this morning. Divine service was held in nearly all the churches on this the third day of the Yankee occupation. So you'll know we haven't disarranged matters very much here. What a blessing to hear the sound of church bells once more. We, (Capt. Ruger and I) went to St. Philip's Church, Episcopalian. There were many citizens, a few ladies, and several "boys in blue," composing the congregation. In a clear, unhesitating voice, the minister read, "We beseech thee to behold and bless thy servant the President of the United States, and all others in authority," and at least some of the people responded, "Amen." The sermon was purely doctrinal, its central idea being that only a knowledge and just appreciation of the attributes of the Deity are required to make all creatures love him. Just think! I am now where I can attend church once more. Only I must hunt up a Presbyterian Church before I feel quite at home. But what a blessing to hear the sound of Church bells once more.

This afternoon I ordered my horse and took a ride through the city. Fine broad streets, lined with elegant shade trees and yards of luxuriant shrubbery surrounding stately residences, and neat cottage homes, in which the owners still remain. Shaded porches and pleasant doorsteps, and parlor windows open to the floor, each occupied by pleasant groups, families and parties of friends gathered together in their "Sunday Suit," watching the sunset. It was glorious this evening, and enjoying the beauty of a most enchanting time, the quiet coming on of a summer's Sabbath evening. (Our summer is hardly gone yet.) Oh! It is almost maddening to be reminded so sharply of the homes we have left behind, and the happiness we must forego. Away in the West of the city I heard music. It drew nearer and soon I recognized *The Star Spangled Banner, Red White and Blue, Yankee Doodle*, etc. A column of colored troops was approaching, and I rode out to meet them. I was not a little surprised to meet a column of Rebel prisoners, a long line of them, twenty-two hundred in all, keeping step to the music of the Union, while on either side of them was flying the Stars and Stripes, the battle flags of the regiments guarding them. They were from Pat Cleburn's Division, the very best fighting division in Hood's Army. This haul of prisoners is a glorious thing for us. They cannot stand many such losses, and such defeats as gave us these men two days ago.

Monday, September 5th: A letter from Crandall. He tells me that Prof. Quimby has become a ψγ, that Gould is making lots of money in the substitute business, and that he never knew what a good fellow I was until he lived with me a year! etc.

I have just been out surveying the Rebel works encircling the town, and a storm came up and gave me a most thorough drenching. I have quit work for today. I went outside the picket lines, to take look at the topography of the country a little and came to the battlefield of July 22d where McPherron was killed. Houses burned, fences destroyed, trees scarred with bullet marks, and everything now as silent as the grave, these tell us of where a terrible conflict once was raged. Many brave boys there brot adieu to life.

September 8: Maj. Sill is quite sick. He has a kind of a remittent fever. He persists in remaining with the regiment, however. I got to see him for the first time since we entered Atlanta.

September 9: Ensyn Conklin came in to see me. He is Capt. in the 66th Ill., and Hd. Sr. Cap'n to Gen. Dodge. His term of service is ended and he expects to go home soon. He is going to Binghamton to live. I sent Eugene Thacher's things home with him, also my autograph book and a few other little things.

Sunday, September 11: Went to the Presbyterian Church. Listened to the preaching of an Army Chaplain, and to the playing of an organ. A letter from James. He is at Harpers Ferry.

September 12: Busy at work in the topog. line. Plenty to do now. Heard today from Preima, from Charlie, Luin, and from Luther Howell. Charlie writes a very friendly letter, and Luther I have not heard from in a year before. He is Capt. now and is home on Veteran Furlough.

Atlanta, Ga., 16th Sept. 1864: We, the 2d Brigade Staff, gathered on the porch of the House, (our Head Quarters), just now to bid "good bye and a good time" to Gen'l Ruger and Aid-de-Camp Lieut. Fay, who are going home on leave of absence. The General goes to Janesville Wis., and Fay to Elmira, N.Y. Furloughs are being granted in this army, but not for me this time. I told Carrie of the compliment paid me by the General in his report a few days since, but I wrote her that I did not care to have it told out of the family, and it is pleasant to know when you give satisfaction to your superiors. After naming the members of his Staff he adds, "Each and all were zealous and efficient in the discharge of duty. To Capt. Thorne I am under obligations for services not pertaining to his particular department rendered on every battlefield, always efficiently, cheerfully and bravely; and also to Lieut. Tuttle for similar services rendered under like circumstances." Says Thorne to me, "let's we two congratulate ourselves." I surely can indulge my vanity enough to write these things to my home folks.

We are doing a great deal of work now. The Generals must have maps and plans to accompany their Reports, and new surveys are ordered besides, so that our Department is the hardest worked now of any in the army. This is the "Month's rest" that Gen. Sherman promised us. Every morning I have an early breakfast and am off remaining at my work until dark. I have tried to take (care) of my eyes, but the fine work I have to do, or perhaps the southern sun glare is ruining my eyes in spite of me. Col. Crane I hear cannot see clearly across the room, and many soldiers are similarly affected.

Just think, two years tomorrow was the Battle of Antietam. And two years ago tonight we made one of the most tiresome marches conceivable. It was after midnight we sunk down, quite wearied out, on the grass and slept so soundly until awakened by the opening volley of the Battle just beside us. I have no memory of what transpired between that dropping down on the grass to sleep, and the passing of a shell over our heads as we were moving into line in the morning.

Luin Thacher has met Maggie Rothrock in Arkansas, and she is a "Savage little Rebel," of course. There are many such here, but they are being sent South very rapidly.

The General and Fay went home on leave in the evening.

September 18: A Grand Review and rain and fizzle.

Saturday, September 24, 1864. Today I received the order for which I have been looking. Here it is *verbatim et [liberatum]*:

H'd Q'rs Twentieth Corps
Army of the Cumberland
Atlanta, Ga., Sept. 23, 1864

Special Order
No 89

(Extract)

II Lieut. R. M. Tuttle 107th N.Y. Volo., Act. Top'l Engineer 2d Brigade 1st Div., is hereby assigned to duty as Topographical Engineer of the 3d Div. 20th Corps and will report to Brig. Gen'l Ward commanding.

By command of Major Gen Slocum
H. W. Perkins
Ass't Adj. Gen'l

I reported this afternoon. Gen'l Ward went home yesterday on leave of absence. I think I shall like him right well. I shall be fully domesticated there by the time he gets back. Col. Dusten 165 Ill. was in command. Was cordially received.

I attended a concert tonight which reminded me of other days and scenes. I send you the program. The hacks waiting at the entrance, the ticket office, the crowded Hall and Galleries, the bright foot lights, the familiar notes of old operas I had listened to from other stages, the applause and encores of the audience, all brought me back to Rochester and the Opera Season. There were a few ladies present, a few citizens, (most of the inhabitants have left Atlanta), a large number of officers and soldiers, Gen. Sherman himself among them. The concert was indeed a success. "Crusty old Sherman" and Gen'l Barry beside him applauded most heartily, as did all. It was all for the benefit of Mrs. Welch, who true to the old flag, has suffered many persecutions under the Rebel rule, and now seeks to get North, her own family and that of her widowed sister dependent on her.

I am very busy now-a-days. Every day I am out surveying, or if at home, busily engaged in plotting up the notes taken in the field. And as sure as I go out I get a soaking. These cold, dismal rains, we have them all the time, are very unpleasant. I have a severe cold which I contrive to add to each day as I get a new drenching.

Gen. Ruger must be having a good time home. We hear not a word from him, though his brother is a member of our Mess. Col. Carman, 13th New Jersey Vols is comd'g the Brigade at present. "John" is sound asleep. I found him in the arms of Morpheus, Murphy as the boys have it, when I returned from the concert. I will not tax my eyes to write more by candlelight.

September 25: While the rest of the Staff went up to the Review of the

2nd Division, I staid at home and kept house. Had a real sick time of it too.

September 26: Moved over to H'd Quarters 3rd Div. They were out on Division Review and had provided no place for me, so I left my goods and went back to Brigade H'd Quarters for the night. Wrote a letter home.

September 27: First day as Division Staff officer, and am not very much prepossessed in favor of the Staff on duty here. Was assigned to a dirty room that had been used as a family cook room, filled with all kinds of litter and with several lights out of the windows. I have not yet been made acquainted with any fellow staff officers. My papers introduced me to the Col. and the Adjutant General, and the Col. introduced me to the Capt. Bearsley of the 20 Corp. That's all. Attended a religious meeting in the evening at the Baptist church. Good meeting.

September 28: Getting very slowly domesticated in my new Home. Evening, paid a visit to the regiment. Wells is a Sergeant once more. Uncle Allen says that the Col. has recommended the Adjutant for Lt. Col., saying that he is altogether the best officer in the regiment. They will try to checkmate this game, Sill and Fox. A letter from Luin. He is in Little Rock, Ark. Has the fever and ague, and hopes soon to be discharged from the service. Says that Maggie Rothrock (now Mrs. Lockman) is a virulent little Rebel.

Good letter too from sister Carrie.

13

The Siege of Atlanta

Atlanta, Ga., Oct. 4, 1864

Besieged! It sounds queerly enough, and yet we in Atlanta are virtually in that condition. It was only today that we came to a realizing sense that the enemy was actually in our rear in heavy force, and that we were virtually cut off from the North. Back along the slender line that was our only connection with our homes, and our only means of support here, we find that our foes have taken position, and captured the supplies they found at the different stations, and are tearing up the track, burning bridges, and completely destroying the road. Something was up. We knew from the unusual movements of the troops around us. Brigade, Division, and Corps have gone, until now the 20th Corps alone is left in the city. We go to the News office for papers and find none, but on the "Bulletin Board" we read, "no trains from Chattanooga since Sunday." "Telegraph working only to Marietta." "Signal Officers report the enemy in force at Acworth! Many fires seen and much smoke, — enemy is presumed to be destroying the Rail Road." "Heavy firing heard and reports of sharp fighting at Lost Mountain yesterday." "No paper or letters need be expected from the North in many days."

For once Johnny Reb has made an astonishingly bold move. He has placed himself exactly in our rear, and is most thoroughly destroying our only line of communication. He has flanked the "great flanker" completely. So far, so good. It remains to be seen what this desperate move will effect. Sherman is on the move with a good part of his Army, and it seems impossible but that there will soon be a severe struggle, perhaps on some of our identical battle grounds of May and June last. The Rebels mean to starve us out here, and to compel us in consequence to abandon Atlanta. But the 20th Corps is left here intact, and in the new and elaborate fortifications we are constructing, can hold out for a long time against a regular siege, supplied as we are with a large stock of food and ammunition, not to speak of tried valor and powers of endurance. We do not fear. Yet we are preparing our minds for what may come. It is unpleasant to be cut off so from the North, to receive no mails and hear no news. Still more (unpleasant) disagreeable would it be to run short of supplies. But we could look starvation in the face for some time, rather than give up this goal, the reward of the long summer campaign we have gone through.

Already we hear facetious remarks about the probable price of mule steaks and horseflesh. Someone was conveying a dead mule by our Head Quarters today and Capt. Bucher proposed to have the animal "salted down." Mule meat might be "good to have in the house" ere long.

Going down the street today I met a ten-mule team drawing along an immense cannon, a 64 pounder, which some curious Yankee had lately unearthed from some "grave" which seemed (and proved) to be much too large for the Confederate soldier it purported to hold. Almost daily we are resurrecting canon, etc., from their hiding places. Did the Rebs think the Yankees would not be cunning enough to find them?

At church in the evening with Capt. Ruger. Thanks to the good Lord for the room-mate I have, whose influence leads me not away from but toward my Savior! The church was crowded as it is every evening, and it is a large one. Many were in the galleries, and in the isles even. There was a short sermon and then a "Conference Meeting." Very interesting were the remarks and narrations of religious experience of the different speakers. Very solemn and impressive the singing which filled all the church, and upon invitation of the Chaplain leading the exercises, many arose, to ask the prayers of God's children in their behalf. God was surely with his children who waited on him there, ah! They cannot cut us off from our God. Only our sins can get in the way between Him and us!

October 5: Morning: No news from "the front." The front now is Northward, and the rear Southward, indeed if it is not all front now. In the meantime our men are busily working at the fortifications, the new interior line. Very heavy details have been at work for some days now. Today the men have brought their arms with them, and their muskets are stacked in line close by where they are at work. It is supposed that while a large part of the enemy have gone to our rear there is still one Corps in front of us. And this Corps we expect will make the attempt to gain the city or at least to ascertain how much of a force Sherman has left here. It will be strange indeed if there is not some demonstration made here on our lines before long. We are rather looking forward to it today. Let them come! They will find the Potomac boys ready to receive them.

Evening: What a rare institution is the Signal Corps! From Marietta to Allatoona it is twenty miles. Our forces hold the Allatoona Mountains and the Kennesaw Mountains at Marietta. Between these points the Rebels have gained possession of the Rail Road, have destroyed everything thoroughly, and have completely cut off communication between us and our friends north of the break. Did I say "all" communication? Not quite. The signal flags at Allatoona have been talking right over the heads of the Rebs to the station on Kennesaw Mountain. They say that they are "all right" there yet, that they are strongly fortified, that reinforcements are coming up, and that they will be able to hold their position. Good. If the Rebel destruction extends no further than between Allatoona and Kennesaw there will result but little inconvenience to us.

October 6: Preparations are being made already for repairing the road damaged by the enemy. By working at both ends of the break, three miles a day of track can be laid. Supposing that the Rebels destroy fifteen miles of the road, five days will repair all damages. But the enemy must first be driven away from the road, and have they been? We cannot hear for certain. But there are rumors to that effect.

At the Depot today I saw a train ready to start out, and loaded with Rail Road iron, and spikes and "chairs" all new. Just think, crowded as the road has been, taxed to the utmost in order to supply this vast army with all its needs, it yet found room for a large quantity of rail road iron, which was piled up in the city here in waiting for an emergency, just like this. I was not a little puzzled, I remember, when I saw trains coming in from the North bringing only iron rails. I thought they ought to hurry in subsistence stores instead of iron. I am convinced now that "they" knew best.

Went down to the Bank building near the Depot where Major Glenn, Paymaster U.S.A. has his office, and drew my pay for September. Deducting the five per cent income tax, he gave me $105.55. "How well the officers in the Army are paid," say our friends up North. "They must be making money like dirt." At the beginning of the war when officers were paid in gold, when prices were moderate, when none of the pay was deducted as tax, when officers were not put on half pay when absent on leave, and when their pay was not stopped by government because of informalities in reports which have to be made out even in the midst of a campaign, then the officers of the army may have been moderately well paid. But now, unless he holds a high position, an officer's pay scarcely exceeds his expenses. If one live well, it will cost for himself and a servant 50.00 a month to live. (If he keep no servant government allows him $22.50 less, per month.) And we must buy our own clothes, a pair of boots cost from 10.00 to $15.00, a hat from $6.00 to 12.00, other things in proportion, uniform, accouterments, etc. A Capt. or Lieut., especially if he be on Staff duty, may be thankful if his pay fully covers his expenses. And as for saving anything, any business almost, is more lucrative than the soldier or the officer's, to say nothing of the peril of life and health, a peril for which no money is sufficient compensation. Let me return to my home after the war is ended, alive and well, with no limbs lost and my constitution uninjured, and my envious friends can have all the money I have saved.

How easy it rains. Yes, it has been raining nearly all day, with scarcely any let up. The poor fellows at work on the fortifications, would scarcely get started at work before a pelting shower, heavy and cold, would drive them to their shelter again. I pitied the Johnny Rebs at work there, sixty or seventy deserters came in a day or two ago, and went right at work on the fortifications. They had no rubber blankets as our men have. Yet old Dr. Calhoun says this is to be a dry month, for the new moon is a "dry moon, so turned up that the Indian cannot hang his powder horn on it." And perhaps it will be clear henceforth. The sun set this evening in a magnificent glory of crimson and gold, giving promise of a clear sky tomorrow! I took a stroll just at (evening) twilight over to the new fort they are building in front of our Head Quarters, and then around three or four squares of the city. All alone, I was, and my thoughts were very busy, putting on an addition I think, to the chapter I read this afternoon in the *Reveries of a Bachelor*. But this climate is delicious, and the evening has seemed truly enchanting.

"Later from the front." Telegram from Marietta says that Signal Flags at Allatoona report desperate fighting there. "Rebels repulsed in two assaults, after which they retired to the West and South." Wonder if that's their last move in these parts? "General Corse badly wounded, cheek and ear shot away, but able to give the Rebs — — yet." (Some of those Signal Flags are very profane.)

The operation at Marietta reports by the army today. "Army of the Tennessee" (15th, 16th, and 17th Corps) on the left, "Army of the Cumberland" (14th & 4th Corps) in the center, and "Army of the Ohio" (23d A.C.) on the right. "Sherman well pleased." I am glad to hear he is "pleased." We went away from here brimfull of wrath and indignation, breathing out threatenings and slaughter; as Doc Pendergast says, "he had a big disgust." I would like to record his remarks on the occasion, so characteristic they were, but no, it won't do to write them.

It's a late evening. One more chapter of the marvels *Reveries*, and then to my own dreams.

October 7: News from the Army today is favorable. In their repulse at Allatoona the Rebs lost heavily. And it is reported that many prisoners were taken. Our loss was quite heavy also. 8,000 head of cattle had arrived safely at Allatoona. The enemy were moving South West, going to Alabama, it is thought, and Sherman after them. The road will be open perhaps as soon as Monday next (10th). This last is cheering news, exciting glad visions of letters and papers from the North.

O! beautiful night! Never was finer than this. All day the skies have been wonderfully bright and clear, and tonight every star glitters as in the keenest nights of winter, while the moon, though only in her first quarter, pours down a flood of light that renders the whole scene magnificent. How could I resist the impulse to stroll out in the moonlight! I have been all the evening in the city's streets enjoying the beauty of the scene. And all the air is filled with music. All soldiers love music, I think, and manage to carry it with them wherever they go. Brass bands are always to be heard. And the drum corps of some regiments far excel any martial music we ever hear at home. Then the bugles of the artillery and cavalry. What music in some of their calls, the rousing reveille and the dreamy tattoo. Ever I hear them I am reminded of the glorious mornings and the magnificent starlit evenings when I heard them first, on the Arlington Place in Old Virginia. And tonight, as I have been walking out, it has seemed as if there was music everywhere. Brass bands in every part of the city, their music came blended, and confused from all parts of the city, yet soft and gentle, not distracting to the ear. Other serenades there were, amateur glee clubs, quartets, and I heard some fine voices.

Near Gen. Thomas' Head Quarters was a splendid quartette, out in the yard, in front of their own offices, were four boys in blue serenading themselves? It seemed so. Singing of home, and the dear ones there, were they not in imagination serenading those far off friends? Each heart recalled a different name, but they all sang *Annie Laurie*. Here a solitary soldier boy was solacing himself with a flute, and there I heard the matchless tones of a violin. Again I passed a house where was a piano, and it was "prentice" hand that was handling the instrument. Something familiar in the strain stopped me. The performer was running through the introduction of some instrumental piece. What it was I could not quite think out, but in a minute it came to me, so like old times, *The Maiden's Prayer*.

So was it whenever I strayed, the spirit of music pervaded all places, as the bright moonlight covered all objects, and this evening stroll has been to me almost enchantment. And not less sweet than impressive, as it quietly came home was the strain that came floating from the church two or three squares away, where a goodly company of worshipers were singing, *Praise God from whom all blessings flow*!

And are not "the heavenly host" praising Him "above"! On such a magnificent night as this, nature herself seems to say to us, "The heavens declare the glory of God, and the firmament showeth his handiwork."

October 8: There's little news today. Little or none from Sherman, and just a little from Grant, that he is pegging away at Richmond again. And a foolish rumor that he has taken it! Why, as the fellow said, I wouldn't believe it, if I knew it. But the fact that we can get news from the North once more is encouragement. The telegraph line is up. Ere long let us hope for communication by mail, unless "our erring brethren" venture on another raid upon the Rail Road.

I have just been reading another novel, *East Lynne*. The *London Quarterly Review* acknowledging the genius of the book denounces its general moral.

October 9: It is a pleasant boarding place that we have. Dr. Grinsted of Missouri, Dr. Bennett of Connecticut, Capt. Ruger of Wisconsin, and myself are the boarders. Dr. G. is a native of England, and a residence of twenty years in the States has not worn off all his English manners, though he is as hearty a "Union man" as ever hated English partiality to the Rebs on Missouri Secession. He has been on the seas a good bit too, and besides a regular sailor walk has a great many sailor-ish ways about him. Dr. Bennett, Medical Inspector of the 20th Corps, is a gentleman and a scholar. A genial, generous souled man whom all the men like, and of high attainments in his profession. Of Capt. Ruger, my roommate, I have already spoken. Suffice it to say that the more of him the better I like him. The family: There is Dr. Calhoun, and Mrs. Calhoun, his wife. There is Mrs. Williams, their daughter Carolina, now a widow, and there is another daughter, Miss Indiana. The rest of the family are away, one daughter in Alabama, one in New Jersey, two in this State, and a son in "Wade Hampton's Legion" of the Rebel Cavalry. One soldier son was killed in one of the battles near Richmond. What names for the girls! "Indiana," "Florida," "Missouri," "Virginia," "Carolina," "Georgia." They are Carolinians all, the family of the genuine Calhoun stock. The Doctor's father was "own cousin to John C. Calhoun." But the Doctor has grown old and wise also. Many doctrines of the chivalry seem now to him utterly wrong and absurd. Said he to Capt. Ruger last night, "If I had my life to live over again, I would never raise a family in the South here." When after a time the Captain asked him why he made such a remark, he said, "I would wish to bring up my children to habits of industry. And here it is not honorable to work." In the course of the conversation he admitted that the structure of society was radically wrong here, and to lose all their slaves would in time be a blessing to them.

Cheers! Cheers!!! Cheers!!! What can all this uproar mean? Forth we go to find out the meaning of it. Down in the city, in the Telegraph Office we hear that Grant occupies Richmond! It is too good news to be true here, and we turn homeward, wishing we could be sure it is true, and discussing the chances of his coming down upon us, transferring the war to the Cotton States.

It is now late in the evening, and in the stillness of the night we can hear that cheer repeated again and again as it is caught up by one regiment after another and carries along the lines, all around the city. It is evident that somebody believes the report. Soon the bands wake up, and now here, now away in the distance we can hear the strains of *Hail Columbia, The Star Spangled Banner,* etc. They seemed to be having a regular jubilee, and I went to sleep to the sound of music.

October 10: Though the enemy has been driven from our communications, the damage they did has by no means been repaired. It will take some days to lay the track again. Until then, no mails. Even the telegraph lines are not up yet. The news from Virginia was signalled to our signal station at Kennesaw. We still have plenty of food, but no forage. Our poor animals are starving. They all go out to graze, but many fall dead on the way. Starving to death by the hundreds, would they not pray, if they could, for the speedy opening of the road? Their prospect for the coming winter is a dreary one indeed. They'll all die, I guess.

A stroll through the town today brought me at last to the cemetery. A beautiful spot it must have been once, so nicely laid out, and so carefully kept. Many fine monuments are there. Some neat and beautiful, some stylish and — for show. Shrubs and flowers everywhere, grass plots and terraces, and lots enclosed by neat fences and hedges, on all sides touching and beautiful reminder of enduring love of bereaved ones for their lost. But what touched me most was a sight of the countless headboards marking soldiers' graves. A large field just east of the cemetery proper, filled with the dead of the Armies. Side by side they lie making long rows that stretch across the field, and so many of those rows! No carefully tended grass plots and flowers there, no trees and no avenues, no room left even to walk among the graves, but closely lain together side by side. There lie Colonels, Captains, and privates from every state in the South from Virginia to Texas, from Kentucky to Florida. Yes, and there are some Northern graves there also in one part of the field., with these words on the headboard, "From Prison Hospital." Poor fellows these, who had not even the poor consolation of dying under the folds of the "Old Flag." Ah! But the old flag now waves over their last resting place, please God it may ever do so! And the sentinel who paces those cemetery walks to guard the place from desecration, is one of the Boys in Blue. I have a deep interest in these captive dead, for a good friend of mine is sleeping among them. We had thought him killed at Dallas (25th May), but here we found his name, company and regiment, the date of his death, June 7, and those three words that mean so much sorrow — "From Prison Hospital."

October 11: Just found out today that Phin Mitchell was in the service, in our own Division, a Lieut. in the 141st N.Y. Volo.

October 12: This is insupportably dull, this life just at present here. Cooped up in the city, for it is unsafe to go outside of the picket lines in any direction, — hearing nothing, from the North or from the Army because the break in the railroad above has not yet been repaired and the Army has moved off northward after Hood. Doing nothing, because there is nothing to do, ah! This is exceedingly dull. But it is part of a soldier's duty to "wait" as well as to "labor." Therefore we slowly and discontentedly accomplish the days of our waiting. In the meantime, the most of the troops are busily at work perfecting the city's defenses.

The repairing of the rail road above us progresses very slowly. Telegraphic communication has at last been opened though, but the only news it has yet brought to us is that they have heard nothing at Chattanooga about the capture of Richmond.

October 13: A day of anxiety. The road is almost repaired again, but an alarming rumor has prevailed that it has been cut again, near Kingston! Woe is us if that be true. Hood seems to have taken his Army on a grand raid. I hope Sherman will be able to defeat his malicious designs.

Evening: All right! Sherman occupied Kingston himself, for we have just recieved a telegram from him containing lots of good news from the North. Our communications are all right yet I guess. But oh! For a mail. They say it will be a day and a half yet before the road is opened.

October 14: A day to be remembered, since it brought us a mail. The first we have had in nearly two weeks. What a sound of rejoicing is heard all through the city. We are not entirely cut off from all knowledge of our friends at the North. Every tie between us and civilization is not yet severed, of this we have the indubitable evidence of these letters and papers. But no. Even amid our rejoicing comes the dark rumor that the Rebs have struck the rail road once more, that they have planted themselves square across our "cracker line" and are busily engaged in a second work of destruction. Now we have cause to begin to fear for our permanence here. It is said that fifteen or twenty miles of track have been torn up, if so it will be many days, it will be weeks before we may expect supplies for this post. If they starve us out, there will be no help for it, we will have to go back. But we have food enough for many days yet, forage for the animals we have obtained, and can get in abundance from the country here, and of ammunition we have any quantity. So! Let us thank God and take courage. It will require a most severe privation to make us give our hold on this place. But for the letters brought to us this day, be a full mead of gratitude. Ah! letters are a blessing, — and to a soldier sometimes the only source of pure enjoyment vouchsafed. All that he has to remind him of what is best and noblest in life.

October 16: Flat Shoals, or Rock. Atlanta to Latimer's Farm.

October 18: Lithonia

October 19: Flat Rock to Atlanta

October 21: Atlanta to Latimer X Roads

October 22: Surveyed into Lithonia with Capt. McDowell. Stopped for the night, at Mrs. Fowler's house at Snap Finger Creek.

October 23: Arrival of 2d Brigade. Moved to Decatur. Stopped for night at Mr. Moor's

October 24: Into the city early. Found a good mail awaiting us. All much concerned about us. To see Miss Hall with Capt. Bennett.

October 25: At work on my plotting. Report of orders to march. Afternoon at Mr. McArthur's. Good letter from home.

October 26: Plotting done. Dinner with Howard. Eve at Mr. McArthur's.

For a long time it has been impossible to send letters North. Gen. Hood is responsible. And latterly I have been out in the country with foraging parties almost constantly.

I send a little account of what we saw and heard in those days of dullness, of the little that interested me. Our foraging expeditions were of a very different character, having so much of interest and excitement, of ludicrous occurrences and romantic interest. But there was even a dark side to the picture, distress and starvation brought upon all the country. God save my home from such a visitation ever, and grant that these horrors may soon be banished from all our land.

October 27: Hard rain all day long.

October 28: Miss Eliza Hall left on the morning train for Adairsville and the North. God be with her and keep her. I had some difficulty in getting her transportation. Visit from Maj. Sill. He has news that his commission as Lt. Col. has been made out by the Gen. Capt. Lamons' resignation has been accepted, and the Maj. wants to know if I want to go in for the vacant Captaincy. Hardy think it proper under the circumstances. Maj. says that Doct Pendergast and Ed Fay had returned, having had a good long visit at Shelbyville.

October 30: Return of Gen. Ward and Staff. Much whiskey drunk. The Gen. says that Gen. Ruger came down today also. Went over to the regiment to see Doct Pendergast. He had lots of news to tell me from Shelbyville, and he had fine pictures of Miss Laura and Miss Helen. Maj. Sill is now Lt. Col. Sill, he having received his commission, and was mustered in today. His campaign is successfully completed. Things look mixed, as tho' something is going to be done.

"Going South to Seek Salt Water"

Is it Mobile or Is it Savannah?

Atlanta, Ga., Nov. 2, 1864.

It is a dismal day, wet and cold and gloomy. Beautiful days were those of the last month, warm and bright, the essence of Indian Summer. Now how changed! And it is not at all pleasing to think that in a day or two we are to start on another campaign. Such weather as this is certainly not auspicious, but we are going, as everybody seems to think, though whether it be to Milledgeville and Savannah, or to Macon, or to Montgomery, Selma, and Mobile, or to Northern Alabama, or back to Chattanooga, or to Libby Prison, none can satisfactorily determine. I suppose we will all know in due time.

At present it is very dull here, there is nothing of interest, to be seen, or described. Of news I can give you none. In my weariness I go down to the Depot every day and watch the heavily laden trains coming in and going out, unable to tell what all these movements mean. Or I go over to the regiment and have a talk with my Uncle Sill, or with Doc Pendergast who has just returned from a leave of absence and who has a great deal to tell me about the people in the North, and about my friends in Shelbyville where he stopped a day or two on his way back. Ed Fay has been home too at Elmira. I have good long talks with my Uncle Sill. He was Captain until we came in front of Atlanta, when he was promoted to Major, and now he is Lieut. Col. of our regiment. I rejoice in his promotion, so deserved, so patiently waited for, so nobly earned.

The regiment is very much changed ever since I left it, and how different from itself when we left Elmira. Then a thousand strong all present for duty, now, after having received many recruits, and five companies from other regiments, numbering but 347 present for duty, and 347 absent, we think we are getting to be veterans, and many are already counting the days that will complete our three years of service. We call ourselves "nine months troops" now as we have only about that time to serve. Yet time is sufficient to use us all up, if we are pushed through an active campaign, and very many, I fear, who are fondly looking forward to a safe return home, will reach only a soldier's grave beneath these treacherous Southern skies. Blessed are they who expect nothing, for they will not be disappointed when they get nothing.

I received a letter from Lydia, yesterday. What a sad affliction to them all must have been the death of Eugene. I am almost glad that I have no dear friends in the army. It is a greater sacrifice and requires more heroism I think to give up one's dear ones than to go one's self. I do not honor the soldier so much as I do the wife or mother who sends him forth with a God speed!

Ere this reaches you the election question will be decided. I have no fear for the result. I have been anxious only to know if we in the army are to be sustained by the people, if the people at home have sufficient patriotism to sustain our fighting by their voting. If they have not, we had better give up both fighting and voting. I have not voted, because I do not think the soldier ought to vote. The armies of a nation should never interfere with politics. If they do, we'll rue it some day.

Evening: We have been having a serenade by the 33d Mass. Band. The first piece they played was *Departed Days*. It is indeed beautiful though very mournful. Did they select it in memory of the season of rest we have been enjoying here, so soon to be ended?

Soon they all came in and we had a very animated discussion as to whither we are to go. The impression is almost universal. I find that we are going "To Seek Salt Water." Is it Mobile, or is it Savannah? If we follow the little rivulet that flows out of one side of the city, it will lead us down the Chattahoochee into the Gulf. If we follow another little stream that takes its rise within the city line, we will find ourselves in due time via the Ocmulgee and Altamaha Rivers on the Atlantic shore. I wish I was there at some federal station. (I'd take some ship for New York)

November 4: Received letter from Father and sister Carrie, and a splendid pair of boots. Carrie says that Charlie and Nelly are married at last.

November 5: At last, and most unexpectedly to us all, the marching orders came today. To start as quick as possible. So out went the troops and encamped about three miles out on the McDonough road. So we're going down to Dixie I reckon. 33d Mass. concert in the evening.

November 8: Attended the "benefit" of Misses Hattie and Sallie in the evening. I never saw the Atheneum more full or the audience more noisy.

November 9: Woke early to hear a sharp popping and cannonading in the out-work of the city. A few Cavalry men attacked Geary's line. The thing was soon over. One Reb. mortally wounded. The rest dispersed. Wrote to Preima, thinking this was my last chance, *"pro tem."*

Atlanta, Ga., Nov. 9, 1864.

Today we expect our last mail from the North, before we start on our campaign. This then is the only opportunity I will have, for some time to send you a letter. How long that time will be, I cannot make the slightest guess at. Where we are going, or how many of us are to compose the expedition, or when we are to start, are most obscure questions to me. I do not trouble myself about the matter because there is no use in it, and because I don't care particularly. This much only concerns me just now, my clerk tells me this is my last chance for the present, for sending letters North.

Three days ago our Corps actually started off on a march, and the next day were recalled. We were very much surprised, as we thought we had bid farewell to Atlanta forever. Perhaps we'll take a fresh start tomorrow, or next day. I only know that when we started out the other day, we took the McDonough road. i.e. We went straight South. By the way, I would really like to find that place they call the "Sunny South." We certainly have not reached it yet. We saw very little warm weather last summer, and there is certainly nothing sunny in the skies that cover us now. I dread the coming on of winter here, especially if it is to find us in the prosecution of a campaign, for a Southern winter means cold rains and mud, instead of the clean cold weather as of the snow of our more northern clime. I have a prejudice against cold rain and all weather in winter time. It looks as if Atlanta will be evacuated and rendered forever untenable after we go. It is not thought this place will ever be of much importance, neither to Rebs nor to Yankees. I never wish to return to it, when we once get away.

Thursday, November 10th, 1864: Atlanta, Ga.

Learned today that we no longer belong to the "Army of the Cumberland," but to the Left Wing "Army of Georgia." The Right Wing is under Howard, and consists of his Army of the Tennessee consolidated into two Corps (15th & 17th). The Left Wing is under Slocum and consists of the 14th & 20th Corps. Sherman commands the whole, I suppose. Williams commands the 20th Corps and Jackson its 1st Division. Gen. Ruger has been assigned to the command of a Division in the 23d Corps, and went to Nashville yesterday. He takes Binny and Fay with him. As Aids-de-Camp.

We were notified that our last mail North would go out today. Wrote to Villie yesterday under a similar impression. Meant to have written home today but had business and was cheated out of my last chance.

14. "Going South to Seek Salt Water" 169

The Railroad Station in Atlanta, Georgia: citizens moving out, box cars loaded with government property, families and goods, and others huddled on top, *sketch by D. R. Brown,* **Harper's Weekly,** November 26, 1864.

Friday, November 11th: It is plain to be seen now that we are going to evacuate this place. The citizens have taken the scare and have been moving out in great numbers for the past day or two. The rail road depot presents an extraordinary scene. The cars loaded first with government property, then chinked in with families, men, women and children, packed in among the old wagons, boxes and barrels, wherever there was a place large enough for a person to sit or stand or lie.

A few box cars were filled with families and their goods. Very few goods could they take with them either, a trunk or two, a little bed clothing and the bundles they could take in their hands. It is sad to think of the amount of furniture that has been abandoned and destroyed in this city. I saw a fine piano lying by the track, whose owner had offered five hundred dollars to any one who would transport it North. It has been cut up for firewood. Indeed a fire had been built against one corner of it. The top of the cars are covered with niggers and their goods. It's a great sight to see, all those nigger women and children huddled together on the car tops. Miss "Maggie" who has been stopping at our boarding place ran away today, in a fit of anger. Poor foolish girl. She deserves great pity.

Saturday, November 12th: The last trains have come and gone sure enough. There has not been a train in today, and not a railroad man to be seen. When shall we hear from our homes again?

Discovered in the afternoon that the destruction of the public buildings of the place had begun. They were tearing up the Georgia road and battering down the stone round house, that had been used as an arsenal. The destruction of the road was complete, all the switches taken up, ties burned, rails twisted, frogs broken up, etc., etc. The tall chimneys of the different manufacturing works in the city were being battered down too. Looks like this place will be no use to anybody after we all have left it. By going up into the East Road Observatory I noticed that there was a line of smoke all the way from the Chattahoochee to Kennesaw. Probably they are tearing up the rail road there. Capt. McDowell told me today that Col. Carman had made application to have me returned to his Brigade. Don't fancy it very much, but it may be done as Gen. Williams is now in command of the Corps.

Sunday, November 13th: Took a ride in the morning to Mc Kel's train, and to our old Brigade H'd Q'rs. Saw Col. Carman, Lindsey, Thorne, etc. Didn't say much about my coming back. Saw a great deal going on in the way of destroying property. The road bed North was being torn up and destroyed most thoroughly. Saw Windship's Foundry burned. Further on they were tearing down the "State Shop," once a splendid building. So everywhere they were destroying everything that could be any use to the Rebel Army or government.

Told Gen. Ward of the application that had been made to have me sent back to the Brigade. He said he didn't intend to have it done. But it may be done in spite of him.

Attended the Dress Parade of my regiment in the afternoon. More men in line than I had expected. It looked good to see all "the boys" together, and to hear our old Brigade Band. Our banner looked old and dirty. I wonder it was not sent home long ago.

Monday, November 14th: Gen. Howard and his Army marched in today, some of them came in yesterday. Everything here looks like our going very soon now. Today the destruction of the public property was continued. The "car shed" was laid low, the Lugrang Depot destroyed, etc.

Evening: Gen. Ward says we are to march at 7 o'clock tomorrow morning. Good! If we have to go let's be off as soon as possible. Bid good bye to "our folks" at Dr. C's, with many expressions of good will and good wishes for the future. Then went over to see Mrs. McArthur and had a farewell visit with her and the family. She is a nice lady!

Got a view at last of a map. It looks like going to Savannah. Heaven guide us safely through!

Tuesday, November 15th: Atlanta to Stone Mountain. A long and hard march. Our Division did not start from Atlanta until nearly noon (being in the rear of the Corps) and not from Decatur till nearly midnight. Took

14. *"Going South to Seek Salt Water"* 171

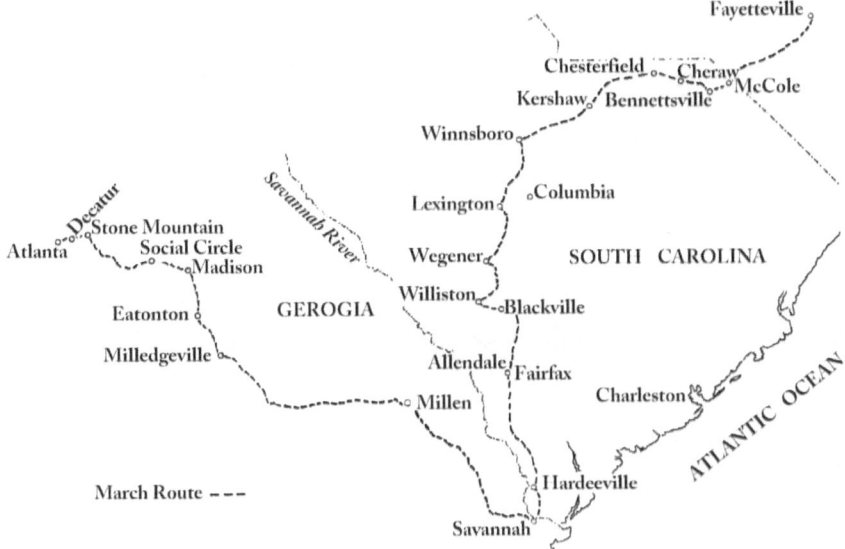

March to the Sea and Northward through the Carolinas

dinner at Decatur and waited until late at night before we could get away. The Western sky was lurid with the flames of the burning Atlanta. I was told by an officer just from the city that not only the public buildings, but also the business part of the city was on fire. If this was done by the order of my superior officer, I have nothing to say. But my private opinion is that such wholesale destruction will load us with merited disgrace and infamy. I have seen scarcely a man who does not condemn the thing *in toto*. Let the railroad be destroyed, say we all, and the warehouses and arsenals etc. but touch no private property, especially that devoted to trade and the common avocations of life, and most of all private dwellings. I sincerely hope the torch will be dispensed with henceforth.

Got tired of waiting for the slow movement of the column, and came on to 2d Brigade 1st Div. H'd Q'rs where I was kindly taken in by Col. Carman.

Wednesday, November 16: Stone Mountain to Rock Bridge. A short march, but we were all day at it.

Went ahead with McDowell and Schilling. Trains were very much delayed again, and the Corps moved very slowly. Beginning to find a better country and get something to eat. Writing home. Warm day.

Thursday, November 17: Rock Bridge to near Alcona Mt. Mail from home. Letters from home with the gloves for Miss Calhoun, and telling me they are all well there, telling me that Col. Crane is home, and that George

Durfy is dead; from Preima; from Crandall informing me that Gould has made $10,000 by the Substitute Broker Business, that Geo. Gardner has been dangerously ill, and that Pattengil was married by the Rev. R. M. Nolt on the 4th of October to Miss Frank Wilson, and from Stillman with the news that T. E. Maxon's brother was recently killed near Winchester, that Ora Rogers and Jarvis Kenyon died in prison at Andersonville, Ga., that Prof Sarkin has gone as common sailor in the U.S. Navy, and that Al Brown is at home out of the service.

Friday, November 18: Through Social Circle to near Madison. A very warm day, with summer clothes on, and tent sides kicked up we were barely comfortable, and that in the woods here.

Saturday, November 19: Madison and vicinity. Letter from Luther Howell.

Monday, November 21: Through Eatonton and Denns to Little River. Near Savannah, Ga., Dec. 16th, 1864.

Yesterday we were rejoicing to hear that communication with the fleet had been opened, and last evening our eyes were delighted with the sight of two New York Tribunes, the first news we have received from the North in many, many days, even the results of the elections were all unknown to us, and you can scarcely imagine the eagerness with which we gathered around the General's tent and listened to his readings of the news. Not the least interesting was a local item which chronicled the sailing of the steamer Fulton from New York with a large mail for Gen'l Sherman's Army—"two hundred and seventy-eight bags weighing over fifty tons." How are we waiting and waiting for that mail! It will reach us tomorrow, we are told. And now we are all writing home, that our letters to our dear ones at home may go with the very first steamer that leaves for the North.

When I have told you that I am here, safe and well, and very impatient to hear from you, I scarcely know what to say next, or when to begin with the thousand things my pen is wishing to write. Our March, from Atlanta here, never was such an expedition known in history, I believe, was marked at every step by scenes and incidents of peculiar interest. I would delight in telling you the history of our expedition, if I could do it, of the awful grandeur of the burning Atlanta, of the beautiful country we passed through, the many fine residences and magnificent grounds we saw, and Social Circle, where a bright little girl kissed me, (the first I had had since I met Aunt Jane in Tennessee), and Milledgeville the Capitol, whose fine library was despoiled by Yankee Vandals, and whose legislative halls were the scene of a most ludicrous event, the mock "meeting of the Georgia legislature," of the Insane Asylum where I had a most interesting visit, and the arsenal which we blew up, we did, then of prison stockades at Millen, where so many thousand of our men were kept in miserable confinement, and the Pine country, level as a barn floor with fine camping grounds 'among the pines,' lighted up by the bright pine knot fire lamps, and lastly of the magnificent scenery we have found on the Savannah River here, the great rice plantations and mills, and the country seats, along the river, beautiful and elegant beyond description, with great groves of the live oak, all hung with southern moss, so thick as to make twilight in noonday, and magnolias and orange trees, and so forth, etc.

How glad would I be could I be with you to tell you all these things. We have had a busy and exciting campaign, not ended yet, and have had no time to think of writing; I seem bewildered now as I take up a pen and try to put my confused thoughts on paper, but we never forget our dear ones at home. The happy homes we saw despoiled by war's ruthless hand, only reminded us of joys left behind, to which we hope yet to return, when war shall be banished from the land.

And now we are in front of Savannah, the end of our journey, but which is not yet attained.

The enemy is preparing for a desperate resistance, and even now is raining shot and shell upon our lines. And we are perfectly quiet. Having inspected the city, our first care was to open communication with the fleet. Soon we will have our supplies of rations, of ammunition, and of clothing, and then perhaps we will do something. Soon we will have our letters and papers once more, and you cannot think how hungry we are for tidings from our loved ones. Once a week, perhaps is all we can ask, on the coast here, of the mail steamers from New York, but even that seems a blessed privilege to us who have been cut off so long from all communication with the "civilized" world.

Entered Savannah

December 21: Entered Savannah.

December 23: Letter from Preima.

December 24: Took a ride with Doc Pendergast and Jackson to find Bonaventure. Went to the wrong place, but had a good ride. Looked all over a large fort on the St. Augusta Creek. Saw Admiral Dalgren on the *Larkspur*. He saluted us as they went by. In the afternoon made a visit to Argyle Island, and to the 107th Regt. on sentry duty there. Was greatly interested in the great rice plantation I saw there. Saw my good friend Col. Kitchen who has just returned from New York. He was elected M.C. while at home. All honors to the worthy and the brave!

December 25: Church in the morning. Heard the Rev. Dr. ...... Christmas dinner in the afternoon. Good one. And then were turned out of house and home by Gen. Easton. Dock found a place at a Mrs. Christian's.

December 26: Mad as fury all day. I wouldn't do a bit of work. Ran around loose. Met Howard at the P.O. He is running a boat. Sent off a package of books by Express.

Orders to be ready to march across the river.

December 27: Survey out the Augusta road. Visit to Jasper Springs. Review of the 14th Corps. Went down to the dock and was greatly interested in looking at the steamers.

Savannah, Ga., 28 Dec., 1864.

The evening of the day we entered this city, I succeeded in writing two pages. (labor lost, I reckon, for I don't know what I did with them) Seated in the front room, second story of a fine, city-built brick house, surrounded by elegant furniture, the costly curtains at the windows closely drawn, and the gas burning overhead, cosily sitting in a grand old armchair and with

15. Entered Savannah

my feet resting on the fender before a bright blazing fire, I started to tell you how comfortable I was — so different from our situation in the swamps a day before. We are having a comfortably pleasant life here in Savannah. Resting from our campaign, preparing for another one.

Savannah is indeed a beautiful city. I am pleased with its situation and plan, wide streets, and a profusion of squares, all having a luxuriance of trees and foliage. Fine public buildings and elegant residences meet the eye everywhere. There must have been a world of wealth and refinement in Savannah before the war. We see it now on every side. I have seen more truly refined society here than I have met in all the south heretofore, and I appreciate the excellence that I find here.

Undoubtedly there have been many Union people here throughout; and as many most-bitter rebels are still remaining here. And a very great part of the people are tied to their property so that they go with the tide, whichever way it may drift, Good Union, Good Rebel, Good Lord, Good Devil, according as the stars and stripes, or the secession rag, float over their city. There was a meeting of the citizens held here yesterday, where they voted Savannah back into the Union, swallowed the Amnesty Proclamation at one gulp, resolved to get at money-making as fast as possible and bring back their former commercial prosperity, passed a resolution of sycophancy, i.e., compliment to the military government here, etc, etc. The whole thing a ridiculous farce. Be sure the government, at least its military arm, puts no confidence in such miraculous conversions to loyalty. Yet, there were some true Union men in the movement who supported these resolutions in sincerity and good faith. I honor all such, and rejoice with them that their side is the winning one here at last. But for the hypocritical weathercocks of that meeting, who a week ago were flaming Rebels, and now are the most faithful among the faithful, away with them! I wish all such might be dead and in heaven, their sins forgiven. Nobody here would have any money on them.

The mails come with the most provoking slowness, or rather they don't come at all, since the one huge mail that came for us when the steamer *Fulton* brought our sixty tons of mail for Sherman's Army. The news that came to me — personal items will interest you. Luther Howell writes from New Orleans, and my college chum, Al Crandall from Niagara Falls, and Jim Stillman from Cumberland, Md. The one tells me J. H. Syphen has developed into a fine military man, and is doing honor to himself, and good service to his country as Colonel of an artillery regiment in Louisiana; and that one Emory Hamilton, who fell in love with Aria Rowe — a long time ago, is now Major of an Engineer regiment at Brazos Santiago. Another tells me that one of my college friends is very ill, that one has $10,000 in the substitute business, that one classmate is dead and another has married. *Sic vita.* And James makes to be remembered to you, and he tells me of the death by starvation and prison torture at Andersonville, of Jarvis Kenyon and Ora Rogers, — and I think of the kennels where our poor men were confined at Millen (not a tent or barrack or shed or house in all the enclosure and eight hundred graves outside), and I long to see the war pushed on with greater sternness and vigor, with a fierceness and a bitterness that shall speedily crunch out hell from rebellion beyond all hope of any resurrection or remembrance even. The women of the South are true to the teaching of the Macon speech. The people urge on their soldiers to fight us, and then when we have taken possession of their towns and cities ask protection of us and want us to grant them special privileges and attentions. See em hanged first! But steady, and band is serenading Col. Barnum's Head Quarters just across the street, and I must listen to the music. Every evening the air is full of music, bands serenading all over the city.

Almost everybody here is from the North, or their fathers or mothers were.

Tomorrow our Corps is to be reviewed. The boys are saying that Gen. Sherman has got him a suit of clothes at last — coming out on Review dressed quite neatly and stylishly. Today I saw Gen'ls Hatch and Saxton from Port Royal. Gen'l Foster and Admiral Dalghren are also in town. This does seem a little like getting East again. Charleston would be a little further, and Wilmington more too.

December 29: Dr. Grinsted went to Hilton after medical stores.

December 30: Review of the 20th Corp. Very large thing.

December 31: Ordered to march across the river. Cold and rainy. After fooling all day got only across. Back and wrote a letter to Carrie.

Sunday, January 1st, 1865. Savannah, Chatham Co., Ga.

Cold but clean. A dull "New Years," yet by no means a Sabbath day's rest for me. All day long I was on Hutchinson Island on duty with Gen. Ward. He is crossing his Division into South Carolina, but until the pontoon bridges are built it is very slow work. I was expecting to pass my New Years in Carolina, but only half of the Division succeeding in crossing today, and tonight we remain in Georgia still. I hope we'll get away tomorrow.

I sent a journalized letter from Atlanta. It may be that beginning with the first day of the New Year, I shall be able to write something each day, describing scenes as I witness them and incidents as they may occur. If I succeed in doing this I'll have some record, I hope, of this soldier part of my life. I am too busy, or too tired to keep a connected journal — you must do it for me. It was late when I finished my last letter, and I went down to the steamer *Canoniscus* and put it into the mail myself with some packages marked "Mail from Gen'l Sherman's Head Quarters." I guess it will go through safely.

But I did have New Year's Dinner today. Are not oyster and canvasback duck good enough for the soldiers? Then I went down to the wharf and boarded the *Planter*, a trim little steamer, and her captain is a nigger. Didn't you read two or three years ago, how the *Planter* was run out of Charleston Harbor, one night and surrendered to the blockading fleet, by her negro pilot? How she was laden with heavy ordnance and stores for one of the harbor forts, which the pilot turned over to the Yankees? Brave fellow, he is, and a very intelligent and gentlemanly man withal, and government employs him as the captain of the steamer he took from the Rebels.

So much for the beginning of the New Year. This evening I have remained quietly in my room, glad to rest after the fatigues of the day.

Monday, January 2d: Another evening closes in and we are still in Savannah. But our Division has all crossed the river, and tomorrow H'd Q'rs Staff and all will go "shoo," to use the General's broad Kentucky speech. Have interested myself chiefly today in drawing any pay for the past two months, a regular allowance of green backs is most indispensable to the soldier's comfort. I am fortunate in being at Head Quarters, where I can draw my pay of any Pay Master I can find, instead of waiting sometimes for six months, as I did when in my regiment, for the Pay Master regularly assigned to that command. Received pay of Major Flemming, up to Dec 31st., '64. Capt. McKel's resignation is accepted. By the way, there is a rumor that our Corps is to be broken up, and consolidated into other commands. If so it may put me into my regiment again.

This evening I passed some women in the street who were elegantly dressed and appeared lady-like enough, except that they were talking as loud as so many drunken sailors would, and as I passed, one of them said, "I don't blame her. He ought to have asked to come into her house. No true Southern lady waits to see a Yankee Officer in her house." I had a notion to tell her I'll see her out of hers, mighty quick. She was "one true lady"! I am certain. But I passed straight on by her and never heard a word she said. Am not well tonight and am going to bed early. Will be all right in the morning I reckon.

Tuesday, January 3: Out of Georgia and into South Carolina.

A late breakfast for I was not well and so was lazy about getting up. Then we had a long waiting at the dock for our boat, but at last it came, *The Planter* and rounded up to the wharf, and the captain Robert Small, told us to bring our horses on board "and take them aft" as expeditiously as possible. I got my horse on board and then gave him to my servant to find out where "aft" was, I didn't know.—It was fun to see the animals loading, some would walk aboard as demurely as a deacon's daughter going to church, some would make a tremendous leap, to the great peril of all who might be in their way, and many had to be blindfolded before they would stir a peg. The pack mules seemed to be especially dubious. They would come just to the edge of the wharf, but no amount of persuasive pulls in the front or abusive kicks in the rear (aft) could induce some of them "to walk the plank." And those who did so had to go side-wise, or backward, as best pleased their eccentric genius. As a natural result some walked off the plank before they could walk in the boat. I had to laugh at the forlorn expression of one mule driver as he lost hold of a halter, the other end of which was attached to a mule that had fallen into the river and "sunk to rise no more." All loaded at last, the whistle blew, the bell rung, the band we had on board commenced to play and out we swung from the dock, into the center of the river, then down, by the steamers and schooners and gunboats that line the busy wharves, and away from the city and the thousands who were watching our departure.

Goodbye Savannah

Savannah to Chevis' House, St. Peters Parish, Beaufort Dist., S.C.

Around the lower end of Hutchinson's Island, in plain sight of Fort Jackson just below, and we came to the "Scriven's Ferry" landing, on the Carolina shore. And just below are the remains of the Ram *Savannah*, burned the day after we took the city. She was a most formidable ironclad, but will never do any more damage I reckon. She is "mustered out."

It was slow work, debarking, but few at a time could be taken from the boat to land by the old scow we had. On shore at last and on the "Union causeway" running twenty miles or more straight back into the country, three miles of rice fields, and one of woods brought me to the house Gen'l Wood has selected for Head Quarters, and where we are at present. Found Col. Case to be a ψγ First night in South Carolina. Busy all day long in Aid duty getting the Division in position, etc.

P.M.: Went down to Red Bluff on New River with Crawford, saw a fine battery there, but not a living soul in all that country. Speed and Jackson over. Col. Robinson here. His Brigade is coming over.

Dr. Chevis' Place, going to ruin fast now, an elegant house where refinement and luxury have dwelt, but now a (beautiful) desolation. We found here printed copies of a speech delivered in Nashville 1850 by the Hon. Langdon Chevis, a most bitter fire-eating, secession speech. Now Mr. C. is dead, fell in front of Charleston, (some say at Fort Sumter, the first man the Rebs lost in this war), and every room of his elegant and beautiful home bears record of the indecency and lawlessness of his own "friends," Wheeler's Cavalry. We found here a little broken furniture, some statuary also broken, a few books, magazines and pamphlets, and a good many old letters written by persons of culture and refinement (some whose names are known to fame). I send you a most interesting one by the gifted poetess Mrs. E. F. Ellet. Is it not worth preserving from the ravages of war?

Wednesday, Jan. 4th, 1865

It was late last night when I finished my story of yesterday's events. The fine band of the 33d Mass. Regiment was serenading us, and I went to the window to hear them. It was a lovely night and the moonlight made strange pictures of light and shade, as it came through the leaves and branches of the forest growth around us. "Think of it," said Lieut. Thompson, "A Massachusetts band playing the *Battle Cry of Freedom* in South Carolina.," and I went to sleep thinking "of it" and all that it implied.

I see I am making too long a story each day. At this rate I shall equal Capt. Speed. He sends a long letter to his wife every other day. And she sends an equal amount of original literature to him. You see, they were married only just before we started our last campaign. Capt. Speed is the Ass't Adj't Gen'l of our Division and a bully good fellow. His father, James Speed of Ky., has recently been made one of the Lincoln Cabinet, as Attorney General of the U.S.

Business all day in arranging camp grounds for the Division, selecting lines of defense, putting the Brigades into position, etc.

We have occupied Hardee's plantation, about five miles from the river, and where we found a good line of fortifications put up at the beginning of the war I should judge, and apparently to repel an advance on Savannah from the Yankees at Port Royal.

In the afternoon went down to Red Bluff, on the New River, where the Rebs had put up a splendid battery, now abandoned, of course. There were deserted houses and empty barracks for troops, and great plantations stretching as far as the eye could reach, but not a living soul to be seen anywhere. We found quite a number of French books here. Wheeler's Cavalry seemed to have no use for them and so left them. French newspapers and music too. Perhaps I'll send a piece of music I found, entitled *"Toi."* Here is a work published in 1691, and a Testament of 1738. In *Le Genie de Montesquieu* 1709 the first sentence that met my eye was *"C'est un malheur pour une femme, de n'être point aimée; mais c'est un affront, de ne l'être plus."* Is it not so?

Thursday, January 5th:

Did I think of writing something every day? I forgot those days when I should be tired and instead of prosy words, I'll send a little specimen of some of the ornamental shrubbery that adorn the place. It comes, mind you from Dr. Chevis' Place, St Peters Parish, Beaufort District, South Carolina.

I didn't go to the city as I was intending to. Eve, wrote to Father. What is the matter with the mails? Don't get the sign of a letter or paper any more.

Friday, January 6th:

Rain. Surveying a little. Finished a letter, and when this minute is made will try to go to sleep again. This must go tomorrow. Just think of it, after going to bed once, Capt. Crawford and I have both gotten up again, having found it impossible to sleep. It is very warm tonight. Is this mid-winter? I sit at my open window and look out at the moonlight, and the air is laden with perfume from the fragrant white blossoms from a tree on the other side of the house. No! This is not mid-winter. Even now I hear distant rumblings and scudding clouds are beginning to obscure the moon. A thunder shower is coming up. And the mosquitoes how they like winter? I can't see it.

Chevis House, S.C. Jan. 7, 1865.

Saturday night and the first week of the New Year closes. If I do as much for Uncle Sam each week of the New Year as I have during this first week, I shall not have lived wholly in vain, for I have done some work this week, some. Making up a plot of this vicinity. Walter doing the work and I playing lazy.

Have I told you about my assistant "Daisy"? He helps me in surveying and in making maps. Corporal Walter H. Howson, Co. C. 73 Ohio Veteran Volunteers, that's him. He's quite young, has bright blue eyes, and cheeks as red as a peach, is always pleasant, and agreeable, and everybody likes him. No one can help liking him. He looks "so young and so fair" they all call him Daisy in his regiment. He has served three years and has re-enlisted. Young as he is, he is a Veteran. But I trust he'll have no more rough service to perform. He has been at work all day in my room here plotting up the surveys we have made during the week. His father resides in Chillicotte, Ohio, and is wealthy, They are an English family, and well bred evidently, for no amount of evil influence can spoil Walter, it seems. He has always been a great favorite in the regiment, and when the captain of his company left the service the other day, he sent special word to me to "take good care of Walter." That I will. I take it as a compliment when they tell me he looks just like me, and that we are just alike. Officers have asked me if we were not brothers. You wished me to tell you of my friends. Please count "Daisy" as one of them.

Good news! There is a large mail for us at Savannah, but (bad news) the pontoon bridge is broken and we must wait for our letters until it is fixed.

Sunday, January 8th: The mail did come. It did bring me one letter from Father.

Savannah, Ga., January 9: "Came to town" today intending to make a few purchases and to return immediately. But ere I was ready to return the pontoniers had taken a notion to repair the pontoons, the bridge would not be ready for crossing until dark, and so not relishing an 8 mile ride over execrable roads in the night time, I turned me back to the city. It has been raining nearly all day, and the town looks dark and dirty and cheerless. What loneliness so great, as that of one who finds himself on such a day in a city where he has neither home nor business, nor acquaintances? Fortunately I am acquainted here and moreover have a good home here at the house of Mr. Henry R. Christian. I have been visiting with some of my friends about town, and went up to the regiment for to see Col. Crane, who has just returned from the North. Now I am at my "home." Have I told you about it? Mr. C. is in the Rebel service, though I believe only as a citizen employee. Mrs. C. is of course very anxious about him. But they are as fine people as I ever met. When our army entered the city Dr. Grinsted and I were billeted here, and though of course they have their own ideas about the war, we have ever been most kindly and courteously treated. Mrs. C. seems to have an idea that she is under obligations to us for services rendered, but certainly the obligations are all the other way. Is it not a good thing to have good friends? And such we are I am sure, spite of the differences this war would occasion between us. Found Dr. Grinsted had returned.

Tuesday, January 10th:
"The day is cold and dark and dreary. It rains and wind is never weary." I was disgusted today after riding clear over Hutchinson's Island through the mud and the storm to find that the pontoon over the "back channel" was still unfinished. Back again. Not feeling well am glad to take refuge in this my Savannah home once more. In today's paper there is an article on "Dark Days" suggested by the gloomy weather that now enshrouds us.

Wednesday, January 11th:
The rain is over, but the winds blow strong as ever, and it is as cold as blazes. This morning I was a long time at Howard's office, at that balconied window overlooking the river and watched the Rebel ladies on the steamer, *S. R. Spaulding*. Flag of truce boat bound for Charleston. Those who couldn't live here under Yankee rule are permitted to depart in peace for Rebeldom, and today two or three hundred have gone to Charleston in the *Spaulding*. What are they going there for? To be captured again? "Wayward Sisters."

Then I ordered my horse and made one more attempt to get over to camp, across the first pontoon bridge from Savannah to Hutchinson Island, 228 paces long, then across the island, then across the bridge over the "back channel" 740 paces long taking me to Penny Worth Island (the wind blew down the river almost a gale! The waves dashed against the bridge, so as to throw their spray quite across it, and it rocked and rolled so that it made me reel like a drunken man getting over it) but we crossed it safely, then across Penny Worth Island and, *disgustibus dictu*, culmination of disappointments, they had just taken up the bridge connecting that Island with the South Carolina mainland. It would take all day to put it down again, so back again I take my way to the city. I am still at my home in Savannah.

Evening: Went to hear a lecture on Pluck by Mortimer Thompson, alias "Doesticks." Had heard most of it before I entered the Service. Rather lame for soldier taste. Rather slate flat and unprofitable any way. But he had a full house. A little chat with Mrs. C., who gave me an invitation to a party at Mr. Reach's, which I shall be glad to accept if I am in town tomorrow evening. I am not forgetting that is the last day of my twenty-fifth year. Thus quietly and prosperously closes another year of life. Hitherto the Lord hath helped me. Col. Wood arrived.

Thursday, January 12:

A beautiful day (as my birthday should be) clear as it was yesterday, but not cold, and no wind. May every year begin as fairly as does this my twenty-sixth.

Started bright and early for the river and received the cheering intelligence that the bridge would be finished by three o'clock. — Over to camp 107th and had a little visit with Col. Crane and then other officers there. Back to town to see the Review of the Cavalry of Gen. Kilpatrick. Waiting for the Review, Col. Sill and I had a fine ride all around the city. The Review didn't amount to much I thought! But there were some distinguished visitors present, Secretary Stanton, Senator Draper and daughter of New York, Adjutant General Thomas, Quarter Master General Meigs, and a number of other notables whose names I did not learn. Gen. Sherman was accompanied by Gen. Logan just returned from the North. He is one of the soldiers' idols, another Joe Hooker — But the Review was tiresome to me, and I was glad when it was over. Another "Goodbye Savannah!"

The islands and the bridges are all safely passed and I am once more on the homeward track. But a more beautiful scene never met my eyes than that of the Savannah river as I saw it from Hutchinson's Island below the bridge. The water was absolutely still and calm, and under the rays of the setting sun looked like polished silver, stretching away for miles above mirroring the mills and the houses and the trees along its banks. The pontoons made a striking and picturesque foreground for the picture. I wish I could find words to fitly describe it, the river, the sky, the islands, the pontoons, the whole scene. It was superbly beautiful. This was the finest birthday present I could receive, this view. It will live in my memory always, more precious than many a costly a gift.

It was after dark when I reached our Head Quarters, glad to be "at home" again. If I ever trust myself to the chances and caprices of a pontoon bridge again, I shall consider myself a candidate for the Lunatic Asylum.

Chevis House, S.C., Jan 13, 1865.

We have received orders to be ready to move at a moment's notice. Now I don't think we will receive that "moment's notice" for some days yet, but it is well "to be ready," as the order requires. All day Walter and I have been at work upon some maps of South Carolina showing the country through which we expect to go. Ho! For South Carolina. I hope it may be for the Northern or Central part of the State. I don't like the climate of this "low country" even now in winter time. And excuse me when the summer shall come.

Gen'l Barnum, Inspector General for Gen'l Grant paid us a visit today, and expressed himself much pleased with our line of defense, etc. As I had about as much to do with the location of the line as anybody, I condescend to take a share of the compliment to myself.

Saturday, January 14th:

Another day of busy work and I get tired of leaning over a table all day long. But we'll soon be on the march, I guess, and office work will cease. "Chip," i.e., Capt. Chipman of this Staff, returned from Hilton Head today with lots of things for our Mess. We are living gloriously now, the supplies we purchase from the North, the fish, etc. we get of the river, and the plunder that we "realize" from the country. Just think of it! For soldiers, butter and cheese and fruits of all kinds, oysters, and chickens, and turkeys, oranges and lemons, etc. etc. We are living very high. How will we ever take up with hard tack and "salt horse"? Of course it costs something, but *diem vivimus, vivimes*. My mess bill for the half month just ended, was $24.65. I paid $50.00 today for a coat. Before the war $15.00 would have bought as good an one. It took $20.00 to get a cheap pair of boots the other day, $4.00 for a poor quality of gloves, and $10.00 for a hat. People at home think that army officers ought to save more money than any other class. They have no idea how much it costs to live. But I'll talk money-talk, a subject I never heard you mention but once.

The U.S. Christian Commission,
sends this sheet as the Soldiers' messenger to his home.
Let it haste to those who wait for tidings.

General Sherman's Army
H'd Q'rs 3d Div. 20th Army Corps.

Chevis' House, S.C., Sunday January 15th 1865.

See what the Christian Commission does for us. There is a large room in Savannah, lined with writing desks, where pen, ink and paper, envelopes and postage stamps are kept for the soldiers' use, *gratis*. Outside is the notice, "Come in and write your letters." I have come home to write my letter, but I am none the less grateful to the Christian Commission for all that it does in our behalf.

Monday, January 16th:
We have orders to march at eight o'clock tomorrow morning. We are going but a short distance but I am thankful for a little time out of service. I have been hard at work all day today making maps. Hurrah for rest!

A mail today brought me a letter from Carrie. They had only just rec'd the first letter I sent after reaching the coast. If the mail's so slow as that, I must not wonder that I get no letters from home.

The Secretary of War left quite a batch of promotions for Generals and Colonels in our Army.

In the 20th Corps Gen'ls Williams and Geary were breveted as Major Generals, and Colonels Kitchum and Coggswell of the 1st Div, and Colonels Barnum and Pardee of the 2d Div. were breveted as Brigadiers. Col. Robinson of the first Div. and Col. Jones of the 2d Div. were made full Brigadiers. Nary a promotion in the 3d Division, nor from any want of merit, however. It is unmilitary for one to speak against his superior officer, therefore I will not write what I think. Everybody in this vicinity very surprised and indignant.

Col. Ross has gone to Washington with his Adj't Gen'l. Col. Wood has received another, for sixty days, and Brev't Brig. Gen'l Coggswell is assigned to the command of our 3d Brigade.

Gen'l W. T. more indignant than ever. "Goodbye" time, on the strength of orders to march.

Chevis House to Hardeeville, S.C.

Hardeeville, S.C., 17th January, 1865.
Well, we did move today, and we're here, twenty miles from Savannah, at the first station from it, on the Charleston and Savannah Rail Road. A little hamlet, in the pine woods, not as large as Arkport, and depopulated. But one or two families have lived, in some months, in the place. We have seen but little today, having left the good plantations, that line the river, and not yet reached the good land in the interior. We passed a few fine places, now deserted, and rapidly going to destruction. The people, except the very poor, have all left the country. Desolation and misery are come home at last to those who first invoked them. So mote it be!

Hardeeville, S.C., 18 Jan'y 1865.
Yesterday we were busied until dark getting Head Quarters established, and I had no time to take a look at the town. Looking around today I have found not one, one thing of any interest whatever, so I went over to Purysburg, three miles distant on the river Savannah, and where one of our Brigades is encamped. The place was settled in 1733 by a Swiss Colony under John Pater Pury from Neuchâtel, Switzerland. A Gazetteer of 1793 says, "It

contains from forty to fifty houses and an Episcopal Church," and *Winterbotham's View of America*, published 1796 described it as one of the six larger towns in the State. I was not a little surprised, when I went there, to find but three or four houses in the place, and they all good similes of John R. Stephen's old house we used to pass, on the Arkport road. "Purysburg is a hilly village," adds Winterbotham. I do not think there is a "hill" over ten feet in all this country. The "bluff" on which Purysburg is built is certainly not twenty feet higher than the lowest land around it. So much for Purysburg. I was chiefly interested in its cemetery, which contained many very old tombs. Heavy brick walls, now old and black and crumbling enclosed some burial-plots, while many tombs were built up and arched over with brick, at once the covering and the monument of the dead. None of the older tombs had any inscriptions. The names I saw would remind one of the foreign people represented here. One whose name was "Lancelot" and one whose name was "Winifred" are lying side by side in their quiet rest. Yet war has invaded even this quiet spot. There are many graves bearing the inscription "15th S.C.V.," and now Gen'l Robinson's H'd Quarters are right among the graves.

Thursday, January 19th:

The First Division, which followed ours in this march, has all gone over to Purysburg. They have had a wet time establishing their camps, in the rain. We have been entertaining many of them today, taking them in, giving them something to eat, and something to drink, and tonight we shall try to lodge some of them. "Entertaining" them, and looking out on the dismal but perpetual rain is about all that I can find heart to do today.

The river is very high and all the low country near it is under water. Our wagon trains between here and Savannah are all water-bound, and it will be lucky for us if the high waters do not carry them off altogether. History tells us of a Division of English troops who were water-bound in this very place, for many days during the Revolutionary War, and here "the American troops under Lincoln" afterwards suffered the same inconvenience. "The American troops under Lincoln" seem doomed to another most disagreeable acquaintance with this detestable region and execrable climate. No more now. I feel too much like the weather, gloomy.

Friday, January 20th:

A steady, unbroken, unvarying rain through all the night and all the day, and still they come, the unfortunates who happened to be on the march when the storm came. Many of my friends from the 1st Division, now the Staff of the Division, with Gen'l Jackson at their head, and at last come Gen'l Williams with all the Corps Staff. Wet and cold are they all, for they have been out in the storm since yesterday morning, and hungry for they have had but one small lunch in all that time, and thirsty too. Never was whiskey at such a premium! And they haven't a blanket to sleep on, for their Head Quarters train, mess wagons, ambulances and everything, is "stalled" eighteen miles back, within sight of Savannah, the water rising all around it, and it unable to move unless some friendly steamboat shall take it in tow, and bring it to dry land. I am busy taking care of the unfortunates.

Hardeeville, Saturday, January 21st.

No cessation of rain, and visitors abundant as ever, and we (supposed to be wealthy Carolinians at home) are entertaining them, (supposed to be distinguished guests from Georgia) in a style of hospitality, if not strictly Carolinian at least quite unique and soldier-like. We feed them up, fit to kill, and give them whiskey, and worm wood bitters, and gin cock-tails for to drink, and lots of blankets and floor room for sleeping. We lends 'em paper collars in place of the soaked up remnants they brought around their necks, and we makes our niggers shine up their boots for them. Why shouldn't one be hospitable when he has servants to assume all the trouble it may make him?

Then we lets 'em use our mash-bowls and towels, our clothes brushes and hair brushes and combs and no, I won't say tooth-brushes. In short we proffer them a soldier's hospitality, which I am glad to say, is accepted as it is offered.

Then we have an occasional visit from Naval officers. The gunboat *Pontiac* is at the Purysburg landing, and the *Sonoma* was at the Scriven's Ferry landing when we were at Chevis House. Ride over to Purysburg with McDowell, Doc, and Burgess. A ride on horseback is a great treat to the sailors, while a visit on their boats is most interesting to us. And a visit from either side is always most welcome. "The Army and Navy forever!"

You must know that the arrival of mail, always of interest to us, is doubly so just now. Pardon me then if I chronicle the arrival today of "another large mail," and it brought to me a last year's newspaper, "only this and nothing more."

Expected naval visitors, disappointed us. Arrival of Capt. Scott. Rain, rain — rain. Over to Cogs Corp H'd Q'rs in evening. Had a sing. Sick.

Sunday, January 22nd:

A man neglects the daily keeping of his journal, sometimes because in the dull monotony of passing days there is nothing to record. Sometimes because the very surfeit of events thick crowding upon his time and multiplying his duties, gives him no time to chronicle the much he would wish to remember. But now both causes are at once at work to prevent my writing a report of each day's events. The never-varying rain comes down as ever, and dooms us all to dull monotony within our tents, while on the other hand our many guests continue to demand our attention. Thus there is little of interest to be told, and little opportunity for telling it.

I have been amusing myself today reading the journal of a trip from Charleston to Boston written by a gentleman of evident cultivation and taste, but with bitter Southern prejudices. He made quite a stay in Philadelphia, visiting the Museum, Academy of fine arts, Insane Asylum, Summer Gardens, etc., and concludes thus: "In leaving Philadelphia, I cannot but remark that any stranger will be astonished to find that although every dwelling is of brick, all are shingled, and moreover that to no house is there a piazza or a porch. The manners of the people I dislike, but their activity and industry merit commendation." Philadelphia thus disposed of, he goes on to Princeton, N.J., where, it seems, he had been educated. Here he had an argument on the slavery question with "an insolent, haughty and overbearing Englishman." At New York he was much pleased with the "City Hotel" where he stopped, but was deprived "of the enjoyment of that great luxury, good Madeira wine, in consequence of its exorbitant price." Through Connecticut and Rhode Island he became disgusted, on account of "villainous and genuine Yankee deceptions" that were attempted to be practiced on him. Hear him, the inhabitants "of both States I dislike, as their knavery and deception are too notorious to be denied. Their principal trade and darling occupation is, the keeping of Taverns, of which there are an immense number and nearly all indifferent, and stabling for horses and cows. Of course a great many of the inhabitants are stage drivers, horse jockies, and tavern keepers. The rest are principally venders of onions, potatoes, fish, cotton yarn and hog's lard, a few noodles, who arrogate to themselves the title of 'Gentlemen of the bar,' are occasionally to be met with." Isn't that heavy on New England?

Then he went to Boston, where the magnificent view to be had from the State House, filled him with wonder and delight. But he could not forget he was in a land of fanatics. "The moment I entered Boston my attention was forcibly arrested by an uniformed company of boys, marching in the streets preceded by a full band of music. At first I eyed them with admiration and delight, as their dignified and truly martial appearance pointed them out to be the descendants of '76; but when I reflected that they were the citizens of a State famed for its steady and unceasing opposition to the constitution and laws of their country, and that their fathers, in our recent memorable struggle, had openly advocated the cause of the enemy and ingloriously refused to aid their countrymen in resisting injustice and oppression, the pleasure at first experienced was removed, and other sensations painful in their nature succeeded. I then remembered that a race of beings, perfectly distinct in nature and disposition from the heroes of yore, at present inhabit this commonwealth: that Quakerish feelings, unpatriotic notions, and a mortal antipathy to fire-arms had unfortunately obtained an ascendancy over the minds of the bulk of the people, and that the Godlike spirit which animated our forefathers on Bunker Hill had probably never to return."

Perhaps this fine gentleman would have more "painful sensations" than ever, could he see his lordly domain here overrun by Boston regiments (perhaps some of the very boys he saw marching), who recovered from their "mortal antipathy to fire-arms." *Tempora mutantun,* and let us thank God for it!

Monday, January 23d:

And still it rains, yet not so constantly as hitherto. Now and then there is a glimpse of sunshine in the sky, but the storm will not yield yet, and again the rain comes down. I shall rejoice when the sun does shine, and I am glad to chronicle the first rays, that herald this coming.

I found a friend today, an intimate friend of some of my intimate friends in Rochester. 'Twas like discovering a cooling spring in the midst of a desert. Down we sat, and had a good, long talk about Rochester.

Our guests are thinning away. The First Division Staff have borrowed a hospital tent from Dr. Grinsted and have gone to keeping house for themselves, and the Corps Staff have domiciled themselves in a house nearby, but continue to board with us. Last night we all went over to see the Corps Staff and to have a sing with them. There was a piano in the house and Col. Asmussen played it well, and we sang — as well as we could. Not a very serious way of spending Sunday evening. I believe there is no sin in music, but still there should be judgement used in the proper selection of music in sacred hours and places.

Evening: The rain has almost ceased; a wind is coming up, and the thermometer is going down, (at least the mercury is). Cold weather will stop the rain if nothing else does. Then welcome cold! Corp Staff going back to Savannah. Our movement evidently postponed for the present.

Tuesday, January 24th:

I have my wish! The rain is gone and the cold is come. Comes too with a sharpness which sets entirely at rest the question whether this can be winter. It is winter now.

The Corps Staff have gone back to Savannah! They came and all bade us goodbye this morning. Gen'l Williams went two days ago, and although he immediately sent back an order that "Division commanders shall remain with their commands," Gen'l Jackson of the 1st Division followed him yesterday. And now we hear that the movement of the whole army is stopped, and that this campaign is countermanded. No movement expected for many days. Was it all on account of the weather? Or did our success after failure at Wilmington disarrange any plans?

Another large mail came today, and (improvement on the last) it brought me two last year's newspapers. I am encouraged.

Later: "Daisy" has just brought me a letter from Carrie, written on my birthday. I am glad to find that communications with my old home have not been entirely sundered. Ten days ago a letter from Carrie appraised me of the reception at home of my first letters from Savannah. This slow "dispatch" of news makes it seem a long ways from home.

Down to the river to see the Corp Staff off. They went on the *Fountain*. Visited Lt. Col. Smith, Col. Dunstan, Hawley's Brigade Staff, and rode home with Beecher and Ford by a new route which I would not recommend for everybody's use. The General quite under the weather. Burgess goes to town.

Wednesday, January 25th:

This cool weather keeps us all in quarters. Ditto the birds, who until now have made the air musical with their songs. And the frogs, I haven't heard a croak from them for two nights; but during the rain the swamps around us were a perfect babel of frog talk. I went to sleep o'nights listening to the multitudinous chirpings and croakings that rose from all directions. But they're mighty quiet now. And so are we all. Cooped up in this little settlement in the woods, it has been rather too wet or too cold for us to do anything, and we are unable to get any letters or paper from the outside world. So we are merely hibernating at present.

But will "man's inhumanity to man" cease ever? A poor woman came a long distance through the cold today to beg the General to save a part of her house for her. The soldiers had driven her and her children into one room, and were deliberately tearing down the rest. When the guard which was sent, finally reached there, the chimney and the entire end of the house had been torn down and mostly carried away, and into the last room was the poor woman and her family driven. The soldiers had taken most of their clothing and their food; and the mother asked our Provost Marshal, when she went home, "Will you please give me a little sugar for my baby?" I am shocked to think there are men in our command who can be so barbarously cruel. I blush to own that the cowardly wretches belong to a New York regiment. They forget that their mothers are women and that themselves have been children, and there is no mercy in their hearts for helpless infancy and womanhood.

Thursday, January 26th:

Gen. Williams and Staff have returned. Hawley's (once Ruger's) Brigade of the First Division was ordered out today to repair the "Augusta Road" and it is supposed that we shall all be on the march up the river in a few days. So our campaign is not countermanded. We are to go on with our movement. The roads are very bad, the army is poorly supplied, especially as regards clothing, and the weather at this season of the year cannot be relied upon, so it seems to me our Generals are a little too fast. But they know best.

Evening: Went down to Purysburg to see Col. Dustin (commanding 2d Brigade). He is as nice a man as you ever saw. Had been about sick lately and was getting gloomy and dispirited, so we went, to drive away the blues. Took the 33d Massachusetts Band and had a grand good time. Music, and story-telling, and singing and dancing, (I almost died a-laughing to see two little darks dance the "walk-round") formed a part of the evening's entertainments, and we cured Col. Dustin, for the time at least. He is a fine singer, as is Lt. Col. Dutton of his regiment, and they two sang some magnificent duets for us.

Very cold. Orders to move day after tomorrow. Letter from Father with $20 inclosed. Clothes are coming now that I do not want them and "Arvilla Goodrich" has written me a letter, and Joe Robinson is home on leave of 15 days.

Hardeeville, S.C., Jan. 27, 1865.

Having nothing else to do these days, I have been reading what old books we have been able to pick up here. *Elsie Venner, Country Living* and *Edwin of Deira* with a host of magazines and reviews from one to forty years old. I took a wonderful liking to *Elsie Venner*, both the character and the story, when I first became acquainted with them, long ago. But *Edwin of Deira* I have never read until now, and I am truly charmed with it. And the magazines, they are all new to us here and just as good as if just published. Anything to pass away the time. Ah! but in a few days we may have enough to occupy our attention, without having to hunt up old magazines and books.

January 28: Ordered to march at 8 o'clock tomorrow morning. Dispatched to M..., to R.T., and to Crandall. Went to bed with head aching worse than ever.

January 29: Hardeeville to J.H. Robert's House, via Purysburg and Ennis Cross Roads 18m.

Robert's House, Jan'y 29th:

Yesterday I was cross and sick all day, with a severe headache, "with a misery in my head" as the niggers say here, and went to bed thoroughly disgusted. Today we have made a twenty-mile march, and my head is still aching. It has been a right cold day, and we started out quite early, making our twenty miles and getting into camp at three this P.M. We came through Purysburg, then to Ennis' Cross Roads and so on, by the "Augusta Road" to this place. It is seven miles yet, to Robertsville, where I suppose the 1st Division is tonight. I guess they have had some little fighting up that way today, and we have heard some cannonading.

We have passed some fine residences today. Residences where were elegant pianos, and harps, costly furniture and china ware, with libraries and valuable paintings, all left by their owners to be destroyed or stolen by the soldiers, (Rebel as well as Federal) who find them. All day we have been guided by columns of smoke ahead, of burning cotton barns, and houses even, the sad and terrible work of our army's advance. War for South Carolina.

January 30: Robert's House to Robertsville, S.C. A visit to my Reg't. and 2d Brig. Head Q'rs. At work all day long on maps for distribution. Staff Bill and officer's Pay Bill passed.

January 31: Fine day. Warm and sunny. Making maps. Ride to see Brigade Drill. Visit of officers of the "Potomac." Orders to march. Letter home.

February 1, 1865: Robertsville to Lawtonville, a little fight at Lawtonville.

February 2: Lawtonville to Duck Branch P.O. Rain struck the Right Wing.

February 3: Duck Branch, Smyrna, Allendale.

February 4: Allendale, Arnold Ch., Hayes X Roads

February 5: Duncanville. Very cold and rainy.

February 6: Duncanville — Springtown M.H.— SCRR, ten miles east of Graham's.

Rain awful.

February 7: To Graham's Station. Tearing up track. Outrageous treatment of citizens by the stragglers.

February 8: Graham's Station to Blackville, S.C. It's as cold as blazes, most disagreeable work surveying. H'd Q'rs at Mr Bennett's. Evening at Mr......, an enthusiastic mason, Miss Helen Hay, Miss Annie Wayne, Miss Pauline Payton. Mail from Home.

February 9: Blackville to Williston, S.C. Troops all the time tearing up track. No enemy visible. Cold and disagreeable.

February 10: Williston to Gingnard's Bridge. Fell in the drink at Yarrow Branch.

February 11: Gingnard's Bridge via Walker's X Roads to near Jefcoats Bridge. Feeding the little ones.

February 12: Jefcoats Bridge to Cedar Branch. This 2d Division skirmish line and after the enemy.

February 13: Cedar Branch to Sand Hills. Wet and cold miserable day.

February 14: Sand Hills to Lexington. (2 m from Lexington) Dark day. A little skirmishing ahead.

February 15: Near Lexington to front of Columbia. Magnificent view of Columbia and vicinity.

February 16: To Zion's Ch. on Saluda River. Very windy evening. Visit to Major Lacey.

February 17: Columbia burned by the Right Wing. Disgraceful scenes.

February 18: Across the Saluda River and to the 16 mile post. (Metz's Mill, S.C.) 14th Corp ahead of us.

February 19: Metz's Mill to Rockville P.O. . Quiet Sunday at Eleagers. March to Freshley's Ferry on Broad River.

February 20: Across Broad River and to Thompson P.O. Magnificent view at the crossing. Song nights march into camp.

February 21: To Winsboro, S.C. Rocks and hills. Fires at Winsboro. A fine place. H'd Qr's at Mr. Laft's. Had to move out two miles to camp. Exploration with Speed.

February 22: By Materee Ch. and Gladdens Grove P.O. to Rocky Mount P.O., 22 miles.

February 23: March over roughest of roads, hills, etc. Eve: visit of Gen. Sherman and Staff. Pontoon laid over the Catawba and part of the Div. crossed in the night. Revolutionary ground.

February 24: Across the Catawba at Rocky Mount Ferry and out five miles toward Liberty Hill.

Rain. Moved two miles and stopped.

Stuck in the mud. Gen. Sherman and Staff took dinner with us and witnessed a cock fight. Rain, rain all night long.

February 25: Up in the dark to eat. Ready to march at 6, when marching orders were countermanded. Rain all day. 14th Corp find it impossible to cross the Catawba.

February 26: Moved to Hanging Rock, a wet, muddy march to Russell Place, then sunshine and better roads. Visit to the Hanging Rock.

February 26: Fine day. Lying still at Hanging Rock, encamped on the battle ground where Sumter defeated the British in 1780.

February 27: The 14th Corp over the river at last.

February 28: March in rain, cold day, 5 miles.

February 28: Mobley's house with white slaves.

Wednesday, March 1st: Across Lynch's Creek at Miller's Bridge and into the Chesterfield District.

March 2: To Little Black Creek. Didn't get to Chesterfield because the bottom fell out of Big Black. Burned my coats.

March 3: To Chesterfield C.H., S.C.

March 4: To Grady's Place (near Sneedsboro, N.C.). A quiet Sunday. Beautiful day. Serenade by 33d Band in evening.

March 5: To Cheraw by the Plank Road. Look at the town. Stopped at Judge Dunkin's, a classmate of Edward Everett. All night crossing the Great Pee Dee.

March 6: To near Joe's Cr, N.C. Tar pitch or rosin.

March 7: Across the Willmington R.R., rain, rain, all day long. Some of the 107th foragers captured.

March 8: On or near Lumber River, raining harder than ever. Into camp, wet and half sick, after dark.

March 9: Lumber River (Drowning Creek) to Rockfish Creek, awful roads, rain and quicksands.

March 10: Rockfish Creek to Fayetteville, a few miles in the quicksands and then 2.40 on the plank road.

March 11: Letters home! Tug up from Wilmington at Fayetteville. Look at the town and arsenal.

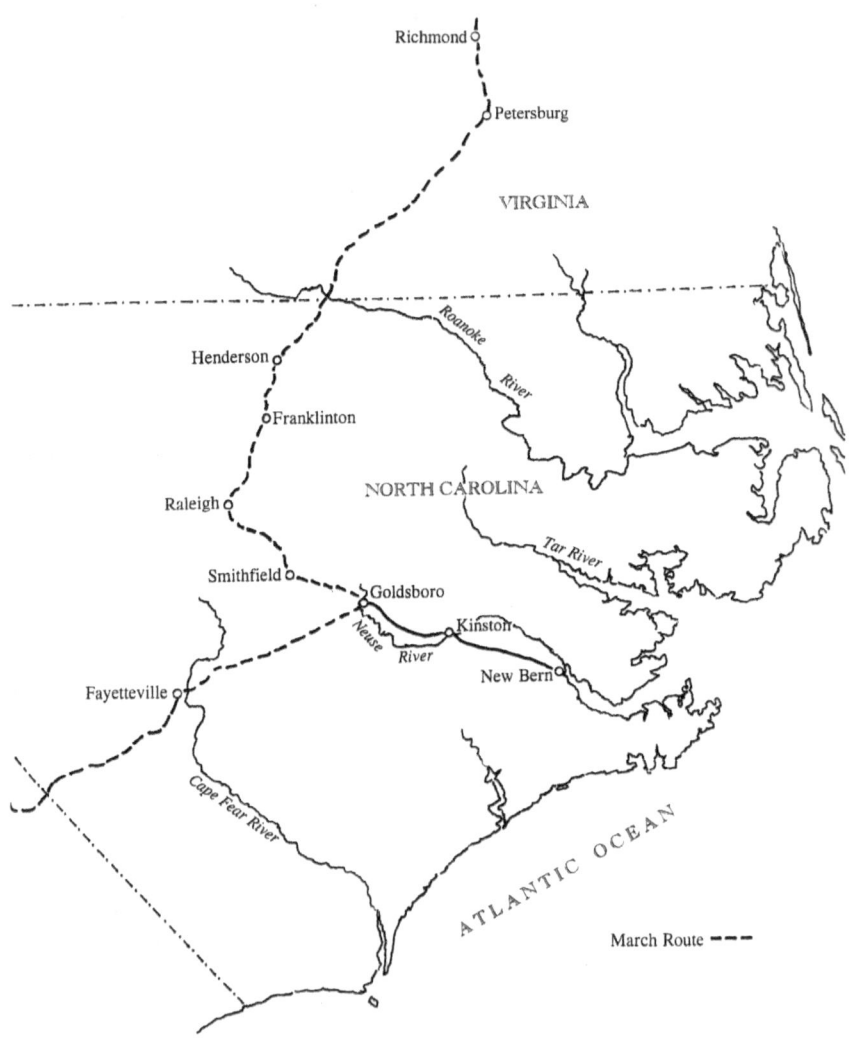

Marching Northward through North Carolina

16. Goodbye Savannah

Fayetteville, N.C., March 12th '65.

"A mail will leave Left Wing Head Quarters at 5 o'clock this afternoon!" A mail! Why, we did not expect a chance to send letters for a week yet. But it must be that our gun boats have made their way up the Cape Fear River to this point. Good! So I will fill up this little sheet of paper, that I have carried clear across the State of South Carolina, with never an addition recorded to the story of our march. As I expected, when we once cut loose from communication, it was useless to try to write any more. And now alas! It is vain trying to go back and tell the story of our progress thus far. I can only say, we are here. Yet, I can give you our route from Savannah. First Hardeeville, and then on through Robertsville, Lawtonville, Beaufort's Bridge, etc, to the South Carolina Railroad at Graham's, along the railroad to Blackville and Williston tearing up track, in all the Barnwell District. Then across the Orangeburg and Lexington Districts to Columbia, which we did not enter, but which was burned by the 15th and 17th Corps. From Columbia across the Saluda and Broad rivers to Winnsboro. Across the Catawba at Rocky Mount and thence, by Hanging Rock, to Chesterfield C.H. From Chesterfield to Cheraw, and thence to this place, which our forces entered, with a little fighting yesterday.

We think we are going to Goldsboro, about sixty miles further, where we expect to "strike a base" and to stop a few weeks for a rest and refillment. Our trip has not been quite as pleasant as that through Georgia, as the weather has been less favorable. But we have come along in good condition, have had plenty to eat, and but little opposition. Sherman is proving most effectually that the Confederacy is but a shell. They could not muster men enough to delay us in the least.

I have been disappointed in the South Carolinians. I had expected a more determined opposition from them, a prouder and more defiant spirit, befitting the noble blood they boast, but they are tamer even than the Georgians, and have disgusted us all with the boasted Southern Chivalry. I should have respected the Carolinians more, if they had not fled so precipitately from their homes, or if when they did remain they had the pluck to stick to their principles, instead of deploring the action of their State in seceding, and of declaring as some did that they had "always been Union men." No one believed them when they talked thus. We expected to find Rebels, refined educated, politer etc, but still resolute and proudly faithful to their cause. A few such we met, but very few.

But the State received a terrible scourging at the hands of our troops. I was pained to see such indiscriminate plundering of the inhabitants and destruction of property. It is heart rending to contemplate the misery and suffering that must have befallen the poor old men, and women and children in the wake of our march. Could I have had my way it would have been different. Of course we had to take food for our sustenance, and it required an immense amount of food to sustain so large an army as ours, but no plea of necessity can excuse the wanton destruction of private property, the pillaging and the excesses in which our soldiers indulged. My regiment seems to be unfortunate. A foraging party of our boys, with the Lieutenant commanding, was captured a few days since, none from my company, for they were nearly in Rebel hands already.

"Order from Gen'l Sherman!" I stop to hear Capt. Speed read it. "Head Quarters Military Division of the Mississippi" (What a Division! From the Mississippi to the Atlantic.) "The Major General commanding takes pleasure in announcing that he is in communication with *Wilmington,* a steam tug having just arrived. It will return at 6 P.M. today with mail, and for some essential supplies. We will, however, have to make a further march in order to reach our true destination." All right. Give us our "essential supplies" and we'll march anywhere you say, is the response of every man in Sherman's army.

This is to tell you where I am, that I am well. It seems a year since I have received any letters. I hope that the tug will bring us letters, with its essential supplies. In the meantime I shall wait patiently, for I have learned that virtue, at least, since entering the service.

Monday, March 13th: Crossed the Cape Fear River. Moved through Fayetteville. Passed in review before Gen. Slocum's H'd Q'rs. Tired and sick.

March 14th: No move, sick all day. Bummers skirmishing with the Cavalry ahead. Captured a brass piece.

Wednesday, March 15th: Marched about ten miles up the Raleigh Road to Kyle's Landing and camped. Rain. Quite sick.

Thursday, March 16th: Advanced to Smithville where our forces had a sharp fight with the enemy. Result favorable. Lt. Starrow killed, also Capt. Grafton of 2d Mass. Lt. Col. Morse, Capt. Woodford, Lt. Wattles, and many others wounded. Took three guns and many prisoners. Sick all day.

Friday, March 17th: Enemy fell back during the night. 3d Div. advanced to Averysboro. Found many Rebel wounded there. A hard day on me. Dr. Rugan says I have Remittent Fever.

Saturday, March 18: Marching easterly. Kept my saddle a few miles when I had to get into an ambulance. Late. Rough march.

Sunday, March 19th: In an ambulance. General sick too and sometimes in the ambulance with me. But word came for the troops to hurry to the front, and he went too. Near Bentonville another fight. 14th Corps at first driven back with loss of three cannon. But as the rest of the column came up a new line was formed and the Rebel assault handsomely repulsed. Things looked very dubious for a time.

Monday, March 20th: In camp on the battlefield. Enemy retired to their works a mile back. Right Wing up and in position. Geary up too. Talk of storming the Rebel works. Taking medicine full blast, but no better of my fever.

Tuesday, March 21st: Sent to the hospital. Put into an ambulance and sent off with a lot of wounded. Terrible roads. Traveled till midnight, and at last had a few hours of sleep in a hospital tent with Maj. Higgins of 73 Ohio beside me under my blankets.

Wednesday, March 22nd: A move of 8 miles more in the ambulance train. Many of the wounded must have died jolting over the horrible roads. Didn't get into a tent until nearly night. Dr. Pendergast gave me a little medicine, otherwise I had no medicine in all day, nor food until Winston brought me some biscuit and coffee from Capt. Lacy's train. Got permission to go with him to Kinston to Gen'l Hospital in the morning.

Thursday, March 23d: Winston came for me early. Got a paper from Dr. Berce and got into one of Lacy's army wagons bound for Kinston. Went through Goldsboro without my knowing it and went perhaps twenty miles. Roads better, but the army wagon jolted me badly.

Camped 8 miles from Kinston. I got a bed in a house and Lacy and Stuart did all they could for me, and Winston took care of me like a father. How sick I was. I had food now, but no medicine.

Friday, March 24th: At Kinston, Lacy left me at the Lenoir House Hospital. I soon made up my mind I would die if I staid there and that I should go to Newbern. Lt. Col.'s Watkins and Morse and Capt. Woodford were going home on leave. I got in with them by the aid of Capt. Young and was taken to the railroad two miles away. Capt. Hopkins, C.S.USA kindly gave me a bed and supper, while waiting, as I had to wait all the afternoon and till nearly midnight for the train. At last we were loaded on a flat car and went to Newbern with a thousand Rebel prisoners.

Saturday, March 26th: 2 o'clock A.M. Winston and I, Lt. Col. Watkins, and Capt. Todd got off the cars and went to the Gaston House. Could get no bed or room so laid down in the barroom until morning. Sadly in need of medicine all this time. In the course of the morning was admitted to Foster General Hospital Div III and felt grateful. Told a *Tribune* correspondent, all about the fights, then went to sleep. Medicine and food and care at last. Thank God! Wrote home of my sickness.

Tuesday, March 28: Wrote home that I was better. Hope they won't get scared about me and come after me.

Div. No.3, Foster General Hospital
Newbern, N.C., March 29th, 1885

I have been very sick since I wrote you last, from Fayetteville, and am under treatment now, but I guess I shall recover if I keep doing as well as I now am. I was taken ill the day we marched through Fayetteville, and crossed the Cape Fear River, (13th) but followed the army in its marches and fightings until the 22nd when I was sent to the rear. It seems a miracle to me almost that I lived through it all. But I guess now I shall recover, and be on duty again in a few weeks perhaps. I have Remittent fever. I hear that a mail has reached the army at the front and perhaps there are letters for me at our Head Quarters. It will be a blessing if we ever have regular mail communications with home again. When wounded or sick one's memories of home become very constant and vivid. And after our arduous campaign from Savannah news from home would be especially welcome. I trust you are all well at least. Newbern I am told is a fine place. I have seen little of it. I have not yet ventured out of the room in which is my cot. Kinston is a poor-looking place. I am told that Goldsboro is a nice town, but I was lying in an army wagon when we came through, and saw nothing of it. I was too ill to raise my head. My Corps is now there I understand, and I mean to get there just as soon as I am strong enough.

Through how many dangers has the Lord brought me safe and alive since I entered the service! I am amazed when I think of all that I have escaped. How thankful I ought to be. I have been all day writing this, I am too ill to write yet. Direct as usual H'd Quarters 3d Div. 20 Corps. Goldsboro. I mean to be there soon, the Lord willing.

Wednesday, March 29: Getting stronger. Walked down as far as the P.O. and bought some things. No news from anywhere.

From *New York Tribune* March 29, 1865

Note: Lieut. Tuttle of the 107th New York, and Topographical Engineer on Gen. Ward's Staff, went to the Newbern Hospital, ill of fever, but is doing well. (The report in the *Tribune* of the 29th is as the Lieut. gave him the facts.)

Friday, March 31st: Wrote a long letter home telling them all about sickness. My room mates, Dr. Samuel Mathers, Ass't Surg. 53d Ohio, Lt. M..... 132 Co. E, N.Y.,Top'l Eng, Lt. Jas Manger 168 Ohio, Col. Zollinger 129 Ind, and Capt. Kickerson 118 Ohio, left for the front a day or two ago. I mean soon to follow them.

Sunday, April 1st: Jack Saltsman came in on his way home on leave, was wounded in the head on the 16th. Said Binny was in town. So I went down street to find him. Instead I found Bill Sutton and Tom Connell at the Gaston House. They have come here to work on the R.R. Andrew, Charles, and Wood, Kimbal are here too. They had been to see the grave of Charles Kinney. Found in the Hospital P.O. a letter from Lon Howard. He is at Moorhead city and has typhoid fever. Call from Sutton, Connell & Andrew, Charles in the P.M. Then Binny delighted me with a call. Sent off some things by Express, and took a stroll up to Cedar Grove Cemetery. Didn't find Charlie Kinney's grave.

Monday, April 2: Morning: Doctor said I could go to the front on the morrow. Went to the Episco Church. P.M. wrote to Carrie.

Procured my discharge from the Hospital and paid my bill of $13.50. Met Capt. Gardner of the Corp and Lt. Benedict of the 1st Div. Staff.

A beautiful day, warm and bright. Quiet and delightful, a sabbath day in springtime.

Tuesday, April 3: Newbern to Goldsboro, N.C. Left the Hospital in a hurry. Was fortunate enough to get in the baggage car and so I had a comfortable ride but it was long and wearisome never the less. At Mosely Hall saw Binney. When I got to Goldsboro could see no one that I knew so inquired for our camp and walked three miles to get to it. Tired me out, but was delighted to be at 3 Div. H'd Q'rs once more.

Saw Gen. Ward, Gen. Coggswell, Gen. Robbinson, Col. Selfridge, and Col. Hawley there. Found a huge mail which delighted me muchly. Concluded to go back to the town, to the Hospital where Dock is, as my valise and blankets are still up town. Found Dock in a pleasant room, and made myself "at home." Very tired but glad to be "at home." Sorry to hear Gen. Williams has been relieved by Gen. Mower.

Having a good time reading and writing letters and reading papers and magazines that came in our accumulated mail. Eat like a horse, take a little tonic medicine, and wait for coming strength. Evening went over to 1st Div. Hospital with Dock and had a good long visit with Pendergast. He read me a letter from Margaret. Joe Thompson had had a magnificent party, and "Laura" had been married by the Rev. Dr. Cunningham to a Capt. Warder. Mamie Fletcher married to Lieut. Martin, etc, etc.

H'd Quarters, 3d Div. 20th A.C.
Goldsboro, N.C., April 5, 1865.

Out of Hospital and at my place again, my "Army Home," our good old Division Head Quarters, among the friends I have served with so long, and learned to prize so highly. Pale, and thin, and weak I am yet, and do not pretend to do duty, but the fever has left me, and I have only to wait in patience for returning strength and health.

One of the chief causes of my anxiety to return to the front was the knowledge of the mail that was waiting for me here. How I have reveled in the perusal of all my letters! Although like as every perfect picture has some shade with all its light, heart has grown heavy as I have read the sad tidings, of the death of intimate and valued friends. How welcome the letters we have received so seldom, yet scarce a mail has come in the past year that brought not some sad news.

I have sent you *Toi*. As I opened my valise to find an envelope yesterday, almost the first thing I found was that music, folded up and directed. So I sent it chiefly in remembrance of the Chevis House, that home of elegance and taste, our first resting place in South Carolina, and now alas! a desolation, under the vandal hands of the 15th Corps.

I had not seen Newbern, when I last wrote. I was yet too ill to walk out, but I became strong enough to stroll around Newbern a little on those glorious bright spring afternoons we had. It was pleasant to wander through the streets of the old town, regularly laid out and lined with grand old trees, whose fresh green leaves gladdened every heart with the thought of summer days, pleasant to look at the fine old residences, and yards full of roses and spring flowers, pleasant to watch the people I met, neat well-dressed soldiers who had been on post duty, and looked so different from Sherman's travel-worn veterans. Citizens, sailors, railroad employees, jew sutlers, contrabands, everybody, a motley crowd. And there were many ladies in the streets tempted out by the sunshine, even as I. Now a stroll to the docks, crowded with steamers and sloops and transports all loaded with supplies for "Sherman's Army."

Then over to the Cedar Grove cemetery, a beautiful place, and back by the old churches of which there are many in Newbern. Last Sunday morning I attended services at the Episcopal Church, a gothic structure I could hardly guess how old. In the yard are old decaying headstones whose scarcely legible inscriptions date back to seventeen hundred and something, and inside, the walls are lined with memorial tablets in honor of former worshippers in that house of God. The music of a sweet toned organ recalled memories of many Sabbath days of yore, when I felt more at home in the house of the Lord than now; and the grand old service you love so much seemed unusually impressive as it was read by the white-haired minister before us. And he gave us a good old orthodox sermon, from the text, "The soul that sinneth, it shall die." Once in Atlanta, once in Savannah, and once at Newbern, have I been permitted to attend church services. When next, and where? I trust it may be ere long, and that at home. But God ruleth.

As I write a band of music is playing at Gen. Carter's Head Quarters, near by. That band has passed by here twice since I have been here, at the head of funeral processions. A sweet, sad dirge they played as they went to the grave, but coming back what do you think they chose? *I wish I was in Dixie*, and *Ain't I glad to get out of this Wilderness*. But they are playing beautifully tonight. It is a beautiful night. Spring has fairly come here. Roses and lilacs and many other flowers are in full bloom, and fruit trees are gorgeous with their pink and white blossoms. I suppose Spring is coming to you also. Your talk of winter storms and of paths in the snow, seems a little strange. I have seen no snow this winter, not a flake. Shall I send a rosebud, herald of springtime in "the old North State"?

We all welcome the coming of Spring, though we know it brings a bloody task for us. And redder than this rosebud may be the fields where ere long the precious life blood of her sons must be shed for our dear country's sake.

We are ordered to be ready to move in five days. Can it be that the campaign will open soon? Or is this but a preparatory movement, to get us in position for works when the time shall come? The latter, I think.

You were wondering how we kept Washington's birthday. That day we made a forced march of twenty-two miles, from near Winnsboro, one of the neatest towns in all our land, to Rocky Mount on the Catawba River. That was when Sherman turned suddenly east, from his northward march, to the great disappointment of the Rebels who were getting ready to receive him at Charlotte. He had anticipated trouble in crossing the Catawba, and all were elated at our reaching the river and securing a passage so easily. A very long pontoon bridge was immediately laid down, and before morning nearly all our Division was across the river. Gen. Sherman took tea with us that evening. It was interesting to listen to his conversation. We were now on historic ground. Many battles were fought in this vicinity in the darker days of the revolution, and this very place, Rocky Mount, was for a long time the post of a British Garrison. He could easily see how it could be a Gibraltar. Had the Rebels been here in any force, they could have bothered us greatly.

Then a dispatch came for him. After looking at it he said, "Here's good news for you gentlemen," and he read aloud the dispatch, from Gen. Howard, announcing that Charleston had been occupied by the Union forces. This completed the good feeling of the occasion. In answer to a Staff officer's inquiry, Gen. Sherman said, "Yes, every regiment in this army can inscribe "Charleston" on their banners, for they took it, though a hundred miles away." "Prettiest thing of a man, to take a city without going near it." And then he told how he had directed the whole thing, the orders he gave to the coast troops, etc. It was late when he left us, all elated at the perfect success of our movements thus far. And all night long the troops were marching by, going down to cross the pontoons, and thus making secure our position on the east bank of the Catawba.

So passed our 22d Febr'y, and surely I can never forget its interesting incidents.

Crawford came back from Newbern in the night; got no pay there of course. Sorry I didn't see Speed before he left. He is appointed Paymaster and ordered to Louisville. Letters bring news of George Gardner's death.

A bummer, in Hospital still. Members of our Staff, here today predict a movement of the army very soon, within 4 or 5 days. What shall I do? Afternoon, paid a visit to Dr. Pendergast, then down with Dock to see

Dr. Bucher Med. Director of 17th Corps. Then back to write to Preima while Dock went down to see Dr. Marsh. Dr. Berce came in and we had a long talk. Then late, Col. Bloodgood 22 Wis. came in and when Dock didn't come back, occupied his place under the blankets with me.

April 6: Tidings come of the fall of Richmond, with the capture of a fabulous number of prisoners. Carl Schurz is the authority. Walk down to town to see McDowell and learn that he has gone up to Left Wing while Schilling is Corps Engineer. Bad!

Afternoon take a ride with Dock to H'd Q'rs. Saw Carl Schurz at Sherman's Head Quarters, and hear that the good news is confirmed. Grand! What next? But we will be soon on the move anyway.

Found all "laid out" at H'd Q'rs, having had a Division Review, and then a glorification over the good news. Beecher said Perkins had spoken of appointing a Topog. in my place. Bad again. All Brigade Topogs. relieved.

Goldsboro, N.C., April 6, 1865.

Something of "good old times" seems to be coming to me again, when I can write something each day, and when the mails each day bring us, if not tidings from home, at least from the world "and the rest of mankind." (I might have enjoyed a good home-letter today had not the stupid boy, who was to bring to me, lost it on the road!) There comes to us today a breeze of exciting rumors, and then a dispatch real and tangible from Carl Schurz to Gen. Sherman, full of glorious news from Richmond.

It has become a settled rule with us to "believe no report that comes concerning Richmond, especially of its capture." So we read the good news, on the bulletin board, with incredulous eyes. But I guess we'll have to believe it. As I rode by Gen. Sherman's Head Quarters I saw Gen. Schurz there, and he says it's so.

Yes, I took a ride today, the first time I've been on horseback these many days. And I went out to our Head Quarters, two miles from town. A dusty road, through the camps, and crowded with horsemen and moving trains. The clouds of dust choked and almost blinded me, and it was a relief to get out in the secluded pine grove where our H'd Q'rs are located. It is really warm weather here, and summer coats and lighter clothing are sought for, but beautiful evenings.

I am at the hospital yet, which is in town, and I stay with the Chief Surgeon of the Division (my tent mate since we left Atlanta) at a neat house, filled with pictures on the walls, and surrounded by a yard full of beautiful flowers and ornamental trees. But it is the house of a secesh family, and tonight the lady of the house, with some friends, has been out praising the beauty of the evening, and as they passed the porch which runs by my door, singing *Dixie, Bonnie Blue Flag* and other Rebel airs, the singing I thought

16. Goodbye Savannah

for my special benefit. Those songs are not unpleasant to me, to hear, but the spirit that leads Southern ladies to sing them at a federal officer, seems to me so pitiful and contemptible. I don't admire Southern ladies as a general thing, and I have no respect whatever for those who consider it their duty to their cause to insult and displease those in whose power they are placed by the fortunes of war. Then many of those who are sensible and ladylike are, in spite of their accomplishments, helpless, like the Carolina friend you had in school. Only half accomplished after all, for not the poorest accomplishments, I take it, are those which pertain to household care and work of which they know nothing, from their life-long dependance on servants. I have many pleasant acquaintances in Shelbyville, of which I sometime told you. There were a great many young ladies there, accomplished, agreeable, good-looking and the society of all was most pleasant. But there were only four whom I learned truly to respect, and thus, really to like, two sisters here, two sisters there.

Intimate as I was with their families, I happened in sometimes before visiting hours, and to my surprise and gratification found my lady friends, as much *au fait* in the kitchen as in the parlor. I did not expect such excellence in the South, but I found in the case of the two sisters I liked best, they were from the North formerly. Their names are in my autograph book. So in Savannah, and before that in Atlanta, and so in Carolina, for (did I tell you?) I made some very pleasant acquaintances coming through the Palmetto State.

Friday, April 7th: My lost letter has come to me! It was from Carrie and I was right glad to hear from home. I had just been out to my regiment with Dr. Pendergast, Assistant Surgeon in the 107th, and just to think of a ride in a buggy, I can recollect all the buggy rides I've had since I became a soldier boy, a very short one with Howard in Savannah, one with Jo Thompson and Capt. Sill in Shelbyville, and one or two when was at home on furlough in the summer of 1863.

And didn't I enjoy this of today, though! and very pleasant it was to meet with familiar faces at the regiment. Of course I had a long talk with Col. Sill, whom I had not seen since I was first taken sick, at Fayetteville. While I was there he received a letter from my Aunt Jane. Good true soul. If saints ever dwell on earth I believe she is one. "Comrades," oh! Yes I have many army friends, friendships cemented by active service shared together, and we will not soon forget each other.

How can we ever forget the hardships we have endured or the dangers we have met? No more can we forget the boys who shared these with us. Even so soon there are only a few college friends whom I still keep sight of. And so with my army friends. Should we survive the war and be permitted to meet in after life, 'twould be with the warmest feelings I know, but should we never meet 'twould be almost as if we had always been strangers, except in the memories that would sometimes return to us of these days.

About that word "comrade." We never use it except in poetry or florid prose. Never hear it in ordinary conversation, yet we have a word in constant use among the soldiers, exactly corresponding to it, in its every use and meaning, "pardner." "Pardner, give us a lift till I get these hams on my shoulder." "Pardner, can you tell me where the Second Brigade is camped?" etc, etc. You hear it everywhere. And "Pardner" is exactly synonymous with "Comrade." And homely as it sounds, it has a wealth of meaning after all. Are we not all pardners in a great and glorious enterprise? I like the idea.

It rains tonight "April showers." But I fear the setting in of a steady rain. It has been so pleasant while we have remained in camp here. Will it be "just my luck" to have the rains come with the opening of our campaign? In these days we expect to march. The time seems uncomfortably near, to me, for I do not feel able yet to campaign it, especially if the weather is to be unfavorable.

Head Quarters Army of Georgia
Goldsboro, N.C. April 7th 1865

Circular.

The following orders and instructions for the guidance of the Topographical Engineer Dept. of this army are hereby published.

I Special order No. 15 H'd Q'rs Mil. Div. Miss. May 27th 1864 is still in force and will be strictly complied with.

II Corps Topographical Engineers will so organize their departments that each Division will have in charge of the surveys, data and information which is required to be compiled during the campaign a competent, active and reliable officer or enlisted man. On Monday morning of each week, the surveys and information obtained will be transmitted to the Corps Topographical Engineers. The Corps Topographical Engineers will consolidate the surveys of Division Engineers and will forward them on Tuesday morning (or at other times if specially required) to the Chief Topographical Engineer, Army of Georgia. The Corp Engineer will denote on all maps forwarded to these Head Quarters, the position of the troops of the Corps with dates of their location; In addition he will forward an "Information Sheet" giving the character of the County marched over each day, soil, timber, the number of miles of road corduroyed, number, length, and kind of bridges built, and the width of streams with their names. The Corps Engineer will aim to render his Department efficient, and will see that every officer and man detailed in Topographical Engineer Department performs his entire duty and in case of the failure of any officer or man, to discharge with credit and ability the duty to which he is assigned, he will at once cause his removal.

III The rules and regulations in regard to making maps and surveys which have been heretofore adopted will be observed hereafter.

By order of
Maj. Gen'l H. W. Slocum
(Signed) Robt. P. Decherd
Major and A.A.A.G.

Head Quarters 20th Corps
 Near Goldsboro N.C. April 8th 1865
 Official
  Chas. Moyer
   A.A.A.Gen'l

Saturday, April 8th: Another pleasant day, and a most beautiful evening. I'll not fear rains yet. Fourth of July in the morning. Can you imagine it, in a large place? Here is a (temporary) population of many thousands, and all seem to have joined spontaneously in celebrating a Fourth of July in the evening. Rifles and pistols popping in all directions, reminding me of the ubiquitous fire crackers that always annoyed Father so much, with now and then a heavier report, where a howitzer or napoleon gun has "spoken," and bands are playing, and large brilliant rockets, furnished by the Signal Corps and the finest I have ever seen, are rushing up against the sky bursting into beautiful stars of blue or crimson or green, that go floating away in the air, and change their colors as they go. And the "boys in blue" are cheering down the streets and in the camps. It all means Good news from Grant. Staff officers are here "just from Richmond," and dispatches have come from Grant bringing truly "glad tidings." Men talk of the end of the war and a near approach of peace. God grant it! In the meantime let us be thankful for the progress we have already made. And I, I have been enjoying a ride out today. I bless God for returning health and strength. I trust I may live till I see my home, in my own loved State.

Letter from Father to Son:

Hornellsville, N.Y., April 6,1865.

Dear Russ,

It is now 4 o'clock P.M. I have been all day up on the flat making fence where the flood carried it away. I am rather fatigued and tired, but will write a few lines. Since I saw that note in the Tribune that Lieut. Tuttle had gone to Newbern Hospital sick of a fever I have felt very uneasy about you, but now since I have read your first and second letter those fears are very much dispelled, and I shall now think, that even now you are nearly well again. Your first letter from Newbern was received yesterday, the 2d today, which is 6th of April.

You will have much to tell us when you do get home, and I am greatly obliged to those officers who were so kind to you at a time when you were in need of friends, and most of all we have reason to thank God that he gave you strength and capacity to endure as well as friends to sustain you in your most trying situation. I will try and write at greater length soon.

Yours truly —
R. Tuttle

Monday April 10th 1865: Goldsboro to Millard, from our camp 13 miles, a disagreeable march of starts and halts, and a rain nearly all day long, men under arms from 5 A.M. to 9 P.M., and all well soaked. Finally at 9–½ when it was found that Gen. Geary's lines could not get across the Moccasin River till morning, we were told we could encamp where we were — 23d Corp just behind us. Rather hard on me, but if I survive this, I think I am good for the campaign. By Millard to near the Moccasin River.

April 11th: Millard to Smithfield. A rainy morning with a clear off at noon, and the rest of the day very sultry and warm. Wearisome riding and very hard marching. Troops were hurried forward, and many had to fall out.

Smithfield is a small old place, but looking beautiful in its wealth of shade trees bright in their fresh garniture of green. County seat of Johnson Co. The 14th Corp skirmished into town a little ahead of the 20th. Saw today Gen's. Sherman, Schofield, Cox, etc.,etc. Visit eve with Schilling and from McDowell.

Wednesday, April 12th: Smithfield to Swift Creek, 15 m. and surveyed it. Met Kilpatrick's Cavalry near the close of the march. Saw Gen. Mower for the first time. As we started out we received the news of Lee's surrender. All were in great glee, and anxious to press ahead, and "close up the war."

Many were talking of a speedy peace and our return to our homes. A little fast I reckon, but who cannot see we're gaining on them.

A fine day and good road. The country is growing better and more thickly settled.

Thursday, April 13: Swift Creek to Raleigh, 18 m. as we came. Had to take by-roads and avoid the road given to the 14th Corp. Arrived in Raleigh at about 2 P.M. Camped on SW side of town. H'd Quarters at the Lunatic Asylum.

Went to see the town, a most beautiful place, pleasant streets, fine public buildings, a wealth of shade trees, and lawns and flower gardens, elegant residences, etc. A few citizens to be seen, some pretty faces, and more old people hale & hearty than I have seen in a long time. This must be a delightful salubrious locality to live in.

April 14: At Raleigh. A fine day. In the afternoon Gen. Ward and Staff took a ride through the town, visiting the H'd Qrs. of Gen. Sherman,

Slocum, Schofield, Howard, and Mower. At Gen. Schofield's we saw Gen. Terry, and learned that Gen. S is to tarry here. Today the old flag is to be raised on Fort Sumter, and at Home they are keeping Thanksgiving in view of our great successes.

33d Band came up and serenaded the Lunatic Asylum. Had a pleasant visit with Dr. Fisher.

Saturday, April 15: Ordered to march at 6, passing through the town in review, but a rain set in during the night, and we were glad to learn in the course of the forenoon, that we could go into camp again. Rained very hard till in the afternoon. All are excited at the prospect of a speedy peace. Wild rumors are afloat of negotiations pending between Sherman and Johnston. It is confidently expected that Johnston will capitulate as Lee did, and it is said that our army is resting here til the affair is decided.

Raleigh, N.C., April 15th 1865.

A mail goes out at 5 o'clock is the announcement that hurries. We have all packed up since morning expecting to move at 6. We were going "to march through the city with our banners so gay" in a sort of review, but a heavy rain set in last night which prevented our review, but it seems, our march also. I am willing.

We left Goldsboro on the 10th, took Smithfield on the 11th and entered Raleigh on the 13th. Our fighting has been only with a few cavalry detachments, and we have not yet been able to find Johnston's forces. I am afraid he will get far ahead of us and lead us a long chase.

Out of our camp and through the woods and fields once more, we have been delighted with the glories of returning summer. How beautiful the fresh green of the new grass covering the fields, and the young leaves of the forest trees, contrasting finely with the deep dark green of the somber pines. The pure white blossoms of the dog-wood tree, and the deep pink of the red-bud and wild thorn and the bright yellow of the jessamine, to be seen everywhere through the woods, added to the charm of the scene. And the birds are out too, among them I have heard the mocking bird, my favorite among all birds of song, and the Whip-poor-will whose song (if it is a song) I have had a perfect horror since Chancellorsville.

Smithfield is a small place, but beautiful in its wealth of magnificent shade trees. County seat of Johnson County, and of interest to us because we heard the enemy had made elaborate fortifications there, but when we reached there we found not a defensive work of any kind, except a few skirmish pits for the cavalry. Crossed the Neuse River at Smithfield, and two days' march brought us to this place. Another State Capital occupied by "the great flanker." As usual Gen. Sherman goes to the executive mansion for his Head Quarters.

Raleigh is one of the finest places I have seen, as fine as Savannah, though different, and as Madison, Ga., but larger. Magnificently shaded streets, and fine public buildings, elegant residences, extensive groves and lawns, and flower gardens, etc. What a healthy locality it must be! The citizens all seem so well and hearty and there is a large proportion of old men and women. If they would only leave the 20th Corps to garrison the town, I think I would be able to serve out my time without any more illnesses, but Gen. Schofield's command is to do the garrison duty along these railroad lines, I believe.

Yesterday afternoon, Gen. Ward, accompanied by his able and efficient Staff, took a ride through the city. To Gen. Sherman's H'd Q'rs where we looked at the flowers in the neighboring yards and talked to the little children while the General went in to see the great Tycoon. Then to Gen. Slocum's where we saw Gen. Carl Schurz, then to Gen. Schofield's where we saw Gen. Terry of Fort Fisher fame, then to Gen. Howard's. He has his H'd Q'rs at the Female Seminary where we took a sly glance at the young ladies watching us from the windows, and then home, stopping on our way at Corps Head Quarters to pay our respects to our new Corps commander, Gen. Mowers. It was a warm day and we were tired enough by the time we reached home.

Though we have had an uncomfortable campaign thus far from bad roads and tiresome marches my health has improved since we started. I no longer fear a return of my illness, and think I shall have better health all summer for the little fever that I had. We think we shall not have much more fighting. Grant, after Lee's surrender says to Sherman, "press against Johnston and let's finish up the work at once." Don't you think our work will soon be finished? I reckon.

Sunday, April 16th: A fine bright day. No move yet. The army is waiting, as all believe, to learn the result of the negotiations now pending. Went over in the morning to the 76th Pa in the 10th Corp to find my Uncle Alonzo, but he had been left behind at Wilmington. Took a ride downtown after supper with Beecher, delighted to see the well-kept lawns and yards and magnificent trees, flower gardens, etc

Monday, April 17th: Last night nearly the whole Corp was holding a grand celebration over the supposed capitulation, or agreement to capitulate, of Gen. Johnstone — a little ahead of their time, but we believe the news we have that Forrest and Roddy have surrendered to Wilson.

But today comes the news that the President has been assassinated and Sec. Seward and son perhaps mortally wounded. What a gloom has fallen, like a pall over the whole army! And liberality toward our enemy changes to bitterness! Sherman and Johnston cannot yet agree. [*Lincoln was assassinated the evening of April 14, 1865. Ed.*]

Raleigh, N.C., April 17th, 1865.

So rapid is the march of events at present, so surprising the revelations of each succeeding day, so momentous the transactions going on around us, it would be useless to think of giving you an adequate idea of our situation, our hopes and fears, our joy and gloom during these most historic days. The sentiments and emotions that prompt one day's letter may be literally changed and falsified on the next. I can only write what I hear and see and think and feel now. At present we are all "in suspense" here. Last night the word came that Gen. Johnston was willing to confer with us in relation to the surrender of his army, and by some mistake the men on the line understood that we had agreed to surrender. If any doubts the ardent, all-pervading desire there is in the army for peace, he would have been convinced of his error could he have listened to the hearty and vociferous cheers prolonged for hours that rose all along the lines. Everybody had gone to sleep, but everybody woke up, bands were out playing *Hail Columbia, The Girl I Left Behind Me,** etc.etc. Salutes were fired, and it is said that many grew wondrously mellow before their jollification was ended. But whether drunk or sober, whether "celebrating" like beasts, or like men, one thing is certain, all were sincerely and profoundly grateful. And with our joy at the prospect of returning peace, all have grown wonderfully liberal toward our fallen foe. There is no vindictiveness, no desire for rigid justice, but a willingness indeed that the most generous terms be given them.

But no! Take it all back. All our joy, all our exhilaration in the hour of victory, all our generosity and mercy also. Then comes the shocking news, impossible to believe at first, but in time repeated and confirmed, that our president has been assassinated. I cannot attempt to describe the overpowering grief and gloom that fell at once like a pall over the entire army. Even in the hour of victory every sound of rejoicing was hushed, not a band playing anywhere along the lines, not a parade or any display of banners, even the ordinary noise and bustle of the camps was stilled, and the men were gathered together in little crowds, their deep sorrow but too plainly shown in every look and gesture, discussing the mournful intelligence. Nor was grief the only sentiment expressed. "Vengeance is mine" was entirely forgotten in the instant desire for revenge that seemed to pervade every heart.

Many expressed the desire that Johnston wouldn't surrender anyway now, that they might not by the cessation of hostilities be prevented from wreaking the vengeance so richly deserved by this last and most atrocious act of the Rebellion. This feeling became so intense throughout the army,

---

* "The Girl I Left Behind Me" was the one song held most dear to the Seventh Infantry. It is a regimental march of old Irish and English origin; melody by Samuel Lover (1797–1868). It is still played at the U.S. Military Academy at West Point at the final Parade before graduation.

that many fear for the safety of Raleigh, and tonight double guards and patrols are on duty in every part of the city. It is night and Gen. Sherman has returned from his all day conference with Gen. Johnston. Nothing effected yet. No troops are to move on either side, and twenty-four hours are given the Rebel leader in which to make up his final decision. So the shades of another night close around us, while the deeper gloom of bitter grief and mourning enshrouds our hearts. The sad intelligence came to Gen. Sherman while he was conferring with Gen. Johnston, and he says that the Rebel leader was as much affected as himself, declaring that "the South had lost its best friend."

Tuesday, April 18: There is hope that the sad news from Washington is all a hoax, or at least there are rumors to that affect. The news that the President was not dead would produce a greater glorification than any other news.

Another day of uneasy waiting, while the chiefs of the opposing armies are endeavoring to settle the points of difference between them. Gen. Sherman's order announcing the death of the President has been received. And with it we read the comments of the papers here, and listen to the sentiments of the citizens. All execrate the atrocious deed, even those who might wish to do it, not daring to show the least sign of exultation or satisfaction. For every man in the army seems ready to sustain the conclusion of Gen. Sherman's order: but woe unto the people who seek to expend their wild passions in such a manner, for there is but one dread result.

There are two papers now published here, *The Standard*, and *The Progress*, continued by the same men who formerly controlled them, and who were all the time as openly for the Union as they could be and live under Confederate rule. How fitly spoken are these words of *The Standard*, "We announce with profound grief the assassination of the President of the United States. Humanity is shocked and the heart bleeds at the announcement. He has fallen at the height of his fame, just as the sun of peace was bursting on his whole country, which he had redeemed by his constancy, his patriotism, and his devotion to the endless existence of the American Union. His name will live always, while his assassin's and their prompter's will be execrated as the basest and most cowardly of human kind. The secession of the Cotton States which commenced in crime has ended in assassination. We thank God that we are not responsible for either the commencement or the termination of this horrid business!" Did not Gen. Sherman once speak of the Rebellion as "begun in envy, perpetuated in pride"? He might now add, "and ended in infamy."

Did I tell you we had our H'd Q'rs in the grounds of the State Lunatic Asylum? We have been talking of moving away, to some house or other, but as yet we keep company with the lunatics, and they are noisy neighbors. A few of the more tractable are allowed the freedom of the grounds and they all like to visit us. Some amuse us, in spite of our pity, and one today has been delighting us with most exquisite music, from a violin. He is a perfect master of the instrument, and plays at ease all the grandest airs of the old masters. A call from such a lunatic would always be welcome. They all love music, they listen eagerly to the bands that come to serenade us, and to every bugle call. And when the 33d Mass. band came to serenade the Asylum they took it as an especial honor and seemed intensely delighted.

Later! A private note from Maj. Andenreid of Gen. Sherman's Staff to Lieut. Thompson of ours says that arrangements have this day been agreed upon involving the surrender of the whole Confederacy, civil and military, which now only await a ratification at Washington! May we not sing *Gloria in Excelsus!* now?

Rode out with Hardenbrook. Stopped at Gen. Ruger's and saw Col. Zollinger 129 Ind. Letter from home. Glad to know that I am improving. At night, dispatches by us of arrangements involving the surrender of all C.S.A. subject to approval at Washington.

Wednesday, April 19: Gen. Harrison has returned from Washington. Brings confirmation of the death of the President. Rode downtown in P.M. Finally reached H'd Q'rs of the Army of Georgia and visited McDowell and Thorne. Saw several Rebel soldiers for Lee and Johnston's armies returning to their homes. All's well.

Another order from Gen. Sherman, confirming the good news of last evening, and assuring us of a speedy restoration of "peace from the Potomac to the Rio Grande." Not the least interesting portion of the order, to us, is the statement, "The General hopes and believes that, in a few days, it will be his good fortune to conduct you all to your homes." He says we will march us to Washington, and it is said that we will make permanent camps there, or at Frederick City, or Cumberland, Md., until sent home. You once fancied you could listen to the coming footsteps of Sherman's Army as it journeyed Northward through the Carolinas, that was the tramp of an invading host. Could you listen now, you would soon hear (I trust) the joyful tread of that same Army homeward bound. May we never more march on any hostile errand. Truly we have seen strife enough, and our march has brought fire and sword, and starvation and misery to homes enough to satisfy the heart of a demon.

I send a copy of some lines, penciled by some of our soldiers, on a tombstone, where some Revolutionary Patriots were buried at Cheraw, S.C. and signed, "Yankee."

"Oh shades of patriots slumbering neath the soil
Know ye the woes of your unhappy State?

> Know ye the turf has drunk your children's blood,
> And your loved homes are spoiled and desolate?
>
> Know ye the farm on which your fathers toiled,
> And which ye guarded as a sacred trust,
> Your wayward sons have entered and despoiled,
> And cast its glorious idol in the dust?
>
> Know ye that treason o'er your sunny clime
> Has blown its breath of perjury and strife?
>
> Know ye, your sons espoused the hideous crime,
> And struck with madness at the nation's life
> Know ye, the haughty and the proud, like slaves,
> Are fleeing to the wood, the cave, the swamp?
>
> Know ye, your mountains, plains, and e'en your graves,
> Are trembling 'neath an avenging army's tramp.
>
> How can ye rest? How can your ashes sleep,
> While man's dread chariot rolls above your head?
>
> Do not your bones with holy horror creep,
> As falls the blood your perjured sons have shed?
>
> Rise! Slumbering patriots, view the rains made
> And bid the traitor anew in shame disperse,
> Bid them restore the Union they've betrayed,
> Or doubly damn them with a father's curse!"

Isn't it good for army poetry? We thought so. A mail at last. Letters from home. I'm happy. Final direction as to my address, send letters to Sherman's Army, via Washington.

A paper from home announces the death of David D. Brownell of Co. K, another victim to Rebel barbarity.

April 20: Morning: Witnessed the review of the 10th Corps. P.M.: Moved into the Lunatic Asylum and established H'd Q'rs in the airy and elegant reception room of the institution. We have flanked Corp H'd Q'rs after all. Eve, another mail bringing me two letters from home. Frank Doty is dead, noble soul, taken away in the very hour of final victory. Gen. Sherman says he will march us home. Bully!

I have become an inmate of the State Lunatic Asylum of North Carolina. I am not in a cell, however, but in one of the spacious and elegant reception rooms, the which Gen. Ward has taken possession of, for himself and Staff. Fine airy, well lighted, well furnished, Brussels carpet, gas, fine library, regular-built bed, pictures on the walls, etc.,etc., and from my window one of the most beautiful views that ever blessed the sight of mortal eye. From the eminence on which the institution is located we can see up and down the valley for miles. Just in front is Raleigh crowning the low line of undulating hills opposite, and half hidden by its luxuriant forest growth. Around it and extending out in all directions, are the encampment of Sherman's men, their white tents and the white canvas covers of the wagons and ambulances, gleaming in the sun. Away down the valley, beyond the town and the camps, the broad green fields stretch away, these in turn by the darker green of the wooded hills beyond.—I cannot describe it so that you can see the beauty.

Gen. Sherman seems to have a mania for reviews. He parades his troops through the principal street of every city or large town he captures. We are about to repeat the operation. Today I witnessed the review of the 10th Corps, Gen. Terry's. But two Divisions were present and one of these was of colored troops. Think the colored troops marched better than the whites. The best part of all was the appearance of Battery E 3d Regular Artillery. But they all marched like veterans, as they are. I was pleased to see, over some doorways in town, the little American flags we used to use in Maryland, in Kentucky, and in Tennessee, and at one house, where a luxuriant geranium half shaded one of the upper windows, there hung amid the fragrant leaves and flowers a miniature "Stars and Stripes," the staff wreathed with the white and black emblems of mourning for our murdered President.

Back again, no news. We are waiting, and still must wait.

Friday, April 21st: Went down to see review of the 23d A.C., but on account of our stopping at "Chez Nous" was too late to see the 1st Division. Tomorrow our Corps will be reviewed, and as usual the glorious old 20th will surpass them all. See if it doesn't! Pleasant during the review, but ever since it has been steadily raining. I can only sit quietly in my room till it is over and be thankful that we are not in bivouac or on the march through it all. The fine library of Dr. Hishen, President of this institution is some consolation to us, and best consolation of all is the perusal of the letters I received this day from home. You have spoken of Goldwin Smith. How rejoiced he must be along with John Bright and Thomas Hughes, and John Stuart-Mill, and all those good friends of America, who have withstood the tide of the English prejudice and envy these four years past. And what will the Rebel sympathizers throughout England say now? I am anxious to see what the London *Times* and *Herald* will say when they learn of Lee's surrender. (April 9th, 1865 Appomattox C.H.) In the meantime it is pleasant to read what they have said in the late years as they predicted the early success of the Rebellion and demonstrated the impossibility of subduing the South. We have been amused at the article from the London *Herald*, which we found in an old North Carolina paper. I send it as a specimen.

Saturday, April 22d: We had our review today and as I predicted we did best anything of the kind that preceded us. The weather was fine and the review a perfect success. Gen. Sherman said it was "a perfect review," and added that he had never seen anything better. After the review we all went up to Gen'l Slocum's H'd Q'rs. I never saw so many Generals together, and staff officers swarmed around, (almost) innumerable. All joined in complimenting the 3d Division.

Evening: Capt. Stuart had a party at his S.D. at which all the Division was well represented. Home again, and listened to the fine singing of Lt. Snyder and T. After piece by Dr. Grinstead.

Sunday, April 23d: This Sunday is indeed a day of rest and quiet. No review today — some went to church, some remained at home reading, writing, etc. Did I not at Newbern, wonder where next I should attend a divine Service? I could not have guessed that it would be in a Lunatic Asylum. Afternoon, attended chapel exercises of the institution. The officers of the asylum and some of the patients were present with a few visitors. The Rev. Dr. Mason of this city preached, and whether or not he enlightened the poor darkened souls of the asylum inmates, I know not, but his remarks were very interesting to us outsiders. It is sad to look upon such an assemblage as we there saw. Only now and then one sees a face that it is not positively painful to look upon. Going through the male department, I saw one man afflicted with epilepsy whose face and head were very fine. He had a noble forehead, and a large black eye, full of expression and power. And there is one young lady whom I sometimes see gazing sadly out of the window, who interests me greatly. She has not the beauty of health, but rather that of the consumptive, wasting slowly away.

Did I tell you of my visit to the Milledgeville Asylum? I saw several there, with whom it was very pleasant and interesting to talk. One, a Miss Forbes, formerly of New Jersey, told me of her Northern birth, and her sympathy for the Union soldiers, and we had a long talk about the war. She was dressed in deep mourning and was ever inquiring for some friend in the army. There was a piano in the room and she offered to play. We were surprised at the excellence of her playing. After several difficult pieces, she began with a strain that seemed familiar to me, *The Pleasures of Home*, playing it soft and slow as I used to love to hear it so long ago. It was evidently one of her favorites.

The 17th Corps (Gen. Frank P. Blair's) was reviewed today, and most important part of it all, Lieut. Gen'l Grant was the reviewing officer. Was it not a sight worth seeing, Grant and Sherman side by side? And then behind them were Slocum, Howard and Schofield, our three army commanders, and Fighting Johnny Logan of the 15th Corps, Blair of the 17th, Mower of the 20th, Terry of the 10th, and Cox of the 23d, Carl Schurz, Gen. Hazen from Fort McAllister, and Gen. Ames of Fort Fisher, with a host of other generals too numerous to mention. We (i.e. a small army of Staff

Officers) escorted the galaxy of stars to the house Gen. Grant had chosen for his stopping place, and then I came home to find — Marching Orders! to start at daylight on the morrow. No more now then.

Took supper with Dr. Pendergast at the 1st Div. Hospital. Col. Crane and Adj't Burdict were also there. Dr. Flood now runs the hospital and gives good satisfaction.

Monday, April 24: Fine day though somewhat cold. Review of the 17th Corps. Gen. Grant was present, and reviewed the troops—the boys who had fought under him at Vicksburg and whom he had not seen since.

Back to find orders to march tomorrow. The agreement made between Sherman and Johnston was not satisfied, I take it, at Washington.

"On April 18th Sherman and Johnston signed an article of agreement embracing the surrender of the latter's army, which was forwarded to Washington for the approval of the government. The papers were returned with the disapproval of the President. On the 26th another basis of agreement was reached, signed, and approved by General Grant. On the 29th a general order was read at dress parade, directing the 14th, 15th, 17th, and 20th Corps to proceed to Washington where they would be mustered out of service." *(History of Slocum and His Men,* W. F. Fox)

April 25: Raleigh to Jones' X Roads, N.C., 13 m.

Bid good bye to Raleigh and to the Lunatic Asylum, but it was nearly noon before we were fairly started on the march. Hot and dusty, bad headache. All kinds of exciting rumors in the evening. "Johnston has surrendered." "Johnston moved off yesterday." "Sherman is relieved." Etc.

H'd Q'rs at the house of Mr Rhodes, a place belonging to Bell Holden. Mr P. has a daughter Narcussa, the soul of simplicity and good sense.

April 26: A most intolerable, dull and tiresome day. No movement. Nobody knows nothing about anything. Dry and dusty.

Thursday, April 27: The warmth has not abated, while the dust has greatly increased. An intolerable nuisance. "Peace on Earth good will to men."! God be glorified that we can welcome now the return to peace. We are ordered back to Raleigh, and we all know what that means.

April 28: Jones' Cross Roads to Raleigh, NC, 13 m.

A dusty march, the boys did march. On our way we met papers containing announcements "hostilities had ceased." Vociferous cheers. Took up our old H'd Q'rs at the Lunatic Asylum, to Dr. Fisher's evident displeasure.

Saturday, April 29th, 1865. Raleigh, N. C.

Today was observed according to order, as a day of mourning for our beloved ex President. Flags are at half mast, salutory, etc.

The glad tidings, for which we have toiled, and waited and prayed so long has come at last. "The war is successfully ended" and we start homeward tomorrow.

Only a "wee note" tonight. Our hearts are full of but one thought. We are going home. We start on our homeward march tomorrow morning, and we can talk of nothing else now, but "home" and its dear ones. "O! Won't it be a happy time, when all the boys come home!" A "happy time" for the "boys" you may be sure. Thinking of all this there are a thousand things I should say — but I must send only the "wee note" that says "We are coming home."

I cannot imagine that the war is over. It seems a dream as I read the words of the general order that "hostilities have ceased," and that "for us" Armies in the East, "the war is ended." I cannot keep pace with the "march of events." The Rebellion has collapsed so rapidly as to surprise even the most sanguine of us. But the end cannot come too soon. I told you once how Gen. Knipe secured a yellow rose to send home. It was at Gen. Hooker's H'd Q'rs, as the Corps was waiting for the laying down of the pontoon (in Northern Georgia) across the Etowah. A large yellow rose bush under our window, reminded me of it all today. And amid the profusion of full blown roses it bore, I found the bud I send in this. Gen. Knipe left us at Atlanta, and now commands a cavalry division in the West. He ought to be with us now, as we are to finish our long journey, from Virginia to the West, from the West back to Virginia again.

I cannot write more now. It is late and we start at five in the morning. Pleasantly to my ears comes the serenaders' song of *The Girls at Home*, and our hearts all say amen, at the closing strain.

> "The Stars and Stripes, the stripes and stars
> for the love of which we roam
> But the sweetest song, and the dearest one,
> Is the song of the girls at home."

Who can blame us for singing home songs now?

Sunday 30th April: Raleigh to Falls of Neuse, N.C., 15 m.

Homeward Bound

Fine weather splendid roads, a beautiful country, and all are in good spirits at the idea of starting for home. Northern papers have come, praising Sherman for his peace notions. (but we believe in Sherman)

Neuse River to Tar River, N.C., 20 m.

A long march through a fine country. It grows better as we go Northward. These people have lived well, as well they might. Crossed the Tar River; and were all very mad at being refused the lead tomorrow. Surveying every day now.

Tuesday, May 2: Short march. Camped by Gen. Slocum's order. Eight miles in rear of rest of Corp. Am satisfied that Gen. Mower does not know how to march a Corp. Interesting talks with the people. They know and feel that they have been thoroughly whipped.

Ellis X Roads to Taylors Ferry, Va., 23 m.

Another long march. Crossed the Roanoke River at the Ferry. Camped a mile north, into old Virginia again. I cannot realize that we have made such a circuit. We are to have the front at last, and will disprove the black guard lies of the 14th Corp.

Taylors Ferry to Suffold's Bridge, Va., 20 m.

Waller and I made the march by half past twelve. The Division was in by three.

Crossed the Meherrin River and encamped at the widow Gil's place.

Fine weather yet. A few more such days will take us into Richmond.

Meherrin River to Big Nottoway River, Va., 18 m.

Another long march, but easily made. Passed through some very fine country. Lunenbury is a fine county to live in. Very large and fine plantations struck the Potomac boys at last. Some of the 6th Corp went out foraging.

Big Nottoway to near Wilson's Station, SSRR, 15 m.

Struck the South Side Rail Road at Black and White and followed it a ways. The 6th Corp is stationed along the road.

May 6th 1865: Nottoway Co., Va.

I take my pen in hand to inform you that I am well, and hope these few lines will find you in the enjoyment of the same blessing. I use the above formula because it expresses precisely what I wish to communicate, that all is well with me even as my hopes and prayers are, that it may be with you. An Orderly is about to go down to the Wellville Station on the South Side R.R. and will take along some letters, to be sent North. I hasten to send a few words. We crossed the South Side R.R. today, will cross the Appomattox tomorrow, and expect to enter Richmond in three days. That will make a ten days' march from Raleigh, eighteen miles a day. How the boys do march going homeward. We have crossed the Neuse, the Tar, the Roanoke, the Meherrin, and the Nottoway Rivers, have traversed some of the finest country I ever saw, over splendid roads and with splendid weather. This has been indeed a grand pleasure march, the great pleasing thought through all being this, that each step takes us "nearer home."

The people along our line of march have treated us with uncommon kindness and consideration. Ah! They know they have been thoroughly whipped; and the Yankees are not the despised race they were five years ago. Rebel soldiers are to be met with everywhere. All express a gladness that peace is established, and all are satisfied that they have had enough fighting. So have we.

But I cannot attempt to tell all of interest that I see and hear. It is a pleasure to travel through this land now. The flowers are in full bloom, the forests and fields are magnificent. The grand views we have at times, the rare perfume of flowers, the songs of birds, the sparkling streamlets and majestic rivers. I hope I may live to tell all of these. I certainly can never forget them.

It is said that we shall all be home by the 4th July next. Sooner or later I shall be satisfied. It is a satisfaction to know that the Rebellion has been crushed, and that we were in at the death.

Now I can go home, when the government shall discharge me from service, feeling that if I have never done any other duty I have at least fulfilled that I owed my country. Continue to write, direct to Washington, I expect to be there in two or three weeks.

May 7. Wilson's Station to Clover Hill, Va., 20 m.

A portion of the road was on the line of Lee's retreat when harassed by Sheridan. The rail barricades, the dead horses, the foot tracks of infantry columns, the bullet-scarred trees, the way side graves, etc. all told of hot

17. Homeward Bound

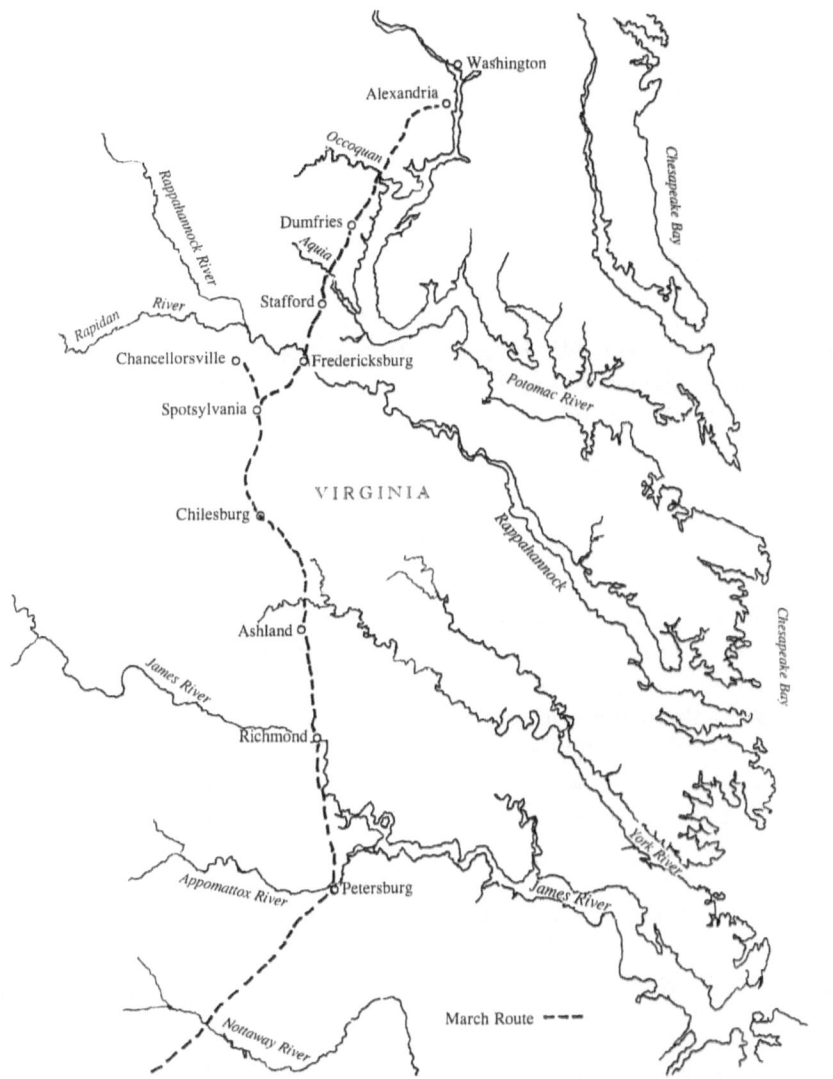

Marching Northward through Virginia and Homeward

work. Coals. Clover Hill is a mining town.
  May 8: Clover Hill to Falling creek, Va. 15 m.
  May 9: Falling Creek to Mrs Fore's House, 2 m.
  May 10: To Brooks Cr., Va. Via Manchester & Richmond, 13 m.
  May 11: Brooks Cr. To near Ashland, Va., 9 m.
  May 12: Ashland to Little River, Va., 16 m.
  May 13: Little River, North Anna River, Chilesburgh, Crutchfields

Wells, 18 m.
> First view of Blue Ridge
> *May 14:* C.M. Spotsylvania C.H. and Chancellorsville.
> *MaY 15th:* View of both battlefields. 17m. (Fredericksburg & Spotsylvania)
> *May 16:* C. to V.S. Ford. Hartwood Ch. Town Run, 21 m.
> *May 17:* Town Run. Brentville, magnificent news, 14 m.
> *May 18:* Brentville to Fairfax Station, 19 m.
> *May 19:* Fairfax Station to Alexandria, 18 m.
> *May 20:* Paid by Major Vellerlip to April 30th.
> *May 22:* Went to Washington with Gen Ward.
> *May 23:* Review of the Potomac troops.
> *May 24:* Review of Sherman Army. New camp.

H'd Q'rs 3'd div., 20 A.C.
Bladensburg, Md., May 25th 1865.

In our new camp, near Fort Lincoln, on the "Bladensburg Road." A pleasant place for Head Quarters, on a knoll, in a little grove, and from which we have the finest views, from Bladensburg with the cavalry camps beyond it, just in front, around to Washington with its magnificent capitol looming up away behind us. And it is a pleasant evening. I enjoy its quiet, disturbed only by the animated conversation of brother officers in a neighboring tent, and by a fine band which is serenading the garrison at the Fort.

How pleasant it is, these quiet evenings, now that the war is over, to think of all the trials and dangers we have gone through, and which have been so gloriously, triumphantly brought to a close! We have been talking of this night one year ago, as many said, the gloomiest, darkest, most horrible night we saw in all our term of service. In the woods, and in the rain, dark and cold closed in the night over one of the hottest, bloodiest conflicts of the war, where dead were thickly strewn, and the wounded in startling numbers were everywhere, along the roads, and through the woods. It was what is known as the field of "New Hope Church," but we remember it with a sort of gloomy horror as the "Dallas Woods."

Looking for Gen. Ruger through the darkness and gloom, I almost ran over four men, carrying back a wounded man, and whom I recognized by their voices as men of my own company. I did not know it was Eugene Thacher they were carrying, until afterwards they told me. Poor fellow. It was a dark scene of horror on which he closed his eyes. But we are sure that when he opened them it was in the ineffable light of the Great Father's loving presence. And we are spared to talk over all these things, thankful yet wondering, that we have been so long and so signally protected from harm.

Were we not near the South Side Rail Road when I wrote last? Away

March Route, Chattanooga to Washington

beyond Richmond? I cannot write now. There are a thousand topics of interest I want to tell about, but I cannot write all the time thinking of so soon coming home when I can tell all this.

We had an easy march into Richmond, one place on our journey will we ever remember with pleasure, a little village, "Clover Hill" by name, peopled by a Union-loving population of miners. (The coal mines are there.) To our great satisfaction we marched through Richmond without being reviewed by General Halleck. (We had never really liked him, and now cherished a special dislike because of his attempts to injure Gen. Sherman.) Gen. Sherman deserves admiration and honor.

From Richmond to Washington, a long and tedious march. Two or three days of their good roads and fine weather all through, except the last day or two when the heat was excessive and the dust multitudinous! At Spotsylvania we looked with a sad interest over the ground where as fierce fighting raged as the world ever saw, examined the bullet-scarred lifeless trees and the trenches now filled with the dead, where Hancock's bloody fighting was done, and gazed with horror on the myriad skulls and bones bleaching in the sun, the scantily buried half-exposed bodies of the slain here, and the never-buried remains of hundreds of Union soldiers, whose bones are to this day lying, untouched where they fell. Chancellorsville also bore testimony of bloody work all over its memorable field. I found the exact places where my regiment had lain, had thrown up works, or had fought, and the trees beside which I had tried to rest through those nights of excitement and horror.

The crossing of the Rappahannock and all the road back to Alexandria was familiar, every house and church and bridge, the same as when we journeyed by them two years before, and the constant thought was, how different is now from then in the situation of affairs in our land.

You will hear all about the Grand Reviews. What more could I write about them? Of course I was there, one of the two hundred thousand boys in blue who made such a long and weary march for the satisfaction of our Northern friends who came to see the great pageant. All that I saw, and said and felt and heard, I will tell when I come. I cannot write it now. Going home from the first review on the boat from Washington to Alexandria, I met Paric McCullum. Capt. Rennée of our Staff introduced us. We had a long talk about the boys and girls we knew at Alfred. He is not a little proud of the success of Angelo, who is now a Lt. Col. Commanding a regiment. And just before our own Review I met James Stillman at the capitol.

This Washington is a great place. It is distinctive to the last degree, with so many excellencies, so many deformities, so much to evoke interest and admiration, so much to excite loathing and disgust. All are anxious to visit it, and that repeatedly, although all are in turn disgusted, and glad to get away from it. But all things considered, I doubt if anyone would ever be made better or nobler by a sojourn in our National Capital.

Now, when returned from active field duty and yet retained in camp, getting a hint of civilization from seeing the people, the citizens, the ladies, the Northern friends I meet when I go into the city, I feel very sensibly the loss sustained in so long an absence from the refining and elevating influences of home and friends. I have never been homesick through all my service thus far, but I must own that I am becoming desperate lonesome here. I have no idea when I shall go home. It is possible that I shall be retained in service, but I mean to go home for a time at least. In the meantime do not forget to write me.

June 4: Quite sick. Visit of James S.
June 5: Returned to H'd Q'rs.
June 6: Washington to Harrisburg, Pa.
June 7: Harrisburg to Elmira & Hornellsville, NY.
June 8: H'ville to Elmira, & to Hornellsville.
June 9: Saw Villie.
June 16th: H'ville to Elmira. To Painted Post.
June 17: Painted Post to Elmira.
June 18th 1865: Elmira, N.Y.
June 19, 1865: Paid off by Major A. H. Hutchins, and discharged from the Service of the U.S.

Mustered Out

Tuttle.— At Hornell, N.Y., May 28th, Hon. Russell M. Tuttle, in the 68th year of his age. He was the son of a leading citizen of the town, and had just graduated in August 1862 when he enlisted in the 107th N.Y. Vol's. and rose through all the grades to a Captain's commission. He was on Staff duty nearly two years with Gens. Ruger and Ward, of Twentieth Corps. Returning home he went into the newspaper business and achieved much success. He took much interest in public affairs, and was President of the village, and represented his County in the New York Legislature. The Hornell papers paid high tribute to him as a public-spirited blameless citizen. He took a deep interest in the G.A.R. and was buried by Doty Post.

National Tribune, Washington, D.C., Thursday October 13, 1908

Russell M. Tuttle. This undated photograph was found among Tuttle's papers.

Epilogue

After the Civil War, Russell M. Tuttle took an interest in public affairs, establishing himself in the newspaper business as proprietor and editor of the *Hornellsville Times* from 1867 to 1879, and as editor again from 1888 to 1906. He was a founder of the Hornellsville Public Library in 1868, and also held the post of superintendent of schools. Tuttle was elected president of the village in 1868, and representative of his county to the State Assembly in 1880 and 1881. He married an Alfred University classmate, Ervilla Goodrich, of Almond, on November 7, 1867. He died in Hornellsville, on May 28, 1908.

Ervilla was an accomplished writer and may have been responsible for having her husband's notes bound in the form in which they were found. Her health declined in her late years. She died in 1920, having outlived her husband by 12 years. There were no children, and no surviving family on either side.

Appendix A.
History of the Tuttle Family

Russell Tuttle's father, Rufus Tuttle, was born in Woodbury, Connecticut, April 2, 1806. Rufus's father died when he was young, leaving his mother with little means, but Rufus and his brother managed to do well, eventually becoming respected businessmen. Rufus married Ann Lester of Mount Pleasant, Pennsylvania, December 1, 1831. Ann died a year later, leaving him an infant son, Rufus W. Young Rufus was employed in civil engineering on the Ohio and Mississippi Railroad at Shoals, Indiana, when he died in his 28th year.

On January 23, 1837, four years after the death of his first wife, Rufus Tuttle married Mellinda Mumford, daughter of Col. Harry Mumford of Mount Pleasant, Pennsylvania. Russell Tuttle, their son, was born in Almond, Allegany Co., New York; the Tuttles also had a daughter Caroline (Carrie). After a short detour to Pennsylvania to take care of family business, the family relocated to Hornellsville, Steuben County, New York, in 1842 where Russell was educated in the local public schools. He began his higher education at Alfred University, where he completed the freshman year in 1858. He graduated from the University of Rochester with honors in 1862, and enlisted in the army shortly thereafter.

Russell Tuttle's wife, Ervilla, was one of two daughters of Dr. Levi S. Goodrich and Laura E. Barnes of Benson, Vermont. They located to Howard, New York, in 1826, the year they were married, and subsequently lived in Hornellsville, Alfred, and Almond, where Dr. Goodrich died in 1846. Laura died at the home of her daughter Ervilla in Hornellsville in 1892.

Appendix B.
A Note on the 107th New York Volunteers

"During its service the One Hundred and Seventh New York Volunteers marched a total of 2,580 miles, campaigned in the states of Pennsylvania, Maryland, West Virginia, Virginia, North Carolina, Georgia, Alabama, Tennessee; passed through Ohio, Indiana, and Kentucky, and took part in the battles of Antietam, Chancellorsville, Gettysburg, Resaca, Dallas, Cassville, Pine Knob, Culp's Farm, Kennesaw, Peach Tree Creek, siege of Atlanta, Sandersville, Redoubt no.3, Argyle Island, Siege of Savanna, Averysboro, and Black River. Loss of the regiment was: died of wounds or killed, 88; died of disease, 107; a total of 195."

From: *History of Steuben County, New York*, Vol. I, 1911, page 400.

Appendix C.
"Health of the Volunteers"

"In a regular army four soldiers die of disease for one that falls in battle. If there are forty-five thousand volunteers in and near Washington on the first of July, it is probable that there might not be more than twenty thousand on the first of October, even if no battle were fought. Of a Southern regiment which went into Mexico some eight hundred strong, only about one hundred and fifty returned, yet not a hundred were lost in the field. The horror of war is not the sudden shot that opens the gate of glory to the soldier, but the fever and wasting disease that slowly eats his life away. At this moment it is not Beauregard, nor Davis, nor Johnson, nor Bragg, nor Lee who most dangerously threaten our soldiers; but it is dysentery, cholera, typhus, and all forms of acute and fatal disease. These are the terrible warriors who fight against each side, and he is the masterly General who defeats them in his own camp, and leaves them to deal with the enemy in theirs."

From George William Curtis's "The Lounger," *Harper's Weekly*, July 6, 1861.

Index

Acworth, GA 129, 157
Adairsville, GA 165
Adamsville, GA 128
Ain't I Glad to Be Out of This Wilderness 200
Alabama 96, 99, 160, 162, 166
Alden 84
Alexandria, VA 19, 21, 23, 24, 61, 63, 64, 65, 66, 85, 90, 93, 148 220, 222
Alfred, NY 10, 11, 49, 113, 222
Alfred Center, NY 144
Alkinson, GA 131
Allatoona, GA 159, 161, 160
Allatoona Church, GA 129
Allendale, SC 192
Almond, NY 77, 141
Altamaha, River, GA 167
America 11
Ames, Gen. 214
Andenreid, Maj. 211
Anderson, Al 99
Anderson, Dr. 110
Anderson, Maj. 83
Anderson's P.O., GA 124
Andersonville, GA 172, 175
Andrew 198
Annapolis Junction, MD 19
Annie Laurie 50, 161
Antietam, MD 32, 42, 51, 59, 73, 132, 150, 154; *sketches by A. R. Waud* 30, 31, 33, 34
Antietam Creek, MD 31, 36, 55
Antietam Ford, MD 48, 55, 57, 71
Appomattox, VA 213, 218
Aquia Landing, VA 70, 72
Aquia River (Creek), VA 69
Argyle Island, GA 172
Arkport, NY 185, 186
Arlington, VA 21, 26, 150, 161

Armstrong, Ed 27
Arnold Church, SC 192
Arvilla Goodrich (Ervilla) 191
Ashland, VA 219
Asmussen, Col. 189
Atlanta, GA 127, 137, 138, 140, 141, 144, 147, 150, 152, 153, 155, 157, 158, 164, 165, 166, 168, 169, 170, 171, 172, 176, 200, 202, 203, 216; *Railroad Station, sketch by D. R. Brown* 169
Atwood, Lt. 58
Averysboro, NC 196

Babcock, Enoch 73
Bachman, Capt. 102, 104
Bacon 11
Baker 97
Baker, Charlie 91, 93
Baker, Mrs. 90
Balcom, Capt. 90
Baldwin, Capt. 20
Baldwin, Maj. 100, 136, 140
Bales Cross Roads 21
Baltimore, MD 8, 18, 87, 90, 148
Baltimore Clipper 28; *sketch, Reading in Camp* 28
Banbridge, Capt. 150
Banks, Gen. Nathaniel P. 27
Barnum, Col. 185
Barnum, Gen. 184
Barry, Gen. 155
Bartlett, Col. 112
Barton 108
Bealeton, VA 90, 91, 93, 144, 148
Beardly, Capt. 107
Bearsley, Capt. 156
Beecher 190, 202, 208

Index

Beeman, Capt. 101, 104, 106
Beers, Lt. 102
Belaire, OH 93
Bell Buckle, TN 97
Belmont, NY 144
Benedict, Lt. 199
Benjamin, Sam 108
Bennet, Capt. 85, 86, 107
Bennett, Capt. 86, 89, 91, 104, 117, 165
Bennett, Dr. 162
Bentonville, NC 196
Benwood, OH 93
Berce, Dr. 147, 202
Big Nottoway River 217
Binghamton, NY 132, 153
Binney, (Binni, Binnie) 105, 107, 112, 115, 149, 150, 198, 199
Binns, Lt. 106
Bishop 120
Black and White, VA 218
Black (colored) troups 153, 213
Blackmore, Dr. 100
Blackville, SC 192, 195
Bladensburg, MD 220
Blain 90
Blair, Gen. Frank P. 214
Bloodgood, Col. 202
Blue Ridge, VA 220
Bolivian Heights, VA 37
Bonaventure, GA 174
Bonney 97
Bonnie Blue Flag 78, 118, 202
Boonsboro, MD 30, 32, 78; *sketch by A. R. Waud* 31
Bosworth 101, 103, 104, 115
Bouton 102
Bowman, Col. 140
Bragg, Gen. 117
Brandy Station, VA 93
Brazos Santiago 175
Brentville, VA 220
Brewer, Capt. Henry 45
Bridgeport, TN 99, 119, 120
Brigham, Capt. 127
Brockwell, Col. 93
Bronson, Lefty 76, 79
Brooks Creek, VA 219
Brown, Al 172
Brown, H.P. 10, 11, 113
Brown, John 45, 57
Brownell, David D. 212
Brownsville, MD 35, 36
Brunell, Olin 35
Bryant's Ford, GA 125
Bucher, Capt. 158
Bucher, Dr. 158, 202
Bucher, Chaplain T.K. 47
Buckhead, GA 140
Buckingham, Maj. 75
Bull Run, VA 24, 25, 61, 141
Bullen, Hornellsville, NY 47

Bunk Ford, VA 83
Burbank 10, 11
Burdict, Adj. 215
Burgess 187, 190
Burk, Miss Molly 104
Burks Station, VA 63
Burnside, Gen. Ambrose B. 27, 29, 30, 54, 59, 61, 62
Burnt Hickory, GA 128
Burrill, Almen W. 41
Butterfield, Gen. 127
Butterfield's Brigade 49

Caldwell, Tom 105, 107, 108, 109, 115, 150
Caldwell, Will 101, 102, 112, 150
Calhoun, Dr. 160, 162
Calhoun, Miss 171
Calhoun, GA 125, 126, 128
Camp Seward, VA 20, 21
Campbell, Charles 69
Canacadeas, NY 10
Canoniscus, steamer 176
Cape Fear River, NC 195, 196, 198
Carman, Col. Ezra A. 118, 155, 170, 171
Carrie (sister Caroline Tuttle) 10, 12, 39, 47, 65, 74, 75, 91, 92, 97, 98, 100, 101, 102, 103, 106, 108, 129, 132, 140, 147, 154, 155, 167, 176, 185, 190, 199, 203
Carter, Gen. 200
Case, Col. 179
Cassville, GA 128
Catawba River, SC 193, 195, 201
Catron, Judge, U.S. Supreme Court 117
Cedar Branch, SC 192
Cedar Grove Seminary, NC 199, 200
Centerville, MD 25
Chancellorsville, VA 93, 123, 207, 220, 222
Charleston & Savannah Railroad 185
Charleston, SC 7, 78, 176, 177, 179, 182, 185, 188
Charlie 24, 27, 89, 96, 100, 101 103 112, 154, 167, 198, 199
Charlotte, NC 201
Chattahoochee, GA 137, 138, 139, 140, 150
Chattanooga, TN 112, 113, 116, 120, 122, 137, 157, 164, 166, 221
Chemung County, NY 52, 53
Cheraw, SC 193, 195, 211
Chesterfield, SC 193, 195
Chevis House, SC 179, 180, 181, 184, 185, 187, 200
Chicamaugians, TN 115
Chilesburgh, VA 219
Chipman, Capt. 184
Christian, Henry F. 182
Christiana, TN 97
Clark, Capt. 20
Clark, Ira C. 23, 86, 87, 89
Claxton, Dr. 10
Clay, Hammond 78, 102, 103
Clover Hill, VA 218, 219

Cobble, D. 115
Coggswell, Gen. 199
Cogswell, Col. 118
Colby, Gen. 71
Colby, Newton T. 20, 66, 67, 69, 70, 76, 84, 92
Colgrove, Col. Silas 118, 140
Colored troups 153, 213
Columbia, SC 192, 195
Columbus, OH 93
Comaco Woods, PA 87
C.S.A. FORCES (Confederate States of America): 1st Maryland Cavalry 78; 15th South Carolina Volunteers 186; 27th Virginia Regiment 62Conklin, Capt. Ensyn 153
Connell, Tom 198
Coon, George 74, 75, 76
Cooper 13, 84, 97
Cooper, Ed. 103
Corman, Col. 143
Corse, Gen. 160
Costen, Gen. 76
Cothran's Battery 42
Cottage by the Sea 50
Cowan, TN 99
Cox, Gen. 206, 214
Crandall 40, 108, 153, 172, 175, 191
Crane, Chaplain 21
Crane, Lt. Col. Nirom M. 12, 90, 101, 104, 106, 108, 118, 136, 149, 154, 171, 182, 183, 215
Craw, Col. 11
Crawford, Capt. 179, 181, 201
Crawford's Brigade 63
Culpeper, VA 23
Cumberland, MD 93, 175, 211
Cumberland Mountains, MD 96, 99, 116, 119
Cunningham, Miss Maggie 108
Cunningham, Rev. Dr. 199
Curtis, Miss 11
Curtis Female Seminary 10
Cutting, Dr. 11

Daisy 181, 190
Dallas, GA 128, 131, 148, 163
Damascus, MD 29
Damon, Capt. 63
Dann, Capt. 87
Davis, Theodore R. 126, 133
Dayton, OH 93
Decatur, GA 165, 170, 171
Decherd, Maj. Robt. P. 205
Decherd, TN 96, 99, 104, 116, 118; *sketch by H. R. Hübner* 95
Dekert, Lt. 104, 106
Delaware 7
Delos 102
Denns, GA 172
Densmore 84
Deserters 73, 78, 92, 160
Destruction of property 152, 159, 170, 171, 185, 190, 191, 192

Dewitt, Ben 77
Dexter 11, 84
Disease 41, 42, 43, 72, 74, 196, 198
Diven, Lt. Col. Alexander S. 42, 43, 67, 68, 70, 76, 77, 81, 84
Dixie 200, 202
Dixon's House, GA 131
Dodge, Gen. 153
Doil, Jimmie 52
Doro, Lorenzo 84
Doty, Bertha 142
Doty, Frank 212
Doubleday's Battery 83
Drabell 101
Drake 79
Draper, Senator, NY 183
Duck Branch, SC 192
Duck River, TN 112, 117
Duck River Bridge, TN 115, 116
Duffried, Lt. 149
Dumfries, VA 58, 59, 61, 67, 68, 85; *sketch by A. R. Waud* 68
Duncanville, SC 192
Dunker Church, MD 34, 36, 51
Dunkin, Judge 193
Dunstan, Col. 190
Dura, Col. 77
Durfy, George 171, 172
Dusten, Col. 155
Dustin, Col. 191
Dutton, Lt. Col. 90, 191
Dysentery 43

Easton, Gen. 174
Eatonton, GA 172
Edwards 11
Eleagers, SC 193
Ellet, Mrs, E.F., poetess 180
Elliot 120
Ellis X Roads, NC 217
Elmira, NY 9, 10, 12, 13, 14, 15, 16, 17, 18 36, 83, 127, 132, 154, 166, 223; *Volunteers on Parade* 16
Ely, Alfred 10
Ely, Dr. Will, assistant surgeon 23, 27
Emmet 91
Ennis Cross Roads, SC 191
Enos 12, 50, 97
Etowah, GA 128, 135, 216
Euhartee, GA 128, 135
Everett, Edward 193

Fairfax, VA 22, 59, 61, 63, 64, 66, 220
Fairfax Seminary 21
Falling Creek, VA 219
Falls of Neuse, NC 216
Fanton, Adj. 84
Father (Rufus Tuttle) 10, 13, 14, 15, 16, 17, 44, 75, 76, 77, 79, 100, 109, 113, 126, 129, 132, 150, 167, 180, 181, 191, 205
Fay, Ed 66, 67, 108, 115, 149, 154, 165, 166, 168

Index

Fayetteville, NC 194, 195, 199, 198, 203
Ferow, George 65
Fisher, Dr. 207, 215
Fitch, Arthur 108
Fitz 49
Flat Rock, GA 165
Flemming, Maj. 177
Fletcher, Chaplain 73
Fletcher, Mrs. Mamie 104, 199
Flood, Dr. 215
Flood, Lt. 101
Forbes, Miss 214
Ford, Prof. Darius R. 92
Forrest 208
Fort Albany, VA 21, 24, 26, 40
Fort Craig, VA 24
Fort Fisher 208, 214
Fort Jackson 179
Fort Lincoln, VA 220
Fort Lyon, VA 21, 24
Fort McAllister 214
Fort Pickens 9
Fort Richardson 20
Fort Smith, AR 140
Fort Sumter, SC 7, 179, 207
Fort Washington, MD 95
Fortress Monroe 71
Foster, Gen. 176
Foster General Hospital 197
Fosterville, TN 97
Fountain, USS 190
Fox, Lt. Col. Charles F. 20, 76, 87, 92, 100, 102, 103, 104, 106, 115, 156
Fox, Charlie 101
Fox, Lt. Col. William J. 136
Frederick, MD 29, 86, 211
Fredericksburg, VA 83, 220
Fremont 54
French 120
Freshley's Ferry, SC 193
Frink, Lt. Col. 87
Fuller 116
Fuller, James 72, 73, 76, 75
Fulton, steamer 75

Gainsville, MD 29
Galbraith, Col. 102, 103, 106
Galbraith, Misses 104, 108
Gardner, Capt. 199
Gardner, George 10, 11, 40, 172, 201
Geary, Gen. 135, 185, 197, 206
Genesee Valley 114, 127
Georgetown, MD 26, 86, 90
Georgia 113, 124, 138, 139, 150, 170, 173, 176, 177, 187, 195, 216
Germanna Mills, VA 82
Gettysburg, PA 88, 148
Gilbert, Carl 14
Gilbert, G.K. 14
Gingnard's Bridge, SC 197
The Girl I Left Behind Me 209

The Girls at Home 216
Gladdens Grove, SC 193
Glenn, Maj. 159
Glory, Halleluyah! 18, 21, 50
Goff, LeRoy 73, 77
Goffs 97
Goldsboro, NC 195, 197, 198, 199, 202, 204, 205, 206, 207
Goodrich, Lt. John M. 48, 53, 54, 58, 64
Goodrich Tuttle, Ervilla (Arvilla, Villie) 168, 191, 223
Goose Creek, TN 97
Gordon, Brig. Gen. George H. 34, 35, 52
Gordon's Mill, TN 123
Gorman, Gen. W.A. 31, 33
Goslings 101, 102, 105, 115
Gould, Ed 10, 11, 16, 24, 27, 153, 172
Grafton, Capt. 196
Grafton, WV 93
Graham's Station, SC 192
Grange & Alexandria Railroad 23, 62
Grant, Ulysses S. 98, 99, 162, 184, 205, 208, 214, 215
Graves, E.P. 104, 108, 109, 111, 115, 136
Gray, Lt. George E. 65, 66
Great Pee Dee River, NC 193
Grinsted, Dr. 162, 176, 182, 189, 214
Grove Church, VA 81
Gum Spring, VA 59

Hail Columbia! 163, 209
Hale, Matt 109
Halleck, Gen. 222
Hamilton, Maj. Emory 175
Hammond, Clay 78, 103, 104, 107
Hammond, Will 83, 87
Hamond, *World*'s correspondent 43
Hanging Rock, SC 193, 195
Hanley, Col. 103
Hardeeville, SC 185, 187, 191
Hardenbrook 211
Harpers Ferry, VA 8, 36, 37, 45, 47, 57, 58, 61, 93, 154; sketch 38
Harrisburg, PA 18, 223
Harrison, Gen. 211
Harrison's Landing, VA 14
Hart, Roswell 10
Hartman, Matt 61, 85
Hartwood Church, VA 81
Hatch, Gen. 176
Hawley, Lt. Miles 65
Hawley, Col. William 101, 118, 199
Hayes X Roads, SC 192
Hazen, Gen. 214
Heintzleman, Gen. Samuel P. 59, 60
Henderson, Adj. 106
Her Bright Smile Haunts Me Still 136
Higgins, Maj. 197
Hillsboro, VA 58
Hilton Head, SC 176, 184
Hishen, Dr. 213

Index

Honey, U. of Rochester 85
Hood, Gen. 164, 165
Hooker, Maj. Gen. Joseph 59, 70, 77, 81, 93, 108, 114, 115, 123, 127, 129, 130, 131, 137, 143, 145, 183, 216
Hope Landing, VA 69, 70
Hopkins, Capt. 197
Horick, Peter P. 80
Horlove, Lt. 87
Horn, Capt. 106, 112
Hornellsville, NY 8, 9, 10, 11, 12, 15, 20, 31, 46, 61, 72, 75, 77, 113, 144, 223
Hornellsville Tribune 8, 1, 31, 113
Horton 90
Howard, Lt. Alonzo H. (Lon) 64, 67, 68, 71, 77, 79, 91, 103, 105, 107, 108, 115, 136, 144, 165, 174, 198, 203, 208
Howard, Gen. 127, 143, 168, 170, 207, 208, 214
Howe, Eugene 83
Howell, Luther 12, 77, 154, 172, 175
Howson, Cpl. Walter H. (Daisy) 184, 190
Hutchins, Maj. A. H. 223
Hutchinson Island, GA 176, 182

Indianapolis, IN 93, 97

Jackson, Gen. 54, 77, 168, 186, 189
Jackson, soldier 174
Jackson, Stonewall 146
James 14, 154
Jamison, Dr., 86th NY 19
Jasper Springs, GA 174
Jefcoats Bridge, SC 192
Johnston, Gen. 207, 208, 209, 210, 211, 215
Jones, Col. 185
Jones' X Roads, NC 215

Kaesin 90
Kamak, Dr. 87
Kellogg, Capt. 149
Kellys Ford, VA 81, 90, 92, 148, 149; *sketch by A. R. Waud* 82
Keme's Brigade 57
Kemps Mill, GA 129
Kennesaw, GA 163, 170
Kennesaw Mountains, GA 159
Kentucky 7, 8, 94, 163, 213
Kenyon 11
Kenyon, Jarvis 172, 176
Ketchum, Col. John H. 118
Kickerson, Capt. 198
Kilpatrick, Gen. 183, 206
Kimbal 198
Kingston, GA 164
Kingwood Tunnel 93
Kinney, Charles 198
Kinston, NC 212, 197, 198
Kitchen, Col. 172
Kneip (Knipe?), Gen. 143, 216
Knickerbacker, Louis 74, 75

Knight, Capt. 108, 112, 141, 149, 150
Knipe, Gen. 77, 86, 135, 216
Knox 79
Koloon 79
Kompton, George 73
Krompton's Creek, TN 116
Kyle's Landing, NC 196

L & N Railroad 64
Lacey, Maj. 192
Lacy, Capt. 197
Laman, Capt. John J. 20
Lamphere, Will 32
Langworthy, Louise 41, 92
Larkspur, steamer 174
Latimer's Farm, GA 164
Lawtonville, SC 192, 195
Lee, Gen. Robert E. 207, 208, 211, 213
Lee, Rutha 74
Leesburg, VA 58, 59, 60, 61
Leonard 10
Lexington, SC 196, 195
Libby Prison, TN 145, 166
Liberty Hill, SC 193
Lincoln, Pres. Abraham 19, 77, 180, 208
Lindsay, John 136
Lindsey, Lt. 68, 114, 115, 170
Lithonia, GA 165
Little Black Creek, SC 193
Little River, GA 172
Little River, VA 219
Logan, Maj. Gen. John A. 143, 183, 214
Loges, Col. 140
Lookout Mountain, TN 123
Lord Fairfax 22
Lorena 120, 121
Lost Mountain, GA 157
Loudan County, VA 60
Louisville, KY 94, 201
Lumber River, NC 194
Luther Howell 12, 77, 154, 172, 175
Lynch's Creek, SC 193

Macon, GA 166, 176
Madison, GA 172, 208
The Maiden's Prayer 161
Manassas, VA 22
Manassas Gap Railroad 24
Manchester, TN 115, 116, 117
Manchester, VA 219
Manger, Lt. Jas 198
Mansfield, Maj. Gen. Joseph K.F. 35
Manson Hill 21
Marcy, Orderly Sgt. 78
Marietta, GA 131, 135, 137, 139, 144, 159, 160; *sketch by Theodore R. Davis* 137
Marsh, Dr. 202
Martin, Lt. 199
Martindale's Brigade 49
Martinsburg, WV 93
Maryland 7, 8, 9, 26, 40, 41, 70, 78, 93, 213

Maryland Heights, MD 36, 37, 47, 49, 57, 72; *sketch* 38
Mason, Rev. Dr. 214
Mason, Capt. Truman 10, 83, 109, 131
Mason, Will 84
Mathers, Dr. Samuel 198
Maxon, Prof. Alfred University 10, 11
McClellan, Gen. George B. 22, 26, 27, 30, 53, 54, 62; *sketch, McClellan's Our Man* 62
McConnell, Maj. 86
McCullum, Paric 222
McDonough Road, GA 167, 168
McDowell, Capt. 141, 165, 170, 171, 187, 202, 206, 211
McKan, Charlie 89
McKel, Capt. 177
McNair, Capt. Jim 27
McNell, Col. 140
McPherron 153
McPherson, Gen. 141, 153
Meade, Maj. Gen. George G. 83
Meherrin River, VA 217
Meigs, M.C., Quarter Master General 183
Mervandervil 76
Metz's Mill, SC 193
Middlebrook, MD 28
Middleton 79
Middletown, Valley, MD 29; *sketch by A.R. Waud* 31
Miles, Capt. 20, 76
Millard, NC 206
Milledgeville, GA 166, 172, 214
Millen, GA 173, 175
Miller, Mrs. 17
Miller's Bridge, SC 193
Mills, Dr. 72
Miners Hill, VA 64, 65
Mitchell, Capt. 102
Mitchell, Lt. Phin 163
Mobile, AL 166, 167
Moccasin River, NC 206
Monocucy River, MD 29, 88
Montgomery, AL 166
Montgomery County, MD 26
Moor, Capt. 44
Morgan, Capt. 20
Morgan, Gov., of NY 20
Morgan, Quarter Master 71
Morris, Theodore 83
Morse, Lt. Col. 197
Mower, Gen. 199, 207, 208, 214
Moyer, Chas., A.A.A. Gen. 205
Mulberry, TN 108
Mumford, Oliver 140
Murfreesboro, TN 96; *sketch by F. Beard* 95
Music 21, 50, 84, 115, 118, 120, 121, 136, 146, 149, 153, 161, 163, 176, 180, 191, 200, 211; bands 10, 21, 23, 62, 84, 100, 104, 117, 127, 136, 137, 138, 146, 149, 150, 161, 163, 167, 176, 178, 180, 193, 200, 205, 209, 211, 220

Nash, Lt. 49
Nash, Mayor of Rochester 8
Nashville & Chattanooga Railroad 113, 120
Nashville, TN 11, 94, 97, 108, 111, 112, 113, 128, 168, 179
Nature: birds 70, 72, 113, 190, 207, 218; flowers 78, 81, 112, 114, 115, 117, 127, 128, 135, 151, 163, 200, 202, 206, 207, 208, 213; moonlight 26, 96, 117, 146, 149, 161, 180, 181; scenery 18, 19, 21, 25, 36, 46, 47, 49, 50, 55, 70, 92, 113, 114, 119, 120, 139, 142, 183, 192, 213, 218; sunsets 46, 117, 149
Nell R. 102
Neuse River, NC 207, 217
New Orleans, LA 175
New River, SC 179, 180
Newbern, NC 197, 199, 200, 201, 205, 214
Nickelson 97
Nikajack Cave, TN 120, 121; *sketch* 121
Nikajack Creek, GA 137; *sketch by Theodore R. Davis* 138
Nin 84, 89, 92, 112
Niven, Robert 93
Normandy, TN 97, 108, 112, 116
Norris, Capt. 103, 137, 140
North Anna River, VA 219
North Carolina 212, 213
Northup, 1st Sgt. Wesley 14
Norton, Charles 83

Occoquon, VA 59, 63, 69
Ocmulgee, GA 167
Ohio 93, 181
Ohio River 93
Orr, John 73
Orr, 2nd Lt. Willie 23, 92
Ors Mountain 114
Orton, Capt. 142, 148
Owen 10

Pacveck, Charlie 24
Painted Post, NY 223
Paling, George 60
Pardee, Col. 185
Pardee, Mr. 77
Parks, Maj. 106
Parlin, John 49
Parma 45
Parmeter 69
Patrick's Brigade 31
Pattengill 10, 23
Pea Vine Creek, GA 123
Peach Tree Creek, GA 140
Peers 107
Pendergast, Dr. P. 101, 102, 160, 165, 166, 174, 177, 199, 201, 203, 215
Penny Worth Island 182
Perkins, Asst. Adj. Gen. H.W. 155, 202
Peters 86
Philadelphia, PA 86, 87, 89, 148, 188
Phrunson, Capt. 103

Index

Pierce, Ed 26
Pikwik 106
Pinch, James 15, 72, 83, 84
Pine Hill 131
Pinhorn, (Pinehorn) 112, 114
Planter, steamship 177
Pleasant Grove Church, GA 124
Pleasant Mt. 91
Pleasant Valley 36, 37
Plimpton, Sgt. Albert. M. 17, 18, 53, 56, 58, 74
Polk, Gen. Bishop 117, 120, 131, 133
Pontiac, gunboat 187
Poormano Creek Bridge, GA 111
Pope, Gen. 22, 23, 27
Port Ellsworth, VA 21
Port Royal, SC 176, 180
Porter 26
Potomac Boys 142, 158, 218
Potomac River 21, 24, 26, 28, 36, 39, 46, 47, 50, 55, 57, 61, 70, 71, 110, 130, 211
Praise God from Whom All Blessings Flow 161
Preima 89, 90, 91, 92, 97, 98, 100, 101, 102, 103, 104, 105, 106, 108, 112, 116, 129, 140, 141, 147, 150, 154, 168, 172, 174, 202
Prentiss, Lt. John 46, 76
Pury, John Pater 185
Purysburg, SC 185, 187, 191

Quantico, VA 68, 70
Quint, Parson 109
Quirk, Lt. 90

Raccoon Ford, VA 136
Railroad 23, 24, 62, 64, 93, 96, 113, 120, 122, 144, 150, 157, 159, 162, 163, 164, 169, 171, 185, 193, 195, 197, 198, 218, 220
Raleigh, NC 206, 207, 208, 210, 212, 215, 216, 218
Ram Savannah (ship) 179
Randall's Plantation, GA 140
Rapidan River, VA 82, 136
Rappahannock River, VA 62, 81, 83, 90, 91, 93, 139, 149, 222
Red Bluff, SC 179, 180
Red, White, and Blue 118, 153
Reekok, Charlie 27
Relay House, VA 19, 93
Remittent fever 153, 196, 198
Rennée, Capt 222
Resaca, GA 125, 126, 127, 135, 136; *sketches by Theodore R. Davis* 122
Reynolds 79
Richardson 67
Richmond, OH 93
Richmond, VA 61, 67, 162, 164, 202, 205, 217, 218, 219, 221
Ride, Ben 13
Ringgold, GA 123
River Ridge Road, GA 140
Roanoke River, VA 217

Rob 88
Robbinson, Gen. 199
Robersville, MD 35
Robinson, Col. 179, 185
Robinson, Maj. Joseph W. 14, 65, 98, 191
Rochester, NY 8, 9, 13, 85, 93, 132, 155, 189
Rochester Democrat 112
Rochester Light Guard Zonar 7
Rochester Regiment 7, 27, 72, 83
Rochester University 10, 21, 26
Rock Bridge, GA 171
Rockfish Creek, NC 194
Rockville, MD 26, 28
Rockville P.O., SC 193
Rocky Mount, SC 193, 195, 201
Rocky Mount Ferry, SC 193
Roddy 208
Rogers, Ora 172, 176
Rogers Mill, TN 114
Rolls, Mak 97
Rorko, Henry 74, 75
Rosecrans, Gen. 99, 116, 117
Ross, Col. 76, 185
Rosseau, Gen. 116
Rossville, MD 36
Rossville, GA 123
Rothrock, Maggie 154, 156
Ruff Station, GA 137
Rugan, Dr. 196
Rugen, Capt. 108
Ruger, Capt. 152, 158, 162
Ruger, Gen. 77, 103, 106, 118, 143, 155, 165, 168, 220
Russell, Capt. 65
Russell Place, SC 193
Rutha Lee 74
Rutter, Nathaniel 21, 66, 83
Ryan, John W. 47

Sage, Martin 42
St. Augusta Creek, GA 174
St. Peter Parish, SC 179, 180
Salem, TN 102
Saltsman, Jack 196
Saluda River, SC 193
Sand Hills, SC 192
Sanders 11
Sandtown Road, GA 137
Sandy Hook, MD 37; *sketch* 38
Sarkin, Prof. 172
Savage 10
Savannah, GA 166, 167, 170, 172, 173, 174, 175, 176, 177, 179, 180, 181, 182, 186, 187, 189, 190, 195, 198, 200, 203, 207
Sawyer, Harris 65
Saxton, Gen. 176
Schilling 172, 202
Schofield, Gen. 127, 138, 206, 207, 208, 214
Schurz, Maj. Gen. Carl 75, 109, 110, 202, 208, 214
Schuyler County, NY 52

238 Index

Seely, Capt. 141
Selestia 141
Selfridge, Col. 145, 199
Selma, AL 166
Seminary Hospital, Georgetown, MD 86
Semmes, Raphael 78
Seward, Secretary 19, 208
Seymour 53
Sharpsburg, MD 32, 33, 35, 36, 46, 48, 49, 61
Shaw (preacher) 10
Shelbyville, TN 99, 101, 103, 104, 105, 106, 107, 108, 109, 111, 112, 114, 115, 116, 120, 127, 136, 140, 165, 166, 203; *sketch by H.R. Hübner* 99
Sheldon 12, 23, 71, 101, 102, 108
Shell Mound, TN 113, 120, 121, 122
Shenandoah River Valley 30, 45, 47, 48, 57
Shepherd 103
Sheridan, Gen. Philip Henry 218
Sherman, Maj. Gen. William T. 150, 154, 155, 157, 158, 160, 161, 164, 168, 176, 183, 193, 195, 196, 200, 201, 202, 206, 207, 208, 210, 211, 212, 213, 214, 215, 217, 220, 222
Sherron, Mike 21
Sickles, Gen. Daniel E. 123, 127
Sigel, Gen. Franz 57, 58, 59, 69
Sill, Allen N. 10, 13, 15, 20, 43, 64, 67, 70, 71, 73, 74, 76, 78, 81, 83 87, 89, 91, 97, 101, 102, 103, 105, 106, 109, 111, 116, 129, 136, 144, 150, 153, 156, 165, 166, 183, 203
Sill, Aunt Jane 12, 13, 104, 105, 108, 129, 172, 203
Skimmeroon 50
Slaves 162, 193, 212
Slocum, Maj. Gen. Henry Warner 20, 47, 59, 60, 69, 77, 84, 106, 110, 113, 114, 117, 143, 146, 155, 168, 196, 205, 207, 208, 214
Small, Capt. Robert 177
Small Pox 78
Smith 17, 25
Smith B. 110
Smith, Goldwin 213
Smith, John 64, 65, 90, 93
Smith, Lt. Col. 70, 190
Smith, O.M. 115, 116
Smithfield, NC 206, 207
Smithville (Smithfield?) NC 196
Smoketown Hospital, MD 57, 58
Smyrna, SC 192
Snake Creek Gap, GA 124, 125
Snap Finger Creek, GA 165
Sneedsboro, NC 193
Snyder, Lt. 214
Social Circle, GA 172
Sondan County, VA 59
Sonoma, gunboat 187
South Carolina 176, 177, 179, 180, 183, 184, 192, 195, 200
South Carolina Railroad 195
South Mountain, MD 29, 49, 86
South Side Railroad 218, 220

Southern Tier Reg. 12
Spaulding, S.R. steamer 182
Speed, Capt. 179, 180, 193, 196, 201
Spotsylvania, VA 220, 222
Spotted Fever 78
Springtown, SC 192
Stafford Court House, VA 58, 69, 71, 73, 77, 83
Stanley, Gen. 127
Stanton, Secretary 183
The Star Spangled Banner 11, 118, 137, 153, 163
Starrow, Lt. 196
Steiner, Capt. 78, 205, 15
Steppenfield 50
Steuben County, NY 53
Stevensburg, VA 92, 93
Stevenson, AL 96
Stillman, James 108, 110, 12, 172, 175, 223
Stone, Capt. 149
Stone, Maj. 108, 109
Stone Mountain, GA 138, 170, 171
Stowe, Mr. 64
Stuart, Capt. 214
Stuart-Mill, John 213
Stuart's Cavalry 48
Stuart's Engineers 45
Suffold's Bridge, VA 217
Sugarloaf Mountain, MD 37
Sukim Gap, VA 48
Susquehana River, PA 18
Sutton, Bill 198
Swan, Lt. 101
Swift Creek, NC 206
Syphen, Col. J.H. 175

Tale of Beauty 117
Tantalon, TN 99
Tar River, NC 217
Taylor, Capt. 10
Taylors Ferry, VA 217
Taylor's Ridge, GA 124
Tennallytown, MD 26
Tennessee 7, 93, 97, 105, 106, 112, 113, 114, 116, 117, 120, 136, 172, 213
Tennessee River 97, 99, 113, 119, 120, 122
Terry, Gen. 207, 208, 213, 214
Thacher, Eugene 15, 102, 113, 128, 141, 148, 153, 167, 220
Thacher, Luin 8, 11, 12, 112, 140, 154, 156
Thomas, Adj. Gen. 183
Thomas, Maj. Gen. George H. 99, 103, 111, 127
Thompson, Capt. Charles A., Jr. 145
Thompson, Joe 199, 203
Thompson, Lt. 180, 211
Thompson, Mortimer 183
Thompson P.O., SC 193
Thorne, Capt. Platt M. 108, 150, 170, 211
Three Fork Mills, TN 115
Todd 11
Todd, Capt. 197

Index

Torrey 97
Tousy 11
Town Run, VA 220
Trembly, T. P., *New York Herald* 91
Tullahoma, TN 96, 97, 99, 103, 104, 106, 107, 108, 109, 111, 112, 114, 115, 116, 117, 118
Turner, Bob 40
Tuttle, Ervilla Goodrich "Villie" 168, 191, 223
Tuttle, Millinda Mumford (mother) 10, 15, 40, 129, 131, 140
Tuttle, Lt. Russell M. 90, 154, 155, 198
Tuttle, Rufus (father) 10, 13, 14, 15, 16, 17, 44, 75, 76, 77, 79, 100, 109, 113, 126, 129, 132, 150, 167, 180, 181, 191, 205, 206
Typhoid 97, 74, 76, 198

Union Forces (Grand Army of the Republic): Army of Georgia 168, 204; Army of Ohio 160; Army of Tennessee 160, 168; Army of the Potomac 21, 25, 27, 69, 70, 83, 87, 93, 113, 123, 220; Army of the Cumberland 155, 160, 168; 2nd Army Corps 27; 4th Army Corps 127, 150; 5th Army Corps 81; 9th Army Corps 71; 10th Army Corps (Gen. Terry) 214; 11th Army Corps (Sigel) 69, 72, 82; 12th Army Corps 27, 69, 77, 78; 14th Army Corps 174, 196; 15th Army Corps (Gen. Johnny Logan) 200, 214; 17th Army Corps (Gen Frank P. Blair) 214; 20th Army Corps (Gen Mower) 118, 133, 214; 23rd Army Corps (Gen. Cox) 214; 4th U.S. Artillery Battery 34; 1st Brigade 18, 131; 3rd Brigade 27; 53rd Brigade, Whipple's Division 24; Cothran's Battery 42; Crawford's Brigade 63; Doubleday's Battery 83; Martindale's Brigade 49; Stuart's Engineers 45; Stuart's Cavalry 48; Co H, 20th Connecticut Regiment 93; 18th Illinois Regiment 102; 165th Illinois Regiment (Col. Dusten) 155; 17th Indiana Regiment 102; 27th Indiana Regiment 27, 34, 48, 82, 84; 33rd Indiana Regiment 100; 129th Indiana Regiment (Col. Zollinger) 198, 211; 10th Maine Regiment 102; 2nd Massachusetts Regiment 27, 48, 82, 106; 3rd Massachusetts Regiment 92; 33rd Massachusetts Band 136, 150, 167, 180, 191, 193, 207, 211; 35th Massachusetts Regiment 24; 16th Michigan Regiment 49; 19th Michigan Regiment 145; 13th New Jersey Regiment 34, 48; 14th New Jersey Battery 115; 18th New Jersey Regiment 155; 113th New Jersey Regiment 82; Battery M, 1st New York Light Artillery 34; 6th New York Cavalry 72, 76; 8th New York Cavalry 44, 72; 9th New York Cavalry 83; 12th Regiment, New York 36; 13th Regiment New York Volunteers 24, 27, 91; 21st Regiment, Buffalo Volunteers 78; 23rd Regiment, New York Volunteers, Patrick's Brigade 31, 46, 76, 84; 27th Regiment, New York 27, 91; 33rd Regiment, New York 27; 44th Regiment, New York 49; 69th Regiment, New York Militia 23; 86th Regiment, New York 19, 73; 107th Regiment, New York Volunteers 16, 27, 31, 32, 33, 34, 42, 47, 50, 56, 71, 75, 82, 83, 85, 90, 91, 93, 97, 101, 102, 103, 104, 106; 108th Rochester Regiment, 2nd Corps. 119, 21, 26, 27; 113th Regiment, (New York?) 23; 123rd Regiment, New York 61, 106; 132nd Regiment, Co. E, New York 198; 134th Regiment, New York 73, 76, 82; 140th Regiment, New York 23; 141st Regiment, New York 46, 65, 74, 75, 93; 142nd Regiment, New York 64; 145th Regiment, New York Volunteers 106; 150th Regiment, New York 91, 106; 29th Ohio Regiment 62; 73rd Ohio Regiment, Co. C 181; 107th Ohio Regiment 82; 118th Ohio Regiment 198; 168th Ohio Regiment 198; 46th Pennsylvania Regiment 34; 124th Pennsylvania Regiment 24; 125th Pennsylvania Regiment 45; 3rd Wisconsin Regiment 27, 49, 82; 22nd Wisconsin Regiment (Col. Bloodgood) 202
University Place, TN 118, 119, 120
Unseld, Mr. 42
Updike 12

Van Valkenburgh, Robert B. 13, 14, 17, 43
Van Valkenburgh, Lt. Ed 90, 103, 111
Vellerlip, Maj. 220
Vicksburg, MS 87, 115, 141, 215
Vining's Station, GA 137
Virginia 9, 20, 40, 47, 55, 59, 71, 72, 93, 97, 116, 127, 136, 139, 150, 161, 163, 216, 217

Wadsworth 53
Walker's X Roads, SC 192
Wallace 137
Wanhatchee, TN 120
Ward, Gen. 155, 165, 170, 176, 199, 206, 208, 212, 220
Warder, Capt. 199
Warrenton, VA 90, 148
Wartrace, TN 97, 99, 101, 103, 104, 106, 107, 108, 109, 110, 112; *Washing Clothes in River* 39
Washington, D.C. 8, 16, 17, 18, 19, 20, 21, 22, 23, 24, 25, 46, 61, 64, 70, 71, 87, 89, 90, 93, 148, 185, 210, 211, 212, 215, 218, 220, 221, 222, 223; *Bridge Across the Potomac* 19
Watkins, Lt. Col. 197
Wattles, Lt. 196
Wauser 16
Webster, Lt. 10, 11, 13, 16, 24, 27
Wellan, 1st Lt. Ed 102
Wells, Gen. 71
Wells, recruit 97
Wells, Sgt. Dave 98
Wellville Station, VA 218
Wheeler 45
Wheiting, Col. 11
Whipple's Division 24

White House Landing, VA 76, 77, 79
Whiteside, TN 120, 122
Whittlesy 115
Wickes, Capt. 145
Wilburn, Litton 90
Wilkinson, Capt. 20
Williams, Brig. Gen. Alpheus S. 36, 63, 77, 79, 116, 117, 143, 146, 170, 185, 186, 189, 190, 199
Williams, Elsie 149
Williams, Maj. 115
Williams, Mrs. 162
Williams, Prof. at Alfred University 10
Williams, (Shelbyville) 150
Williamsport, PA 18
Williston, SC 192, 195
Wilmington, DE 87
Wilmington, NC 176, 189, 194, 208
Wilmington Railroad 193
Wilmington, steam tug 196
Wilson 208
Wilson's Station, VA 218

Winchester, TN 118
Winston 197
Wisener, Judge (Shelbyville) 140
Wolf Run Shoals, VA 59, 67
Woodford, Capt. 197
Woods, Col. 141, 183, 185
Woods, Mr. 53
The World, periodical 129
Wright, Cpl. 69; *sketch, Writing Home* 134
W.S.M.R.R. 64

Yankee Doodle 153
Yarrow Branch, SC 192
York, PA 18
Yorktown, VA 14
Young, Capt. 197
Younger 10, 11, 41

Zanesville, OH 93
Zenia, OH 93
Zion's Church, SC 192
Zollinger, Col. 198, 21

www.ingramcontent.com/pod-product-compliance
Lightning Source LLC
Chambersburg PA
CBHW051219300426
44116CB00006B/642